Shakespeare Comes to Broadmoor

'The Actors are Come Hither'

Shakespeare Comes to Broadmoor

'The Actors are Come Hither'

The Performance of Tragedy in a Secure Psychiatric Hospital

Edited by Murray Cox

Foreword by Sir Ian McKellen

Jessica Kingsley Publishers
London and Philadelphia

First published in the United Kingdom in 1992 by
Jessica Kingsley Publishers Ltd
118 Pentonville Road
London N1 9JB

Copyright © the contributors and the publisher 1992
Cover/jacket photograph of Brian Cox as King Lear © Neil Libbert
Cover/jacket photograph of Mark Rylance as Hamlet © Richard Mildenhall
Cover/jacket design by Christopher Ranger

British Library Cataloguing in Publication Data
Shakespeare comes to Broadmoor: "The actors are come hither": The performance of tragedy in a secure psychiatric hospital.
I. Cox, Murray
365

ISBN 1–85302–135–0
ISBN 1–85302–121–0 pbk

Printed and bound in Great Britain by
Billing and Sons Ltd, Worcester

Contents

Foreword

There is a commonly expressed view amongst professional drama critics that there are too many productions of Shakespeare in the United Kingdom. When I played Hamlet in 1971, there had been ten other productions that year in and around London. More than one critic wrote that they were bored with the play. To adapt Samuel Johnson – a great Shakespeare critic: 'When a man is tired of Shakespeare he is tired of life; for there is in Shakespeare all that life can afford'. That is, in part, the message of this book and it's significant that no drama critic has contributed to it.

Instead, we can read here the reactions of actors and their audience, the essential participants at any theatre performance, whose views are nevertheless rarely recorded. All of them have presented their feelings with an honesty which is more authoritative than most drama criticism, whether journalistic or academic. There is no need to apologise for this unique addition to the flood of literature about Shakespeare.

Other books have analysed the plays from every possible standpoint, discovering in them a confirmation that the writers' own interests, expertise and prejudices are shared by Shakespeare. Through the last 400 years, some of his plays have dipped in and out of fashion, but there has been a remarkably constant acceptance that Shakespeare knew more about ourselves than we could ever have discovered without him.

A senior member of the House of Windsor, after seeing *Richard II* in 1969, told me she had learnt something new about being royal, which she wanted to discuss with her family. In 1977, when Harold Wilson saw *Macbeth*, he was most intrigued by the minor character of Ross, who reminded him of the type of civil servant he had worked with as prime minister. Soldiers, too, are astonished by Shakespeare's grasp of the details of their professional lives: so are sailors, lawyers and gardeners. He is a mirror reflecting all our lives, now as much as ever.

Perhaps more than any other group, theatre-people regard him personally. He is one of us. After all, he could have just written poetry or essays or treatises or sermons. He could, surely, have invented the novel. Although he didn't invent the tenet that all the world's a stage, he certainly lived by it and there it was, as a text above his Globe Theatre – *Totus mundi agit historiem*. Every one of his plays uses the metaphor of theatre and of acting, to illuminate their meaning. Let others despise us for escaping the real world for a career of disguise and pretence. Shakespeare reassures us that acting is close to the heart of human experience.

So whatever our discipline, we feel we are personally represented in the plays, encouraging us to try and imagine the man who wrote them. Caroline Spurgeon (1979) even believes that details of his life, taste and physical appearance are revealed in his clusters of imagery. That sort of enquiry is why so many actors and audiences like to be in his hometown. For all of his working-life he was in London, where his theatres have been destroyed. Looking at the fragile remains of the Rose and Globe Theatres recently uncovered in the water-logged mud on the south bank of the Thames, it is difficult to imagine their original state. But in Stratford-upon-Avon, renovated and adapted maybe, so much looks as it used to – the birthplace, school and church and plan of the streets where he walked and played. There as a child, the touring actors introduced him to theatre. All of us who sense him as a man and feel grateful to him, keep returning to Stratford and the Warwickshire landscape that bred him. It's not surprising that the farsighted plan for Shakespeare's first visit to Broadmoor should have been suggested in his hometown.

The reports in this book are, without exception, enthusiastic about the outcome. Some actors, perhaps too apprehensive for their own safety, didn't join in. Nor did every patient, for reasons unrecorded, want to see the plays. But it is moving that the rest of us all felt we were beneficiaries of those performances in Broadmoor. I wish there were fuller reports from patients – there's certainly a need for a further book, if other productions take place. Their nurses and therapists have written in detail. So have some of the actors: and there's no need for me to add much to the insightful impressions of my colleagues.

Was I alone, however, as I peered round the audience, in being unable to work out who was a patient and who was a nurse? Was the man who sat silent through *King Lear*, his slack jaw down on his chest, really asleep or just listening intently? Like Brian Cox, I can never forget as he asked the audience, 'Is there any cause in nature that make these hard hearts?' to see beyond him, the rapt attention of the young woman who slowly shook her head in sympathy with the question. I suppose in Broadmoor, more than anywhere else, there must be faith that there can be an answer.

As Deborah Warner astutely observes, much of the experience of playing in Broadmoor was not out of the ordinary for some of us. Touring actors are used to adapting themselves to a wide variety of theatre-spaces. Anyone who has worked in the open-air or in a very small theatre knows the challenge of seeing the audience as clearly as we could in Broadmoor. Performing *King Lear* in everyday clothes, we recaptured the freedom of an exploratory rehearsal. What was incontrovertibly special was the nature of the audience. Some of them might be expected to have a unique sympathy with the violence of the action. Others had never seen a Shakespeare play before. Clare Higgins expresses the most extreme revelation, when she wants, in future, to rehearse Shakespeare with Broadmoor patients. She and the rest of us, were reminded of the purpose of playing, which can too often be obscured by the pressures of first nights and of long runs. Who do we do these plays for? Anonymous audiences whom we never meet, directors whom we meet all too often, or drama critics who sometimes tell us they are bored with *Hamlet*? I hope all these groups will read this book and be as grateful to Murray Cox as I am for inspiring and compiling it. He will forgive me if I end by thanking an actor, Mark Rylance, for realising before anyone else that 'it would be good if we could bring *Hamlet* to Broadmoor'.

Ian McKellen

Sir Ian McKellen
January 1992

Acknowledgements

'Your visitation shall receive such thanks
As fits a king's remembrance'

(Hamlet II.2.25)

These words so aptly convey the gratitude of the entire Broadmoor community towards those members of the Royal Shakespeare Company, the Royal National Theatre and the Wilde Theatre Company whose 'visitation' – in their own time and at their own expense – prompted the cry 'The actors are come hither'. And, together with the actors, came directors, stage-managers, musicians and others who likewise deserve our thanks. Nevertheless, in addition to those who took part in the performing 'visitation', there were those who spent much additional time giving extended interviews about acting or directing, when the plays were performed to an audience consisting largely of Broadmoor patients. Indeed, these interviews form the main substance of Section I – *'Dramatis Personae'*. Our indebtedness both for the time spent and the degree of personal disclosure involved cannot be exaggerated.

It is always invidious to mention names on such occasions. Suffice it to say, that from the first tentative planning explorations to those crucial details which can only be dealt with at the last minute, a hospital-wide collaborative enterprise was activated. It involved staff from several disciplines, and called for advice and practical help from many patients. We are grateful to them all.

Overall encouragement from senior management was matched by the skilled know-how of the electrician and others working on both sides of the 'footlights'. There was scarcely a discipline within the hospital which was not involved, either on-stage or off-stage, in one capacity or another.

As this was a pioneer venture, it called for many decisions for which there was no precedent. Calculated risks were taken, but only after the fullest discussion at every level with all concerned. *Hamlet* was therefore the prototype, which tested new ground. This meant that subsequent performances became easier to plan and to set in motion. Though it still seems scarcely credible that I should receive an enquiry as to whether *Romeo and Juliet* would require 'the usual RSC arrangements!'

This statement of grateful acknowledgement is Janusian, and faces in two directions simultaneously. It is both an expression of thanks to all those who 'came hither' on behalf of those whose lives are, at present, in

Broadmoor. It also conveys the personal thanks of an editor who could not have been surrounded by more congenial support.

I am particularly grateful to my Broadmoor colleagues whose contributions to these pages speak for themselves. But they can only do so because of their energetic personal assistants whose 'secretarial over-load' was increased still further.

Past and present colleagues at The Shakespeare Institute, The University of Birmingham, offered stimulus, friendship, and professional resources on many wavelengths. Again, generic gratitude must suffice. There is both a formal necessity and an inner obligation, that I should state that the editorial views here presented are personal, and do not necessarily represent those of the Special Hospitals Service Authority. But, having the full support of management, and the contributions of several colleagues, including that of the Director of Medical Services, such a disclaimer can also serve as a further opportunity for the expression of thanks. There is however a word of apology that needs to be made. I refer to the fact that several patients, whose comments appear in Section III 'This Tempest in my Mind' had expressed the wish that their names should appear in print. Nevertheless, after extensive discussion and consultation, it seems wisest for such contributions to remain anonymous. The reasons behind this decision are given in the ensuing section on 'The Horizons of Possibility'. It is no accident that this issue takes its place under the heading 'Acknowledgements'. This is because one of the predominant concerns, shared by all the Broadmoor staff, is to acknowledge and maintain the privacy of that which a patient may disclose within the bounds of professional confidence. Therefore, any details which might suggest identification have been changed. The amalgamated responses of members of the audience are presented as a stream of corporate consciousness in 'This Tempest in my Mind'. These, when inter-woven with statements from members of the cast, form one of the solid foundations upon which the entire edifice rests. For this, and for many other reasons, we are indebted to all those patients who willingly opened windows overlooking their inner worlds.

In addition to the actors themselves, there are others who came from the world on the other side of the wall. We are collectively indebted to the distinguished contributors who have written on various specialised topics in Section IV under the heading 'Wider Horizons'. Their chapters considerably enlarge the scope of the book and will augment its relevance in several related fields of study, which run alongside theatre studies.

There are, however, two names which appear on the cover and expressly call for our thanks.

Sir Ian McKellen who kindly agreed to write the Foreword was, himself, one of the actors who came hither. He came with *King Lear* as Kent. We are indeed fortunate that *Shakespeare Comes to Broadmoor* comes with his blessing. And came with his presence.

It is literally true to say that without Jessica Kingsley, the publisher, this book would not be the book it is. Jessica willingly took a risk and encouraged us all to follow suit. Once again, she proved both firm enough to keep the pressure on and sufficiently relaxed to convey the impression that I would know when the right time had arrived! This unusual amalgam of attributes turns a publisher's deadline into an opportunity. To successfully copy-edit a book with so many contributors demands the clinical equivalent of simultaneously monitoring more than 25 pulses. Yet Helen Skelton achieved this with ease and still remained cheerful, efficient and unruffled.

There is, of course, one other acknowledgement to be made. Though, in a sense, it is implicit in the very title of the book. Shakespeare, and all that he stands for, actually 'came' to Broadmoor many years ago. In an existential sense, he has been there all the time. But our deepest acknowledgement is that his influence, through rehearsal and performance, workshop and informal discussion, gives his words from *Troilus and Cressida* a heightened meaning. In the pages which follow they will be invoked again:

'One touch of nature makes the whole world kin'

(III.3.175)

In an inspired moment in 1876, thirteen years after Broadmoor received its first patients, an American Shakespeare scholar and enthusiast, Joseph Crosby, changed one word in this line, so that it reads:

One touch of Shakespeare makes the whole world kin

(Velz and Teague 1986)

Murray Cox
Editor

The Friends of Broadmoor Hospital

As previously stated, the actors performed free of charge and in their own time. From the earliest negotiations about publication, it was agreed that any royalties should go to appropriate charities.

The charities originally decided upon were as follows:

1. The Friends of Broadmoor Hospital

2. Charities directly linked to the Royal Shakespeare Company and the Royal National Theatre

3. The Institute of Dramatherapy

As the day for publication drew closer, the hospital became an even greater beneficiary than before, as both theatre companies generously agreed to donate their proportion of the royalties to The Friends of Broadmoor Hospital. It was stipulated that such royalties accruing should be directly channelled into funds connected with the furtherance of drama, music and other creative arts in Broadmoor Hospital.

That the actors came hither has been of enormous help to the hospital, in so many ways. It seems fitting that such an act of generosity should not take place 'behind the scenes'. On the contrary, it should be publicly acknowledged in these introductory pages.

Horizons of Possibility and Ethical Boundaries

The publication of a book of this nature opens up extensive horizons of possibility. It represents a confluence of two major realms of discourse, these being the world of drama and, in particular, Shakespearean tragedy; and the world of psychiatry and, in particular, forensic psychiatry and psychotherapy (see Appendix A p.253).

Ever since the idea was born, there has been considerable pressure from non-clinical colleagues to 'be courageous'. This tends to imply the detailed description of the way in which various individual patients responded to the psychological and physical proximity of enacted tragedy, especially if their 'index offences' matched, say, Gertrude's poisoning or the enucleation of Gloucester's eyes. But such disclosure – even with the signed consent of named patients – would run directly counter to all the tenets of clinical confidentiality. These can never be less than important. But, for obvious reasons, they need to be jealously guarded in a special hospital, such as Broadmoor, to an absolute degree. In my view, there is nothing negotiable about this position. Furthermore, opinion about in-formed consent may change over the years; whereas a book, once publish-ed, does not. This book will inevitably attract a wide readership, for a variety of reasons. And even at this early stage, the reader will find the question of his motivation coming under the audit of self-scrutiny. The search to identify patients by name-hunting in the index will prove abortive, and the voyeuristic, the prurient and the salacious will remain frustrated. But those interested in the creative potential of drama in a secure therapeutic setting will find much to think about.

The *raison d'etre* of this book is clear and unambiguous. Yet it needs to be stated that it is neither a text-book of forensic psychiatry nor one which comes under the capacious umbrella of 'Shakespeare studies'. Both fields are already over-flowing. Though, should it come to a competition, Sha-kespeare would easily win. I have it on the good authority of Susan Brock, librarian of The Shakespeare Institute, The University of Birmingham, that there are now nearly 5000 Shakespearian publications each year! (see Appendix B p.259 for reference to an interdisciplinary meeting on Shakes-peare, Psychiatry and the Unconscious.)

This book exists primarily to set on record certain crucial events which transpired when two worlds met. The horizons of possibility seemed almost infinitely extended when, for a brief period, 'the other side of the wall' and 'the other side of the footlights' seemed to merge, so that both location and perspectival worlds were reversed. Such standing in the shoes of 'the other' when it is both transient and reversible, can be looked at from two points of view. Clinically, it is one of the necessary hallmarks of empathy; a *sine qua non* of all psychotherapeutic work. Dramatically, it is in line with Gloucester's injunction to Edgar:

> 'Set me where you stand'

> (*King Lear* IV.6.24)

Many who attended the performances did not send in written comments. Their reticence must be respected. For this reason, there was no hint of any formal 'follow-up' in the form of structured interviews or questionnaires. Nevertheless, we are all indebted to those performers and patients who felt able to say something about the impact made upon them when Shakespeare came to Broadmoor. We have been given so much. The rest that is silence must remain so.

These pages will tell how Hamlet's description of the actors took on a startling new relevance. As far as their time in Broadmoor is concerned, they indeed became 'the abstract and brief chronicles of the time' (*Hamlet* II.2.520) thus providing a unique and eloquent voice with which to report [the] cause aright to the unsatisfied.

Murray Cox

Style and Notation

A large proportion of the book is devoted to interviews and unstructured comment. I have tried to balance the need to convey the staccato, off-the-cuff quality of dialogue, with a presentation which is both readable and untiring. The interviewers had a free hand to write as they wished. Some of their questioning is explicit. Some is implicit.

I have adopted the conventional mode of gender reference. 'He' can refer to individuals of either sex. I would equally willingly opt for 'She' embracing he. But he/she, his/her on each occasion is tedious. It ruins any sense of linguistic cadence and referential rhythm. In a book on Shakespeare this is *anathema*. Imagine:

> 'He/she that outlives this day, and comes safe home,
> Will stand a tip-toe when this day is named,
> And rouse him/her at the name of Crispian.'

> (NOT *Henry V* IV.3.41)

The Arden edition of the plays has been used throughout, apart from Chapter IV.2.ii 'That Secret Voice' by Cicely Berry, who used the Penguin edition. Detailed references to quotations have usually been given, except when they seem to disturb the flow of a sentence, and have already been quoted.

Although 'audience' is a collective noun, it sometimes seems more natural to speak of 'their response', rather than 'its response'. This was a chosen occasional option and not a sign of editorial neglect.

Prologue

'How these things came about'*

Murray Cox

This book sets on record a significant event. Or rather, it takes note of the beginning of a series of events. For reasons which I do not entirely understand, it feels right that these opening lines wrote themselves at Stratford. As far as Broadmoor Hospital is concerned, this is on the other side of the wall. Furthermore, the date of their writing is important, it being a Sunday morning in May 1991. This is two years to the day since Mark Rylance – who was currently playing Hamlet – had casually remarked over a cup of coffee: 'It would be good if we could bring *Hamlet* to Broadmoor'. That was how it all started. That, in brief, was 'how these things came about'. We had met at a symposium in Stratford. Little had I realised, as I prepared a paper entitled 'The therapists are come hither', that it would lead to a meeting resulting in the decision that 'the actors [would] come hither', the first 'hither' referring to Stratford, the second 'hither' to Broadmoor.

Here is Shakespeare in Performance with a difference, the unusual feature being that it is concerned with the performance of tragedy which is both setting-specific and audience-specific. In *Players of Shakespeare* (Brockbank 1988a, Jackson and Smallwood 1988) players were invited to describe how they approached a particular interpretation. In the present volume players and directors describe how they approached their already well-established roles and productions in a particular place, before a particular audience.

These pages attempt to convey an impression of all that went on, in 'the hatch and brood of time' (*II Henry IV* III.1.86), before and after Hamlet Day (6 August 1989).

---

* (*Hamlet* V.2.385)

But most of all, they hope to present something of the kaleidoscopic impact of Hamlet Day itself, and of its liberating effect on the creative life of the hospital. For the insurgence of the *Hamlet* company and its non-judgemental energies opened doors of possibility which have not closed. They came as an approachng tide shortly to fill the hospital's reasonable shore.

Admittedly, the 'phone message I received from 'The Gate':

'The actors are come hither'

(Hamlet II.2.388)

had been rehearsed. Though no amount of preparation or rehearsal could possibly have predicted all that ensued.

Was this enterprise taking too many risks? Was it to be a once-off, isolated special occasion? What kind of preparation would the patient-audience need? Would the actors need a mirror-image briefing on the other side of the wall? And, if so, what would the briefing be about? Should weapons be used? Could *Hamlet* be *Hamlet* without weapons? What kind of special security measures, if any, would be necessary? What about props and costumes? What about blood – albeit 'stage' blood? What of the attention-span of chronic hospitalized psychiatric patients? What of the period language? What of the possible representation in the 'dramatic mode' of life-and-death events from episodes in the personal 'clinical mode' memories of the audience? What of the physical and psychological proximity of performing 'in the round', with little opportunity for mem-bers of the audience to take refuge in the safety of distancing? These are a few of the questions which were endlessly discussed in both formal meetings, and casual encounters, on each side of the wall.

A brief glance at the contents page will indicate that other days also acquired new assignations; as *Romeo and Juliet*, *Measure for Measure*, and *King Lear* followed in *Hamlet's* wake.

What, frighted with false fire?*

After weeks of indecision, it dawned upon me that I had been 'frighted with false fire' when it came to preparing this prologue. The mountains of books on my desk had grown higher and higher as the day to begin writing approached. After all, it was no small challenge to attempt to link Shakespeare studies and the psychology of performance, or to try to weave theatre and therapy into a purposeful pattern. How great was my relief when Prospero caught me surveying the scene and whispered:

---

* *(Hamlet* III.2.260)

'What see'st thou else?

(The Tempest I.2.49)

It was not only into 'the dark backward and abysm of time' – time without limit in a special hospital – that I had been peering, but also at the overwhelming everlasting now of unfolding therapeutic possibilities. Prospero reassured me that the heaviness of endeavouring to link such topics as psychiatry, psychology, psychotherapy, theatre and tragedy could become a 'heaviness that's gone'. He made me realise that my task was to introduce a book which described 'happenings', occasions and, above all, events. Remembering that an event is a 'coming-out'. And a great deal came out of the coming-in to Broadmoor of a group of actors from the RSC.

I also seem to remember something else he murmured, about *Macbeth* and the 'seeds of time'. Perhaps he also pointed forwards (it is now 1991) towards *Scenes of Madness: A Psychiatrist at the Theatre* (Davis 1992).

Metaphors Competing for Attention

Knowing the plays, knowing the audience and having carefully read and re-read the 'several tales', that constitute the substance of this book, there is a bewildering array of major metaphors which permeate the whole. Some are unavoidable because of their familiarity and specific relevance; such as 'To hold as 'twere the mirror up to nature' (*Hamlet* III.2.22) or 'Is there any cause in nature that make these hard hearts?' (*King Lear* III.6.75). Others seem so surprisingly up-to-date; such as object-relations theory – the dynamic psychological emphasis currently in the ascendent – finding its roots in words referring to Cordelia: 'She, whom even but now was your/best *object*' (*King Lear* I.1.213). Or again, audit, the topical ubiquitous preoccupation of professional, administrative and commercial enterprises finding its roots in language about Claudius: 'How his *audit* stands who knows save heaven?' (*Hamlet* III.3.82).

Nevertheless, it seems to me there is one metaphor which could be mutative. That is to say, one metaphor which could change our perception of what took place when Shakespeare came to Broadmoor. Taken together, these sequential performances became a non-judgemental transfusion of life-giving energy which flowed into the hospital. At this point, I have in mind a question I was asked by the *King Lear* cast during a pre-Broadmoor discussion at the National Theatre:

'What's in it for them?'

I replied, among other things, that it could never be wrong to be present during a performance of a great tragedy, such as *King Lear*. Great art must ultimately be its own justification.*

The performances would be 'straight' dramatic performances, with only the minimal necessary modifications dictated by the unusual features of the setting. They would be 'therapeutic' in the widest possible sense, in the way that all creative arts tend towards healing. And, though linked, they would not assume the more focused and professionally controlled 'modes' of therapy such as dramatherapy, (see p.229), or psychodrama (see pp.201,205). And I spoke of the numerous beneficial sequelae to Hamlet Day, which these pages will recount.

What is this metaphor which seems to thread its way throughout the four 'Broadmoor' plays – which we tend to regard as four tragedies? Wherever *Measure for Measure* is formally placed in the Shakespearean canon, it certainly has much tragic material. The interview with the director (see p.97) shows how difficult it was to speak some of the lines, while being aware of the offender-patients in the audience. And all the actors knew that the members of the audience must come within this category. Though they knew no more – 'Seek to know no more' – is a *Macbeth* echo and an imperative here. Our major metaphor is already implicit in this paragraph. It is perhaps epitomised in the *Hamlet* closet scene, when Gertrude says:

'Thou turn'st my eyes into my very soul'

(*Hamlet* III.4.89)

Turn, turning – (and other variants) – and eyes feature prominently in each play. The turning of the eyes into the soul is a paraphrase of how the play-within-the-play will catch the conscience of the king. Eyes, blindness and eyelessness, sight and insight, vision and foresight, hallucination and imagination are all interwoven. And eye-contact features prominently in many of the actors' comments.

Psychologically, it is easy to reflect upon the way in which the play-within-the-play-within Broadmoor will 'catch the conscience' of the offender-patient audience. Such is the projective aspect of performance (see p.163). Voyeuristic bells may ring at this point. No-one is immune. 'How his audit stands who knows save heaven?' And the reader of this book cannot escape the self-scrutiny of why *Shakespeare Comes to Broadmoor* has caught his attention.

---

* I have subsequently read *Truths the Hand Can Touch* (Vandenbroucke 1985, 206) and came across this sentence: 'Great works of art are intensely affecting not because they contain something new, but because they create experience anew, thus confirming what is already known somewhere deep within us.'

A Mirror – A Moving Mirror

Clare Higgins refers to 'a very active mirror'. A patient speaks of 'a very strong mirror'. Presumably, a strong mirror can imply both one that is unbreakable and also one which gives a strong reflection. For our metaphor to be complete, for it to be mutative, it needs a moving mirror; a mirror that will turn.

Mirabile dictu, even at this point Shakespeare's creativity does not fail us. The Fool might say *'Mirrorbile dictu!'* Because his intuitive knowledge embraces the understanding that a mirror is something which faithfully reflects or gives a true picture of something else; something worth imitating. He would have guessingly known that the French and Latin root of 'a mirror' is both 'to look at' and 'to wonder'! We do so with special intensity when Shakespeare comes to Broadmoor. Taking a look at the four Broadmoor plays from a more distant perspective, we find these words in *Julius Caesar*:

> 'And it is very much lamented, Brutus,
> That you have no *such mirrors as will turn*
> Your hidden worthiness into your eye,
> That you might see your shadow'

(I.2.54)

The Mirror-Globe: 'Such Mirrors as will Turn'

Hamlet's famous metaphor of holding 'the mirror up to nature' cannot be bettered. But, for our purposes, its relevance was enhanced by a curious detail of hospital history, which would have 'much amazed' the original architect! On Page 108 there is a description of some aspects of the history and architecture of the hospital. When it received its first patients in 1863, the Central Hall was the main meeting area where all the patients could assemble at the same time. It was here that 'public' announcements would be made and staff meetings took place. In those early days it must have seemed incredible that such a 'congregation area' would subsequently be used for regular dances. More particularly, it would have 'defied augury' to have imagined that suspended over the central dancing area would be a 'mirror-ball'. Such an object certainly dates its installation; it almost sounds as though 'disco-dating' is a new scientific technique, alongside carbon-dating, for ascertaining chronological precision! Though it certainly has another connotation, nevertheless, for those not familiar with these things – and this prologue is concerned with how these things came about – such an object as a mirror-ball needs to be described. It is a spherical, multi-faceted mirror, approximately 18 inches in diameter, which is suspended above the dance-floor. Whenever the DJ wishes, it can be made to rotate so that the multi-coloured lights, which are aimed at it from a variety of projection points around the hall, can bathe the entire area in all the kaleidoscopically changing colours of the spectrum.

If ever there was a tailor-made metaphor, this was it. Because, on Page 116 the reader will learn that *Hamlet* was performed 'in the round'. This meant that the centre of the acting area was, *ipso facto*, usually the centre of the dance floor. In other words, the mirror-ball was suspended immediately above Hamlet's head. More precisely, when he was speaking of 'holding the mirror up to nature' he did so beneath the myriad mirrors of the mirror-ball. The mirror with multiple moving faces seemed the precise psychological metaphor. Within the hospital the mirror-ball is also sometimes described as the mirror-globe. This, because of its multiple-connotations, is an even better Shakespearean refinement. When *Julius Caesar* offers us a reference to 'Such mirrors as will turn', we could not ask for more. We all see ourselves – from every possible angle – in the mirror that will turn. Such is Shakespeare's capacity to make us reflect upon reflection.

Images of the eye, looking and reflection abound in both *Hamlet* and *King Lear*. Hamlet's words to his mother 'Look here upon this picture, and on this' seem peculiarly apt. And their significance is intensified by the multiple reflections possible in the mirror-ball. But before Gertrude is made to look upon the picture of one husband after another, Hamlet has already offered her a mirror where she may see 'the inmost part' of herself:

> HAMLET: Come, come and sit you down, you shall not budge.
>   You go not till I set you up a glass
>   Where you may see the inmost part of you.
>
> QUEEN: What wilt thou do? Thou wilt not murder me?

> (III.4.17)

Whether or not a particular production chooses to use a real tangible mirror, or whether the whole scene is construed as a metaphorical mirror, there is no doubt that she found herself before 'a very strong mirror'. Words which we shall encounter (p.135) are forcefully resonant at this point:

> All of a sudden [Hamlet] opened doors I preferred to keep shut. And from that point I encountered the turmoil and struggle with things that in the past I've buried.

When Hamlet's terrified mother shouts – or whispers in frenzied fear – 'What wilt thou do? Thou wilt not murder me?' she demonstrates a reaction which is so often encountered in forensic psychotherapy. I refer to the fact that a potential victim will often name the attack which is presumed to be imminent ... 'You're not going to rape, strangle, murder me ... ?' Sometimes this can stop a potential assailant in his/her tracks. Sometimes it serves as a spur to action. There are echoes here from the end of *Othello* when Iago's wife says 'And your reports have set the murder on' (V.2.185).

What we see mirrored in this mirroring scene is the way in which Hamlet is making his mother see 'the inmost part' of the memory from which she has turned away. There are many clinical parallels here. This exemplifies Shakespeare's paraclinical precision – a theme to be explored in *Shakespeare as Prompter* (Cox and Theilgaard,1993). It is a huge metaphor of seeing and reflecting on reflecting (Pines 1982).

In the productions at Broadmoor we were asked to 'look here upon this picture. And on this.' And beneath the mirror-ball one wondered if the 'distracted globe' could contain so much? This phrase may refer to the globe of Hamlet's head, 'Whilst memory holds a seat/In this distracted globe'. Today our clinical concerns often centre upon the adequacy of the cerebral hemispheres. But we also speak of the ocular globes and the orbits. Which, by association, takes our thoughts to Gloucester's eyes and the cosmic chaos of Lear's extremities. When he rejects Cordelia, he swears in the text 'By all the operation of the orbs/From whom we do exist and cease to be'. He remembers Gloucester's eyes 'well enough', even though the only place they could exist is in his memory. And his memory was patchy, inaccurate and failing. He confessed to Cordelia, what she had known from the beginning, that her father was not in his 'perfect mind'. Whereas *Hamlet* is set in a specific location – even though Hamlet's Elsinore is not recognisable from the geographical description (see p.171), in *King Lear* the location is not 'local'. The scene of greatest disturbance is on 'a heath'. A subsequent scene is in 'Another part of the heath'. Perhaps not a long journey from a broad moor. Or another part of a broad moor. Perhaps on the other side of the wall. And even stage directions have a curious ambiguity. 'Storm still'. This could mean a continuous storm or a storm which has become still.

Our mirror-globe, the distracted globe, the orbs and the orbit, and the huge container of so much lived and unlived life brings us, in this associational flow, to the great globe itself; the great predecessor of Broadmoor's Central Hall, The Globe Theatre situated on the South Bank near Southwark Cathedral.

But to return to the beginning. What was the aesthetic imperative that called for these early pages to be written in Stratford, within a few yards of the doorway through which Shakespeare went to school? One of the reasons is that there seems to be a particular blending of inner and outer worlds, of fact and fantasy, past and present, actor and character, personality and role persistently present in the streets of Stratford. Yesterday I bumped into Falstaff in a pub and chatted with Prince Hal in a doorway. Or was it Robert Stephens and Michael Maloney? Yet it is encounters like this which serve as constant reminders that there is always 'the other side'. On Hamlet Day the other side of the wall, and the other side of the footlights took on a new meaning for a while. And the theme of 'the other side' is one which will permeate these pages. Hamlet is Mark Rylance, just as much as Mark Rylance is Hamlet. Mark says (see p.29), 'He, (Hamlet) wanted to go and see if he had brothers there (Broadmoor)'. And this brings us to mention Becker's (1963,33) notion of the 'controlling identity', which is a sociological term for an aspect of an individual's identity which seems to over-shadow other personal attributes. It was extended by Matza (1969,160) to include 'ancillary identities'. Thus, to say 'I met Hamlet in the Post-Office' would convey certainty, about a recent encounter, to a fellow member of the audience. Meeting Hamlet implied meeting Mark. Because, in the world of the theatre, roles influence recognition. Such controlling identity for an actor may be transient, or enduring, depending on the run of the play. But Becker's original description was in relation to those whose deviant behaviour had been defined by a controlling identity: a rapist, an arsonist, or a man or woman convicted of homicide. This means that, for example, Bill Brown has the controlling identity of being a rapist. He may also be an excellent father, a poor singer, a first-class tennis player, but his controlling identity – which tends to determine how others perceive him – is that of being a rapist. One of the poignant facts of working in a secure hospital such as Broadmoor is that 'the index offence', which influences the 'controlling identity', is often evidence of a minute fraction of all the life that is Bill Brown. For obvious reasons the ominous significance of such offences must never be trivialised, though it is equally ethically essential that the horizon of therapeutic possibility should not be restricted.

Among the many enriching aspects of Shakespeare's legacy to us is the fact that he rarely over-emphasises the 'controlling identity'. He tends to offer us the whole person, for better or worse, so that his characters are neither wholly good nor wholly bad. Taken together, they usually represent the 'centre' of humanity, from which, individually, we all deviate in our own idiosyncratic way. The following phrase once arose casually, *en passant*, in a group therapy session:

People like us . . . and that means everybody.

Did this refer to everybody in the group, everybody in the ward, everybody in the hospital, everybody in the South of England? Or was this a
statement about an essential aspect of humanity, so that everybody means
exactly what it says? It is reminiscent of Falstaff's:

> 'Banish plump Jack, and banish all the world'.

> (*I Henry IV* II.4.479)

Such a comment has many implications about individual similarities and
differences, about 'perspectival worlds', which imply that everyone sees
the world from a different point of view.

We have now considered some aspects of that which is normally kept
at a distance from us 'on the other side of the wall'. We have observed that
this may be an architectural wall designed to enclose 'a place of safety'. It
may also be a psychological wall by which we distance ourselves from
that of which we would prefer to be unaware. We may be frightened of
what may lie on the other side of the wall. We may have an ambivalent
attitude, taking the form of wanting to know about that area of life of
which we would prefer to be ignorant. A voyeuristic impulse may confuse
our motivation and make us doubt even our best intentions. Above all,
our appreciation of that which lies on the other side of the wall will make
us aware that much of our own experience also lies on the other side of a
psychological wall. The experience of being put 'in touch' with one's
feelings is both part of psychotherapy training and part of the psychotherapeutic process itself. For psychotherapy can be defined as 'a process in
which the patient is enabled to do for himself what he cannot do on his
own. The therapist does not do it for him, but he cannot do it without the
therapist' (Cox 1978,45). Referring to psychotherapy, Kathleen Raine has
observed 'The experience of the arts is, after all, the more ancient avenue
to self-knowledge' (1976). It is for this reason, above all others, that the
opportunity of experiencing great drama, in the heart of the hospital, was
an almost miraculous possibility for all those present to take advantage of
this 'ancient avenue to self-knowledge'. For a time, the wall seemed to
cease to exist from a psychological point of view. Paradoxical and illogical
though it is, both 'other sides' of the wall met. It was a moment in time
(*chronos*) which was the right time (*kairos*). So that W. H. Auden's (1976)
words about the other side of the wall were strangely appropriate:

All the rest is silence
On the other side of the wall;
And the silence ripeness,
And the ripeness all.

(*The Sea and the Mirror*)

So much for walls and such mirrors as will turn. Our gaze is now upon the *Dramatis Personae* who will herald the things which came about.

Broadmoor and Stratford

I

Dramatis Personae

Introduction

Dictionaries and reference books are in broad agreement about the nature of the *dramatis personae*. Some draw distinctions between the characters themselves and a list of the characters in a play. Some point to a secondary reference under the heading of 'Cast List' which supplies the actors' names. Sometimes a wider frame of reference is implied so that *dramatis personae* includes all those assembled for the performance. In other words, it includes both the actors and the audience. All are 'persons of the drama'. For reasons which are self-evident, it is clear that from the beginning of the performance on Hamlet Day to the final words of *King Lear*, there was heightened reciprocal interest between actors and audience as they engaged in the dramatic space within Broadmoor Hospital. All in Broadmoor are 'persons of the drama'. We shall look at the general theme of the place of drama in custodial settings in Section IV. But now our attention is upon the Broadmoor audience, those who played the title roles and those directors who were able to be present in Broadmoor during the performance. Unfortunately, Terry Hands who directed the RSC *Romeo and Juliet* could not attend the performance, though we corresponded about the production. He was concerned to establish the fact that such a visit would 'help [therapeutic] work, properly and profoundly'. It is not easy to resist extensive quotation from a recent book which deals specifically with the topic of theatre audiences. Indeed, its title *'Theatre Audiences: A Theory of Production and Reception'* (Bennett 1990) is of great interest, even though there is no specific reference to the general issue of drama in custodial settings, or the more specific topic of the performance of tragedy to psychiatric patients. However, bearing in mind the nature of the present volume and the fact that the reader is about to learn about the Broadmoor audience, the following quotation from Bennett creates a tension arc of augmented anticipation:

> The spectator comes to the theatre as a member of an already-constituted interpretive community and also brings an horizon of expectations shaped by ... pre-performance elements – or, as Herbert Blau describes it: 'An audience without a history is not an audience' (1987: 34) (149)

Such a sentence is steeped in allusive implication, for the Broadmoor audience will not only be an audience with a history, that is to say it will have a history of witnessing previous productions in the Central Hall; but each member of the audience will have personal memories re-ignited by that which is presented to him. Though this applies to any theatre audience, it takes on added significance for both patient and staff witnesses to the play within the hospital, and to the play-within-the-play-within-the-hospital.

The Broadmoor audience being an 'interpretive community' when witnessing tragedy is a statement which almost defies commentary. *Res ipsa loquitur*. These things speak for themselves.

Writing of Shakespeare's technical skills, Honigmann (1976,15) says 'Shakespeare exercised his skills . . . as an "impressionist" artist: like Bacon he understood perfectly "what things are to be laid open, and what to be secreted and what to be showed at half-lights".' He ends the chapter by referring to Shakespeare as 'an expert in half-lights'. This comment serves, with precision, to throw lights and half-lights upon the response of the audience to that which takes place before them. Dramatic space and therapeutic almost coalesce at this point. At times even a half-light is disconcertingly exposing. At others it is insufficiently illuminating. In the interests of clarity Claudius calls 'Give me some light. Away.' And Polonius shouts 'Lights, lights, lights' which sometimes becomes a cry on behalf of those too disturbed to speak. In a subsequent passage Honigmann observes 'even when revealed spontaneously the inward self only reaches us in refracted glimpses, inferred from the emotion that bodies it forth'(15).

'Half-lights' evokes an echo from a poem by Yeats which refers to dreaming and ends with the line 'Tread softly because you tread on my dreams'. Always a cautionary reminder to a therapist.

This is another bridging metaphor – and *metaphor* means that which 'carries across' – between the aesthetic world of poetry, the aesthetic/action world of drama and the world of psychotherapy which endeavors to link the inner and outer worlds of the patient. Dreams, the process of dreaming and all the other attributes and reservoirs of unconscious life are the 'hatch and brood of time' and the working place of therapy. In one sense they are closely linked to the aesthetic and romantic connotation which Yeats' poem invokes. Yet such associations may also be far removed from the central significance which dreams and fantasy life hold in psychotherapy. Here they may be concerned with the many-headed hydra of destructiveness, fear or the three root causes of anxiety described by Tillich (1952,50); death, guilt and meaninglessness. Yet Shakespeare's paraclinical presence enables an individual member of the audience to face his own music in safety. He helps us to adjust the half-light to a level which illuminates adequately, so that exposure only occurs when the patient is ready for it. So much so, that when the time is right, he actually invites it. Watching a play allows us to recall personal tragedy (as either agent or victim), so that we learn how much of our hitherto banished experience we are ready to tolerate.

The links between the *dramatis personae* of dramatic spaces and those of therapeutic space are brought out by Pedder (1977). He refers to the necessity of ensuring 'that there is a safe space' (219) in both theatre and therapy to allow play to take place. Indeed his play opens with an exploration of 'common links between psychotherapy, play and theatre; especially *where* they take place and what *conditions* are necessary to bring them to life' (215). (See also Pedder 1979 on Transitional Space in Psychotherapy and Theatre.)

Beckerman (1990) in *Theatrical Presentation: Performer, Audience and Act* has this to say on 'Actor to Audience':

> while the audience may accept any fancy thrust upon it, unless that fancy catches the audience at a subliminal level, it will not take it to heart. Indeed, the most effective communication with the audience occurs when it is accepted for itself and not asked to assume a persona. (127)

There can be no doubt that the Broadmoor audience was 'accepted for itself' and, because of this, 'the most effective communication' ensued.

Pfister (1988,37) has written on the social psychology of collective reception and observes that 'the collective aspect increases the intensity of the reception.' This was certainly true of the Broadmoor audience. He also comments on 'the intuitive, rhythmic form of synchronisation between actor and audience' and 'the effect of the audience's reactions on the production itself'. The ensuing pages amply support these observations.

It is on this audience that the curtain now rises.

M.C.

The Audience
Broadmoor Patients and Staff

Trevor Walt

It was the afternoon of Sunday 12 September 1971 and it was my first experience of employment at Broadmoor Hospital. I was then a student psychiatric nurse, with dreams and aspirations of a successful career in mental health, who had been drawn to Broadmoor by the chance sight of an advertisement for nurse training which had been placed in a national daily newspaper. Twenty years on, my employment record remains unbroken, even though, after years of working as a student nurse, qualified nurse and teacher of nurses I now, amazingly, find myself as whole-time Church of England chaplain. I have had, during the last 20 years, the great privilege of working with, and for, both patients and staff. And now have an even greater opportunity – that of relating to the whole hospital community, at every level, as pastor and counsellor. I aim to minister to all patients, all staff and their families; indeed, to all the people of Broadmoor. So who are they?

Those Who Enter Centre Stage

Broadmoor exists for the detention, care and treatment of approximately 500 men and women who are mentally disordered. They have been judged by society and due process of the law as being a danger to others. Our Victorian professional predecessors were quite clear in declaring their purpose in creating an asylum, not a prison (no prison of the same era compares in design); but a place of ultimate refuge for those found to have committed serious crimes whilst influenced by mental disorder and requiring long term care in a secure setting.

During the almost 130 years since its creation, Broadmoor has undergone many phases of change and development. There have been great advances in the development of specific psychiatric treatments, including the selective use of medicines; there have been many changes of nursing strategy; there has been much development and updating of mental health legislation. Socially, the hospital community has evolved as part of, yet set apart from, the wider community of Crowthorne. However, Broadmoor still exists and has maintained its central function of providing a refuge for those who are severely ill and are exhibiting dangerous behaviour, related to or caused by mental disorder, which warrants detention within a secure environment.

The facts leading to each individual admission to Broadmoor Hospital will often have horrified the local community in which the patient lived or in which an offence may have occurred. Each patient's admission will have given the local, and often the national media a great opportunity to report the human suffering both of the patient's family and that of any victims involved. Exploitation is an ever-present risk. This may also lead to the patient being shunned, not only by society, but also by his or her own family.

Broadmoor patients come from all social and ethnic backgrounds, all walks of life, all adult age groups and all levels of intelligence. On admission, many are found to have long and complex histories of a gradually developing mental disorder, while others may have suffered a sudden onset of symptoms which have quickly and dramatically changed their behaviour. Most, but not all of the patients have committed criminal offences whilst being disordered in mind. Crimes range from relatively minor breaches of the peace to the most serious and horrific offences against the person. Many patients have been the subject of front page newspaper headlines. In our society, there is a popular view that the average Broadmoor patient is nothing less than an evil homicidal maniac or child abuser, who should be hanged or at least locked away for a very long time. Someone who should be incarcerated, not cared for, a worthless human life with no hope. Someone who is beyond rescue and for whom rehabilitation is an impossibility.

In reality, Broadmoor is indeed a place of much hope. It may often be clouded by the uncertainty of an individual's ability to reach sustained improvement. Nonetheless, a hopefulness exists which is plainly evident amongst patients, their families and the staff who care for them. Broadmoor is not an evil place. It is a veritable storehouse of human tragedy, aiming to offer solace, care, treatment and the hope of eventual rehabilitation to those who pass through.

A Broadmoor patient is a person whose very being, often already disrupted by painful life experience, has been broken by the intrusion of mental disorder. Such disorder has led to behaviour which is dangerous, violent or criminal. However socially unacceptable this may be, it still remains within the bounds of human brokenness. Broadmoor's function is to restore and rehabilitate those with broken minds, in the same way that a general hospital aims to restore and rehabilitate those with broken bodies.

If all the world is a stage and Broadmoor part of it, then those principal players, the patients, who enter centre stage, are those who may have played leading parts in previous tragedies. Broadmoor is a place, where, with time and support, many of these players may be able to look self-critically at earlier behaviour with a view to making radical revisions, before future performances on the stage of life.

Those Who Enter Side Stage

Broadmoor Hospital employs approximately 890 men and women of many disciplines and grades, with job titles essentially those of any health care facility. Although the hospital environment is surrounded by obvious physical security, there are no staff who are employed directly and solely for the custody of patients. Contrary to popular belief, there are no prison officers (Broadmoor is not a prison) and no guards. All staff, whatever their disciplines, carry security keys and have the dual function of the designated job and the maintenance of necessary levels of physical security in the hospital.

The hospital is managed by a general manager and a team of directors with their relevant support personnel. The treatment ethos of the hospital is based on a multi-disciplinary approach, with teams of professionals, led by a consultant psychiatrist, working together to assess and meet the individual needs of each patient. The care-giving staff are supported and serviced by a full range of ancillary staff, all carrying out essential tasks for the benefit of all.

Staff are attracted to work in Broadmoor for a variety of reasons. Professionally qualified staff may be attracted by the particular challenges posed by the patient group or by the possible personal development and training opportunities which may be gained from work experience in a secure psychiatric hospital. Some staff may have been attracted by the prospect of a secure job or a career change in mid-life, having been made redundant elsewhere. Some work for a few months or years and leave for pastures new, while others tend to stay for long periods of time and become integral parts of the living history of the place. Most are drawn to

Broadmoor with a clear and genuine desire to be gainfully employed in rewarding work. As in every other place of employment, some would admit to working simply to pay the rent.

However, the vast majority of staff have, within them, a firm foundation of care values which is reflected in their consideration of employment at Broadmoor at all, let alone their ability to stay for any length of time. All members of staff, at some time, will have met someone who will have declared 'I don't know how you could work in a place like that. I couldn't.' Whatever personal motivation there may be, each individual member of staff has chosen to work in the hospital and consequently meets the fundamental employment criteria of being able to accept equally its purpose and the people it cares for.

All members of staff will admit that, because of the closed nature of the hospital, they went to work on their first day with apprehension, a fear of the unknown. Wise and experienced staff will also admit that, however confident and relaxed they have become, they could, at any moment, find themselves in a volatile and frightening situation, due to the unpredictable behaviour of a patient in their care.

The largest group of staff employed are psychiatric nurses. There are 530 qualified nurses and nursing assistants who effect the greatest part of the direct care given to patients. They are both agents of treatment and custody. Although there are times when these two roles may directly oppose one another, nurses are able to develop and maintain excellent therapeutic relationships with their patients. As the average length of stay of patients is measured in years rather than weeks, nurses have great scope for relationship development and a 'primary nurse' system operates. This ensures that each patient has a key worker to relate to, with regard to his or her individual plan of treatment. These same nurses, if and when necessary, need to be able to quickly control any dangerous or violent behaviour with the minimum of intervention, and without compromising the therapeutic relationship in the long term. Nurses are expected to be compassionate in their acceptance of those whose behaviour and mental state has led them to be found unacceptable by society, non-provocative in their application of control and diligent in their attention to physical security.

If all the world is a stage and Broadmoor part of it, then the staff are those who enter side stage and play a variety of supporting roles – some prominent, some less so, but all crucial to the plot. Good supporting actors are those who by both performing at their best, and becoming an integral part of the setting, provide the backdrop against which the principal players will do well. Good principal actors are those who recognize the full benefits of a good supporting cast. Such is the relationship between Broadmoor staff and their patients. Each is dependent upon the other.

Those Who Come to Watch

In addition to the patients and staff, there are many others who come to Broadmoor to watch and thus offer 'audience participation'. Large numbers of patients' relatives visit the hospital day by day, providing a vital link between the patient and the outside world. Equally large numbers of professional visitors of all disciplines are in constant attendance to carry out the specific tasks related to the work of the hospital. Many people from the local community of Crowthorne have strong relationships with the life of the hospital. This is seen particularly in the work of the League of Friends which, among many other activities, provides a visiting service to patients who have no family contact. All these people provide something of a live audience for the hospital's performance.

This audience effect is magnified by the constant attention of the local and national media. Because of its closed nature, Broadmoor, like its sister hospitals, endures the pressure created by the microscope of media attention; a pressure which is corporately felt and absorbed by staff, patients and their families. Broadmoor is a refuge set apart and established by the public conscience, although it is always subject to public scrutiny.

If all the world is a stage and Broadmoor part of it, then those who come to watch are those who come to support the cast or to adopt the role of amateur or professional critic.

Epilogue

These, then, are the people of Broadmoor as I perceive them. Some living in; some going home each night. Some arriving by due process of mental health legislation; some by the provisions of employment legislation. Some receiving help; some giving it. Some wanting to be there; some not wanting to be there. Some experiencing a brokenness and an 'index offence' which most would find difficult to imagine; some – for a variety of reasons – needing to work closely with brokenness and breakdown. Not some, but all being part of humanity. All needing to be there for one reason or another.

If all the world is a stage and Broadmoor part of it, then the people of Broadmoor are involved in the production of a complex human drama, which in itself is just a reflection of the global drama of life.

I - 2 & 3

Actors and Directors

The Royal Shakespeare Company
The Royal National Theatre
Wilde Community Theatre Company

Honesty, Body Language, and 'a different discomfort'

A rapid glance through the first drafts of the interviews with both actors and directors gave unmistakable evidence of a thread of coherence, which through each contribution, and also pervaded the whole. I suppose it is similar to Stanislavski's 'Through-line'. As an editor, I am tempted to keep quiet about this, so that the reader has the chance to see whether he reaches the same conclusion. On the other hand, he may conceivably get more from this almost overwhelmingly rich material, if given some kind of signpost. Perhaps a better analogy is that of trees marked by a colour-code to guide a forest walk. Even then, some of the markers seem bafflingly remote.

Of the many possible opportunities for guided exploration, I have chosen to use only two marker colours.

The first is the colour of honesty. Through direct statement, inference and allusion, the theme of honesty is one which permeates this book. So that Hamlet's question to Ophelia, 'Are you honest?', is one which can be almost infinitely extended in terms of integrity, authenticity, motivation for performing within Broadmoor, working in Broadmoor, being part of the audience in Broadmoor and, of wondering about the honesty or motivation in reading these pages. Even though Hamlet's 'honesty' implied chastity, its wider connotation still holds. There is, however, a variant, on this marked walk. And this takes us to the inevitable paradox of acting, seeming, performing and how this relates to the authenticity of acknowledged pretence. In this context 'pretence' and 'presence' are so closely related. There are also many clinical echoes to be heard about the nature of psychotherapy (see Appendix A p.253). At this point the enigmatic comment of a Finnish colleague, Martti Siirala, comes to mind 'Does the therapist have the delusion of having no delusions?' (Cox 1978,xiii).

The other marker takes us along the route of the direction of gaze. The topic of direct eye-contact between actor and audience is a recurrent theme with variations. For obvious reasons, it was especially significant when members of the audience sat so close to the action, and there was an implicit awareness that their *presumed* predicament might closely match that of the character speaking. This meant that the actor felt compelled to trust the text and the audience to an even greater extent than usual. It also endorsed my impression that actors are always interested in discussing the psychological significance of gaze-patterns and sequences. Shakespeare so often gives explicit reference to such key componants of non-verbal communication as gaze-pattern, so that the text actually directs our attention. The evidence Horatio gives about the ghost is so incredible, that Hamlet cross-questions him. One of his direct questions is:

'And fix'd his eyes upon you?'

(Hamlet I.2.233)

Not a glance, but 'fix'd' eyes.

There are many other facets of body-language description and emphasis throughout the Shakespearean canon. Sometimes sensory modalities are crossed. This phenomenon is known as synaesthesia and the *locus classicus* is in *King Lear*:

'Look with thine ears'

(IV.6.149)

Sometimes motor functions and the voice of the body – always vital aspects of life on-stage – are expressly described in the text:

'There's language in her eye, her cheek, her lip;
Nay, her foot speaks!'

(Troilus and Cressida IV.5.55)

Georgia Slowe (Juliet) said that she was 'aware of a different discomfort' (p.48) when performing in Broadmoor.

Perhaps this phrase is as near as we can get to tapping a seemingly universal stratum of what came to be known as 'the Broadmoor experience'. Virtually everyone present was aware of 'a different discomfort'. Yet inextricably linked with such discomfort was a sense that new doors of possibility were opening. In itself this book is a testimony to this process.

Here, for once, we seem to be reversing Shakespeare's lines. In *Macbeth* we read:

'So from that spring, whence comfort seem'd to come,
Discomfort swells.'

(I.2.27)

But our comfort springs from awareness of a different discomfort. Remembering that com-fort means 'with strength'. Different discomforts speak of honesty and Hamlet's question.

Now for Hamlet, himself.

M.C.

Hamlet and Romeo

Mark Rylance
interviewed by Rob Ferris

RF I understand that the idea of bringing the production of *Hamlet* to Broadmoor was yours. Can you say how that idea first entered your mind?

MR I went along to a Dramatherapy Conference held at the Shakespeare Centre in Stratford where Murray Cox, whom I had never met before, was attending as part of a panel, with Paddy Godfrey, Clare Higgins and myself. We were talking to a group of people there for a dramatherapy weekend. We got talking about how the plays created *catharsis* or healing or transformation, and what our feelings were about this. Afterwards Murray came and talked to me and was remarking on things he had found interesting in the performance and saying how he wished his patients could see it. He told me how some of his patients had written about *Macbeth* for an 'O' or 'A' level exam. In a discussion a patient said, 'When I killed someone it wasn't like that, or it was exactly like that'. In any case, the patient's comment was from his own experience. It was an odd comment the patient had made, very understanding of the play, and I was struck by the notion of an exam paper, with no mark or indication of it coming from Broadmoor, going to the Examiner's Board alongside those of ordinary 15 year old students. I thought to myself – these people really have experienced some of the things that we as actors pretend to do in plays. It is a shame that they are not able to see them. Murray Cox agreed and I said 'Well, we could come to you. It would be good if we could bring *Hamlet* to Broadmoor'. That was all. So from that chance conversation the thing came about.

The play had always worked very well in the dress-rehearsal period in rooms. It worked very well with a big audience also, but I knew that it was actually very good for us as well to do it just in a room. I wanted very much to go to a place where perhaps people's fates are that they descend into some sort of underworld, as Hamlet consciously does, to see what they made of it and to see if the play spoke to them.

RF Having heard Murray Cox express interest, how did things proceed from there, in your recollection?

MR He wrote to me and asked if I was serious. I said 'yes', made some enquiries and asked Ron Daniels and later a company meeting whether the company would like to take part. There was some debate over whether it was a good idea or not. I think there were perhaps one or two people who had a moral reservation concerning whether they wanted to perform for people who had carried out such violence. There was fear on my part as to whether or not we would be patronising them.

RF Did you have a moral feeling about it?

MR No, other than that I wanted very much to go. I think I was excited by the credibility of the audience in a sense. I imagined they would be less than usually credulous. It's lying, basically, acting – we lie and convince other people that we are someone we are not and that we are doing things that we have not done and it's challenging when you have people in the audience who you think will see through lies. It's challenging to make them believe you.

RF So that if you could lie, as it were, tell the very important lies that are contained in *Hamlet*, to an audience like that, the very reverse of a credulous audience, then . . .

MR Then we would feel that we were doing well. It is like robbing a bank, I suppose. We are thieves in a way. We are trying to steal people's conceptions of the limitations of their lives on a certain level. Trying to take away something that is locking someone up, and the more secure that system is the more intriguing it is to see if you can penetrate it.

To go back to the practical side, we had meetings with the company and there was a very positive feel about it. But also a lot of uncertainty about what would happen. To our knowledge, it had not been done before. For instance, we weren't sure whether people would get very upset during the performance. I wasn't absolutely sure of what I felt, but I thought hard about it and decided it would be for the good. I had to do that, I had really to check because, I thought, it's no good to just go in there and mess everything up.

RF So in dealing with those almost clinical anxieties, whether your performance might disturb and upset the audience and be counterproductive, you really left those worries to the people who were responsible for the care of the patients?

MR Yes, I thought we had no power over that anyway.

RF And what sort of response did you get from them? Did you sense that they were in any way hesitant or did they seem unequivocally positive?

MR I only realised afterwards the great debate that had taken place. I heard that some staff had been very fearful of it, but that others had said by all means come and upset the people – the sooner they get upset, the sooner they actually calm down and so can move away.

RF And what did you make of that sort of notion?

MR I could see the sense of it. A lot of things are locked away – you know the first thing is to actually feel the pain of that before it starts to heal, like alchemy. The water is the first thing that moves the hard heart. You have to take the hard heart of stone and put it in some water, in some solution.

Going back to your earlier question again, I remember now feeling that Denmark is a prison and feeling that there was something of Hamlet in me that wanted to go there. There was something – you know, if you do something eight times a week you take on the character's objectives and their desires and passions. They do infiltrate your own life a bit. And at the time I think it was largely unconscious, but there was in Hamlet a feeling that there are brothers of mine there, of wanting actually to go somewhere where there is chaos, utter chaos internally, and so I think in a sense he wanted to go and see if he had brothers there.

RF The part of you that was playing Hamlet?

MR Yes, that sounds mad. I will end up in Broadmoor.

RF Well you did, albeit temporarily. What happened when you got there?

MR Something strange. I was very frightened before we started. More frightened that I had been. Earlier in the run, when it first opened, I would be frightened about whether I would get through it, whether I would be able to do it. That is still to do with the audience, I guess, whether they will accept it and believe it; but this was a different thing. I was very frightened that I would be patronising them and upsetting in the wrong way. You know – they would think, well, who are these actors coming here pretending to be mad or pretending to murder or to rape and to get into that place where I have actually been and where I have actually suffered all this pain because of being there. I suddenly got very frightened about what I was doing. What right had I to come here and portray things like this to people who had perhaps experienced these things in their lives? And that feeling is like a fire that burnt away any excess of ego and all the tricks you would rely on, and I just felt I have to be absolutely honest here. The Hamlet must be absolutely acid, honest. In a sense, out of that fire rose the character much more strongly than I had felt it before and I felt absolutely free, and not there actually myself. It was one of those wonderful moments which I chase after all the time, when you feel you are a conductor and something is coming through you, rather than you are doing anything. And I didn't feel that I had played the part at all. I felt they played it. Something collective came through me, through the words. There was very little 'doing'; the 'doing' got burnt away and there was more being. That was how it felt.

RF So your fear was that they would see through your tricks or pretence?

MR That they would see through my lie, yes. But what happened was the line between reality and fantasy was much more fluid than normal. The amount of belief was much more there than not there.

> 'Foul deeds will rise,
> Though all the earth o'erwhelm them, to men's eyes.' (I.2.258)

I said this line to a man who I didn't know, but who had looked at me with such clarity, with nothing but an absolutely straight gaze. It just felt immediately as if there was a very sensitive group of people there, that one had to tread very carefully and not abuse, not take advantage, just give them it as simply as one could. That was the feeling that rose during the performance and I had a great feeling of suffering and pain that I hadn't experienced before, of torment coming from them.

RF From them?

MR I felt so, yes.

RF But you were somehow able to reflect that back to them or express it in a way that perhaps they couldn't?

MR I suppose I thought that afterwards. I like to think of all the characters in a Shakespeare play as different aspects of one being, as well as different aspects of a society. Usually there is one conscious element, there is one who talks to the audience and who is the audience. He or she is like the consciousness, like the one taking you through. And then there is the higher consciousness or the soul, for example, Ophelia. There is Polonius, the old adviser, kind of the mind aspect, or the analytical mind; there are the king and the queen and the different aspects they reflect. And so you have different aspects of a single psyche, so that when you play the conscious one, it is you who are in a sense the spokesperson to the audience and deciding whether the door is a big door or a little door, or whether it is a little window that would best suit these people to come through. It is as if you are a filter, and though all the characters do it to a certain extent, as the conscious character in a Shakespeare play, you determine the aperture as in a camera, where there is an aperture to get the image to get the story. So you do adjust. I found I got more relaxed about playing the part, I adjusted enormously to the different audiences, because it is a conversation really. If it is just a one-way presentation then it is dull. It is dead, it's got to be a two-way thing. If you have a Saturday-night tourist audience in Stratford, a different kind of performance will get that play across to them. Different from the one we gave in Broadmoor.

RF So you anticipated speaking to this group, who, because of their unique qualities as an audience, might put you on your mettle; might be harsh and unforgiving, might be antagonistic, might be upset . . .

MR Incredulous.

RF Incredulous, and as a result upset and disturbed because of what you were doing. But you didn't find that at all?

MR No.

RF You found something quite other, really.

MR Yes, yes I found something very different.

RF And you realised that quite early in the performance?

MR Yes.

RF So everyone who was there accepts that it was a tremendously powerful experience. As a clinician, I spent a lot of time afterwards trying to understand how it was so powerful, and to a lesser extent why it was so powerful. There is a danger here of trying to analyse something out of existence, of reducing it merely to its elements. Perhaps it is not really a sensible notion to think too much about it, but nonetheless, just accepting for a moment the idea that it was an enormously powerful experience, would you agree with that?

MR Yes, oh yes. It was the most powerful performance of the play I think that I was ever part of. You know plays depend on the imagination of the audience, on the level of their audience; they don't happen otherwise.

RF Does the question of why it was so powerful interest you or exercise your mind?

MR Yes – it's a question I suppose I think about all the time, with every play I do. How to make it more powerful, how to make the experience one of transformation or liberation for people who come. Liberation from whatever thing you might wish to be free of, even if it is just the day's telephone calls. That is certainly what theatre did for me and it saved my life by doing that – not perhaps in a healthy way at first. It freed me of myself in that I found myself.

RF Broadmoor is a place attempting to change people who are defined as being disordered and dangerous in some way, or more particularly, to help them to change so that they may no longer need to be locked away.

MR Now we are getting on to something interesting! How do you do that? My mother is a therapist, so I have some idea about that, of what you actually do. It was interesting when I went back to talk to some doctors there and we got to speaking about the ghost and what you would say to someone like Hamlet who came to you and said he had seen and heard the ghost of his father. The room went very quiet. Is it a hallucination, a disorder? Does the spiritual side exist or not? You tell me. I heard of a man in high security who kicked a steel door off its hinges. Can it just be physical energy that does that? I was just aware that in my view there was a lot of spiritual stuff that was going on there with those people, and that is the level where adjustment is needed.

My point is that in a play, in a fantasy, in a theatre, you can talk about those things and for three hours believe and say that this man is not hallucinating, he is not a fool, believe that he can actually be the hero of the play, in the sense that he is the main character you follow; and he talks to ghosts or, as in *The Tempest*, he has an angel and controls the elements. There are all kinds of spiritual things which in the last 400 years or so we have denied. And so for me, going there is not to do with religion and not to do with the state and all the repression that goes with it. It is to do with this great and amazing libertarian Shakespeare, shaking his spear at ignorance and talking about spiritual things, but in such an Open University fashion, such an open way, that you can take it as you like it. Or, if you want, you can say it is just a play and Hamlet is mad anyway. So you can take it whatever way you want. That is the really marvellous thing about going there, because in my mind there are spiritual things that need adjusting as well as the practical things of how better to order your life.

RF Like getting a job or where you will live when you leave Broadmoor?

MR Yes, things like that. But I think there are actually mythical levels that the plays work on or were constructed to work on to change things unconsciously in people.

RF From my perspective as a doctor, there is a workaday sense in which we look at people's experiences and try to categorise them fairly crudely and bluntly as normal or abnormal, as part of the process of diagnosing mental illness and deciding about treatment. Perhaps it might be said that this process actively avoids the spiritual aspects or dimensions which something like the play taps.

MR I know how to say it. Someone descends into an underworld of unconsciousness; of doing things that we would assume a conscious person would not do, because of the destructiveness to life involved, your own life and others' lives; he descends into an area that we would call mad. It would be enough even in this society to say 'Well, we won't punish them, we will put them in a hospital where they can be cared for in high security'. How do you touch on that area and that fear? I could see that you must talk to people and you must come out of the room and think how can such things happen in the world? How am I going to go home and get a cup of coffee? How do you keep your centre, how do you get out again from touching on these areas without losing yourself as well? That is what I imagined was really difficult. You must actually go down into the underworld like Orpheus, to touch, to get to, to rescue Euridice, to rescue the soul or rescue the heart, the real rational centre that is the heart. So how do you do that? How do you do that without getting lost, without not coming back yourself, with all the dangers that are mythically described in the journey inside yourself? Well, you can do it in plays of course. You could go down there with that character, that part. You could go down there, and be there, and come out. And they can go with you and you can leave them, perhaps, in an area that doesn't make any rational sense.

Perhaps that's why there are so many books written about *Hamlet*; yet none of them could explain what some of the lines meant. It took me eighty or ninety performances before I learnt what some of them meant. Because you could learn it, but you couldn't make sense of it until you experienced it; until you got to a certain point where you were so frustrated and tormented that finally a funny flip happened and you find yourself saying something to someone and realising that's why I am saying it. There is no way you can do it with a dictionary or rational thought. It is only through play that you get there.

RF There are certain lines in the play that have an obvious and particular resonance with the audience, with the patients. Did you find that actually happening during the performance?

MR Yes, funnily enough speeches like 'To be or not to be', which I thought might be very powerful, I didn't feel so much. Some of the exchanges with Rosencrantz and Gildenstern were quite potent there. This speech was amazing too:

'O what a rogue and peasant slave am I!
Is it not monstrous that this player here,
But in a fiction, in a dream of passion,
Could force his soul so to his own conceit
That from her working all his visage wann'd,
Tears in his eyes, distraction in his aspect,
A broken voice, and his whole function suiting
With forms to his conceit? And all for nothing!
For Hecuba!
What's Hecuba to him, or he to her,
That he should weep for her? What would he do
Had he the motive and cue for passion
That I have?' (II.2.544)

Now there is such a weird loop of reverses going on there; me saying that to them – me being a player – about other players. Take some of the letters that the patients sent in; the thinking in them was so amazing, and I thought, reading them, 'Well, my God, the loops of rationalization that were going on in that performance; it's like you don't want to analyse the thing away. They were beyond understanding'. You know there is stuff going on here that is angelic.

RF What do you think that the audience got out of the experience, particularly the patients? How do you think it affected them?

MR I imagine it gave them putty to play with, something to talk about that wasn't themselves and maybe was more liberating than talking about 'Why did he do that?' or 'Why was she like that?' And it was maybe useful in that way, I would have hoped, giving a reference point that is not personal but imaginary, and therefore has no threat in it. I imagine it was something in itself just to feel that we came and gave that performance to them. If I was somewhere like that and someone came and did that for me, I would feel that perhaps there was something good in people or they thought I was worth it. Many people there may feel that they are not very worthy, so I thought that was maybe good, the fact that we came. One of them said to me as I was leaving the curtain call, 'You were really mad – take it from me, I should know, I'm a loony'. I thought it must be odd for them if someone can transform themselves, someone who is not mad, to a level where they look completely mad – well, then, what are the limits of what human being can do? Can they transform? Any play if it is done well, and particularly a Shakespeare play, breaks down our conceptions of the limitations of human beings. You can change. You can be something different.

RF And those human beings, of course, have been judged to have profound limitations, limitations so great that an 18 foot wall is required
to keep them apart from the rest of us. What about, then, the notion of
catharsis, which I have seen described as purgation through pity and
terror. If this is a true description of *catharsis*, then here are people
greatly in need of it. Did you have a sense of that?

MR I don't know, because I haven't seen them so much. I went back to see
two plays that they have put on and we went back and did *Romeo and
Juliet*, so I went back three months ago, I think, and saw a few people.
A few of the patients were very friendly, but then they have always
been friendly, so I don't know if that is anything that is different, really.
I suppose I can only speak about my own *catharsis* which certainly is
happening all the time. It is a very difficult thing to give proof of, or to
give an example. I don't know what evidence I can give you of *catharsis*
happening. It rarely if ever happens in a single moment. I don't think
that we were anywhere near a level of instant *catharsis*. I think the
effects would be gradual and may not be noted, but I would think that
we would be a big step towards balance.

I do think it had an enormous effect on us as a company of actors,
in that there wasn't one member of the company who did not sense in
his or her heart the situation and rise to it, and play with, or attempt to
play with, as much honesty as they could muster. But it wasn't that
situation alone which made it. That added to lots of things that we as
a company had gone through together. What it means, I think, is that
when you come to experiences of trouble or things that might fracture
or separate the company, the bond is stronger – to bond together as a
group. Maybe it has that effect also with reality; perhaps when you see
a play and in fantasy go through experiences in the play which are
horrific, as they are in *Hamlet*, if you then were to come to that situation
in reality, you could have an experience or memory that would help
you from fracturing or separating. It might give you a unity somewhere
that may make you feel more conscious and balanced in a frightening
situation.

I think that the plays were structured on the same principles as the
old plays of the mystery schools in Greece and Egypt, in which initiates
into the mysteries would go to a temple and not be shown the plays so
much as actually go through experiences set up for them. *The Tempest*
describes such a one; Virgil was one of the first people to write about
these secret schools for princes of initiates. I think the wisdom gained
from actually experiencing such things is something of a different order
of knowledge from that obtained by learning about something from a

book. So I think that in a sense that can be a kind of *catharsis*, preparing you perhaps for psychic experiences that will come up in your life, but you will already have been there. That's why I don't think critics have anything useful to say about plays, because they stay in the rational, critical mind and that's completely not the point. The point is to go into fantasy. Then you really want to check that the story you are telling is true, is as true as you can – you know with your heart – to what he wrote. Because then I think you will actually tell a story that is to do with the movement from desires, to thought, to action through death and birth and back around that cycle.

RF And did you feel that it was a good story, a true story that you were bringing and were telling?

MR Yes I did and he – I mean Hamlet – felt vulnerable. I remember the experience of coming into that room, coming in through the little kitchen entrance with a knife behind my back. And Clare, as my mother, standing there in her nightie. I don't know what any of those people did and why, but I am imagining in my mind that there may be someone out there that has been in this position; who has really been here and you just think, 'How am I going to act this?' I felt so responsible. I wasn't sure that someone wasn't going to jump up and say something or shout out, that the bounds between fantasy and reality wouldn't go totally. I wasn't frightened that I would get killed or anything, or that any danger would come to me. It was more like it was a tornado we were creating and wondering whether that would suddenly just ignite.

RF So that was one of the dangers or risks that everyone perhaps felt and to which, in retrospect, we overreacted as the responsible clinicians, though perhaps understandably.

Something else that strikes me, as a doctor working in Broadmoor is the profound and deliberate way in which society has set the patients apart. It is said to them, 'You will not do, or this will not do – you are a disordered person – you are dangerous – you are violent – you are beyond the pale – and you are going here'. So the barriers between them and the rest of us are very great and one constantly has a strong sense of these barriers. But to me, one of the things that the performance seemed to do was to strike them down. Maybe because of who you are – and the part you were playing particularly – the barriers between you and them were not perhaps as great as they are for other people.

MR They had so much within themselves that they couldn't control, but they seemed very loving people. I didn't talk to all of them, of course;

there were only 80 or so. But they just seemed ordinary people and that was something I had imagined but hadn't experienced until then.

RF Maybe you were more or less confirming something which you felt or expected already. But I think for other people, for all sorts of reasons, those barriers are very real. They need to be real. And one of the things that the play did was to show that, at least in fantasy, they can be removed and nothing terrible happens.

MR Absolutely. In that imaginary world, nurses, audiences, actors, everyone joins in the world of Elsinore for those three hours, to the varying degrees that they want, but especially the patients. There were very few people sitting about, eating crisps, making fun, or taking it down. Everyone was in this world which is a place where anything can happen without disastrous effect.

RF That reminds me that some of the performers said afterwards that they felt the audience to be the most attentive they had perhaps ever experienced. What was your feeling about that?

MR There was no gap between their attention and ours – I felt they were as much players as we were. Usually, the concentration of the actors is very strong; but their concentration was equal, if not more so, to what was happening. Normally, the actors lead an audience, of course, by their concentration and, through the actors' imagination, the audience takes part. But their imagination was so strong, that it was for us to let go of – our holding on – our belief that this was just a play, just a performance. We had to say 'Hell, let's go there, let's go with them because they are going'. It seems that when you come from a child to an adult, your imagination comes that way too, you get more solid – the longer you act the easier, perhaps, it comes to just simulate the game, rather than play the game; and I think that was nice for the actors to say 'What's the point of simulating, let's play'.

RF Was it their imagination or their memory of psychological places they had been, because of the things they had done and the disorders they had suffered? Why was their imagination so powerful?

MR Well, of course, they are bound there by society because they have gone across certain boundaries that you and I might not cross. Or haven't crossed yet, other than in our minds perhaps, of murdering someone or burning something down or raping someone. They have actually crossed that boundary and done it, so they already have experienced what it is to have no boundary. Maybe they had things happen to them when they were children that crossed boundaries so their imaginations are already freer. I think that, perhaps because of their experience, that's why they were able to go there. I don't know.

RF Theatrically speaking, you have talked about the effect of the performance on you and the rest of the cast. What was the carry-over to the rest of the season?

MR It was awful going back to Stratford after that. It was awful going back to the audiences. They felt much more in prison, the audiences, funnily enough, in Stratford. You felt they were more into the material aspects of having a drink, of having a night out, of coming to the theatre. I always imagine that you are talking to people on the level on which they want to communicate, and that is fine; but it was difficult after Broadmoor, where we thought we had had a wonderful conversation. There was much more to talk about in this play in a funny way and it was like people didn't want to talk about it at that level. They wanted something different. Of course that is a projection onto the audiences, but I just kept in my mind the imprisonment of those people in Broadmoor. The harshness of the fate of being a 'curséd spite'; as in the line in Act I:

'O curséd spite, that ever I was born to set it right!' (I.5.189)

That's the situation that Hamlet is in. Not all those patients were in such a situation, but certainly they had been handed hard fates in terms of life. Maybe they had made bad choices, but I wouldn't think they were easy choices and probably they are learning more from this life because of it. But Hamlet has actually got to organise some harmony out of all these different sides of himself, who are the different characters in the play. A lot of them are going to have to die for him to be able to go on into a new hopeful situation, the marriage of the man of action and the man of thought. And he really is handed by his father this terrible anger and depression and he has to deal with it. I suppose I felt that at a more profound level, having met people and feeling such sympathy or empathy for the fates that they have had to deal with, the situations they have had to deal with. They were given no escape from that; they had to be there in that hospital until they faced themselves. There are little things that I find hard to face about myself, so I suppose I felt that I could play more truthfully and if you give up on something and say 'What's the point of playing a part truthfully?', then it is very difficult to do it eight times a week. I got the feeling that I owed it to these people to tell this story truthfully, to play this character of Hamlet truthfully, because it's them, it's their character.

RF And of course it is everybody's story. Yet you still had a sense back in Stratford that the people in their comfortable lives weren't so attuned or ready to hear it, or in need of hearing it perhaps.

MR Well you just come out and I suppose you think of your own self-righteousness compared to people who are locked away or incarcerated. The company felt there was a lull about performing back there at Stratford, after the buzz of performing in front of the Broadmoor people who were spending their whole lives – well, eight years on average – dedicated to looking at themselves, and to getting over the grief or taking responsibility for themselves, which is so often what the Shakespeare plays are talking about. It was difficult after that to go back to people who were not; whose lives were dedicated to making enough money to go on holiday.

RF That's very interesting. As a clinician, the principal problem for many of these patients seems to be that they can't or won't face up to themselves and take responsibility for what they have done. Maybe because they are too ill or disturbed or whatever – the fact is they are not doing it. And that, in many instances, is the reason why many of them stay so long, because in order to leave they must do that to some extent and be seen to do so by us. The problem is they are not being honest; maybe for reasons that are all too understandable because many of the things they have done are absolutely awful. We watch and wait for some evidence as time goes by that they are facing up to themselves. We attempt to help them to do it but generally that task in a place like Broadmoor is a difficult one. If you went to the hospital ordinarily you would see them day after day and sometimes you could talk to them once a week and see them set in that comfortable routine and find and see no evidence of that sort of facing up. In contrast, the play, through the telling of that story seemed to have a remarkable power to get people to look at those things. It is difficult to over-emphasise what a dramatically different atmosphere was generated by the performance in comparison with daily life.

MR Really?

RF Of course you have to work there and see the play to realise that, but that is undoubtedly true, I think.

MR We added some lines to the performance at Broadmoor. We added the full apology to Laertes. It stayed from then on and made an enormous difference, because it is his one redemptive point; the fact that he takes responsibility. It is such an amazing apology, it's worthwhile quoting it:

'Give me your pardon, sir. I have done you wrong;
But pardon't, as you are a gentleman.
This presence knows, and you must needs have heard,
How I am punish'd with a sore distraction.
What I have done
That might your nature, honour and exception
Roughly awake, I here proclaim was madness . . .
Who does it then? His madness. If't be so,
Hamlet is of the faction that is wrong'd;
His madness is poor Hamlet's enemy' (V.2.222).

I kneel to him and he has this terrible thing of being bound to kill me. But he accepts my apology. He has all this trouble about doing it or not doing it. It is terrible for Laertes, that thing of taking responsibility for himself. Hamlet is someone who loses himself so much, but comes back and gains such wisdom from that experience. He does gain good from it and is able to go into his fate as someone who can deal with these things that his parents created, without fear of death. He goes into the duel, saying: 'Now I am ready, I would do what I am expected to do – I know the king has set it up – I know that they are going to kill me. I won't run away from this. I'll go. I will do what I need to do.' – and he does. So that was a profound thing for me playing it there.

RF Were there technical problems involved in the performance there for the company? Or was that small space in fact an advantage from a purely theatrical point of view?

MR Well, from the start I had not wanted it to be a blocked production. I wanted everyone to feel free to move in different places within the limitations of the objectives of their character, not to get into visual patterns. Of course we did fall into certain patterns, but they came naturally rather than being imposed. We were perhaps a bit loud at first, because we had been playing in a 2000-seater where a lot of energy was needed to fill that big memorial theatre. It took us a little while to come into the space properly and not just blast it. It was very shocking to turn to someone no further away than you are and speak to them and see all their faces; after I had been talking for a whole summer to people I could not see and people who generally needed more of a pull into a different reality than this particular audience. In fact it was more for me to join and just say 'I am here too'.

RF What about the question of weapons? There was a lot of discussion about the use of weapons and the use of stage blood, and in the end certain things like blood were omitted.

MR Well it was fine. You can rely more on imagination. It didn't make any difference to me. What was nice was that everyone didn't wear their full costumes. We wore just bits of our own costumes and bits of our own clothes. That is all you have to work on – your imagination and your experience and so that's what makes it wonderful. Every different production is the bits that people have brought of themselves; some people playing more boldly than others, others following a traditional line. Everyone does different things; so it was nice to see the characters wearing partly their own clothes.

RF A bit of the honesty peeping through. This is me, these are my clothes.

MR Yes, it was much more informal. It was nice also that there were some understudies, as some people couldn't make it that day. Russell Enoch, who played the old king, couldn't make it and the understudy gave a wonderful performance – better than he had ever done before, and that was very nice.

RF What about the workshop? At the end of the performance the play had finished, there were interesting group conversations, but then the actors just went away. It seemed that people were unhappy to leave things there and that was one of the reasons why the workshop happened. What would you say about that?

MR Oh, that was marvellous, yes. That was a very good experience. The thing I remember most about it was doing the graveyard scene and allowing everyone to take part, and just to imagine they were part of the society of Elsinore and had come to the funeral of Ophelia. It was an improvisation with the lines and we said, 'Come and stand around and imagine you are present and you haven't been there before and react - if you want to say anything or do anything, just go ahead'. One person fainted, I think, and sat down in a chair. There was an amazing moment when I said to Laertes:

> 'I lov'd Ophelia. Forty thousand brothers
> Could not with all their quantity of love
> Make up my sum' (V.1.273)

and one of the patients stood forward and said 'I believe you'. And it was extraordinary because my heart really choked up and tears flooded into my eyes and I thought – oh I really needed someone to say that. I didn't realise how much I needed to be believed. I thought about it afterwards and I always felt in that scene, when playing in front of an audience, while saying that line, that the women in the audience must think that I am such a prick. I had been so awful to the feminine in this play – to Ophelia, to Gertrude. I have transferred so much shit onto them and been so unreasonable with them and the feminine side of myself. I always expected someone to stand up and say 'Fuck off, you self-indulgent little bastard'. I jump into the grave, having already killed her father and led to her accidental death; then, to jump in and claim that I loved her more than anyone – I always found it difficult to play that. As myself, Mark, I felt 'How can you say that?' So when this man stepped forward I felt yes, only someone like you would understand. Perhaps that is part of why I wanted to go – or Hamlet in me wanted to go; a feeling that people would understand. If anything, Hamlet wants to be understood. He makes great efforts towards the audience in order that they understand and that he himself understands what is happening. So that was quite wonderful, that moment. Funnily enough, that was one of the lines that many people asked me to write down, immediately after the performance, too.

RF Some months later you came back and did *Romeo and Juliet*. Are there any comparisons you would make between the two productions?

MR One thing I wanted to mention. One of the doctors was sitting with three of her patients watching *Romeo and Juliet*. Before the fight scene with Mercutio and Tybalt, Mercutio describes three reasons that one might kill a man: because the bows on his shoes were not the right colour, or because he woke your dog up or because he insults your clothes. Now I was told that the first of these patients had killed a man because he had taken some shoes back to a shop and the guy had refused to give him his money back; the second had killed a man because of something to do with his dog and the third patient had killed a person for the third reason; and so the play went; bang, bang, bang. The doctor came up to me and said 'Did you change the play, did you rewrite it?' I said 'No' and she said 'You have done in a moment what couldn't have been done in years of therapy. I couldn't have spoken so directly to them and shown them the outcome of temper'. It was quite extraordinary.

[*Editorial Comment*. During Mark's initial visit to the hospital, we crossed a rather grim, high-walled courtyard which separates two buildings. I have never heard anything good said about it; until Mark spoke there. 'Couldn't we perform here in the open-air? The acoustics are terrific!' As an example of 'selective perception' this could not be bettered. M.C.]

Juliet

Georgia Slowe
interviewed by Ann Barker

AB Taking Juliet to Broadmoor unearthed for you preconceptions – and perhaps prejudices – that you did not realise were there?

GS It's embarrassing to have to admit it; I didn't realise I had the prejudices. One never likes to think one does have them. But judging by my reaction when I got there, I suppose I must have had, otherwise the experience would not have felt like a revelation.

Broadmoor is a place that has infamous patients, names we all know, people that you have seen written about as 'monsters' in newspaper headlines. There is a line in the novel *Silence of the Lambs*, where the FBI chief says to the Jodie Foster character, 'I want you to go in and talk to Mr Hannibal Lecter', and she replies: 'Ah, Hannibal the Cannibal'. Then comes the line: 'There was a brief silence that always followed that name in civilized company'. In 'civilized company' there *is* a sort of morbid fascination with notorious characters. So I suppose that one of the preconceptions, the fears and anxieties, I had before I went there, was that it would be humiliating. I was anxious that perhaps the men would think we had come as voyeurs, to get a cheap thrill like watching a horror movie; I thought they would view us like that and that would be humiliating for us and for them.

Nothing could have been more different. It brought home just how much rubbish we are fed by the gutter press. We only ever see headlines that read 'the monster who did this', or 'the monster who did that'. We never hear about why someone ended up in a situation like that, and what happened to them to become the person who could do this. Not hearing anything about their lives and background makes it difficult to feel any sympathy for them, or even to think of them as human beings to be related to. Somehow no one ever seems to show any curiosity as to why the person should behave like that. When you read in a newspaper of just the event, without any of those personal facts, the person who was violent is portrayed as just a monster, not as a human being at all.

I suppose going to somewhere like Broadmoor and actually talking to the patients, right at the beginning, was the most extraordinary thing about the whole day. We sat down, had a cup of tea, and chatted about this and that; they asked questions and we answered. It was a normal, completely normal, tea-time situation; memorable for being in Broadmoor, but in any other way entirely unmemorable. And what was 'scary' about it, in a very different way, was the realisation that people who end up behaving in such ways are no different from you or me. It was the circumstances, or something they lived through, that trapped them in a situation, where in the end, they behaved in that way. People aren't born murderers or whatever; it is something that is forced upon them by situations that they have to live through. I suppose it was a little unnerving to see that 'normality', and suddenly to lose the assumption that anyone who is capable of such violent behaviour is instantly recognisable.

All the people I spoke to when I came away, friends, asked, 'Was it depressing, didn't you come home and feel miserable?' I said 'No. I was very heartened, because I didn't expect to see all the care that I did see'. I didn't think of it at all as a hospital before I went. I thought it was a sort of excuse; you read that it's a 'cop out', sending a person to somewhere like Broadmoor, or 'he should have been thrown in a prison'. We are lead to believe that it is a prison where life is made just a bit easier. I came away realising that it is basically a secure hospital.

It looked a lot nicer than I had expected: I expected it to be a lot more depressing. I especially hoped that it hadn't been cleaned up or done up for us. [It hadn't! M.C.] I think the thing that affected me most was the atmosphere. A place can be painted with flowers all over it, but if the atmosphere is depressing it will be a depressing place, like some children's wards in hospitals. Broadmoor didn't have an 'atmosphere' and it certainly didn't have the atmosphere I was dreading. Afterwards I told one of the actors who did not come for that reason how wrong she had been: it had been a most heartening day.

In particular, the grounds are beautiful. I remember talking to one of the doctors, who told me how he used the beauty of the landscape in his work with patients. He would speak of time in terms of springtimes with the flowers blossoming, and the autumns with the leaves falling. We became very aware of the language we were using, and the care that was taken not to talk about the place as if it were a prison. I was aware of what words were used, and how no one talked about cells or guards: it was striking how the words like doctors, wards, nurses and patients, made it natural to view Broadmoor as a hospital, rather than the prison I had thought of before.

On arrival, I think the thing that made the strongest impression was the lack of door handles. When we walked in I immediately became aware that there were no door handles; with that came the thought of living every day in a place where you don't have the choice about whether to open a door or not. But I suppose I had imagined more evident signs of security, and I was very pleased to find that there weren't any. When you arrive in certain countries, for example, there are men walking about with big guns, and you are so aware that someone might get shot. Things look somehow uncontrolled when all the signs of security are visible, like a panic situation. I thought Broadmoor had a feeling of being secure, with a security of a much higher level, because it is so ingrained into the daily life that you don't actually see it.

Another thing that struck me was how extraordinary the nursing staff were. They were jolly, without being jolly in a sickly way. They showed genuine kindness to the patients, and we often saw the patients and nurses talking together in a completely relaxed and informal manner, without the enormous barriers between them that I would have anticipated. I wouldn't have thought that they could have been friends with each other, or take on a paternal role, like the father that the patients might not have had. There was a joke at the end. When it was time for us to leave, one of the nurses asked: 'Right, who would like to go down to the gate now?' One of the patients put up his hand and said 'Me please', and there was a lot of laughter, with genuine good humour. There didn't seem to be any resentment that we were coming in from the outside world, with our nice jobs and our preconceptions about how they live, to look at their lives for a day, and at the end of the day to get in our cars and drive back to our homes and families. I had assumed that going home would be really difficult; and it wasn't; they joked and laughed about it. That feeling of closeness added to the feeling of security and safety about Broadmoor.

The patients' need for security came across clearly to me, especially from talking to a man I met at tea. He was going to be moved, and was worried about leaving. He had earned a certain amount of respect at Broadmoor; he had a job and was allowed to earn money, and to spend it in the shop as he pleased. He could walk around by himself in the gardens, and was given errands to do. He was very proud of the respect he had earned, and worried about having to start all over again in a new place. I asked him how it would be if he were free to walk out on to the street now. He told me: 'I'm sure I'm institutionalised, I've been in institutions all my life. I'm sure I'll learn to cope, but I'm not ready now; I would feel frightened and vulnerable and unsure of myself'. He was quite aware that he was not ready to walk out, and wouldn't have wanted to, which I thought was marvellous because he obviously had a great deal of self knowledge, and the years at Broadmoor certainly had not been wasted. I later found out why he was at Broadmoor, which didn't affect how I felt about him at all. I liked him enormously and it seemed to me that what he had been through had led him into a situation which must have been quite unbearable. I think if I had been told what he had done, and never met him I would have come to a very different conclusion. Of course I prefer to believe I wouldn't have been prejudiced, but I'm fairly sure I would have been.

One instant really stuck in my mind. Jenny, who played the nurse in *Romeo and Juliet* is a very tactile and maternal person with lots of children of her own. She was in conversation with someone, and a patient came up to her and asked her if she would like a cup of coffee. She turned round absent mindedly and stroked him on the arm, saying 'No thank you, darling', and then turned back to her conversation. She would automatically treat everyone like that. I was behind watching the man, and it was his expression that struck me, when this lovely maternal woman stroked him and called him 'darling' in an absent minded way; it was just a wonderful expression. In that moment it struck me, that had he had Jenny as his mother, he might never have been in there; his whole life might have been very different. Meeting people, talking to people, realising what they had done, and to some degree getting a glimmer of understanding why they had done it, was very important. With that glimmer of understanding came an enormous amount of sympathy and regret that something need never have happened, and the realisation that it had happened because of the way we live our lives in this country, and the kind of times we live in. I think that understanding was something that I picked up during the day, and I don't think I would have picked it up in such a personal way by reading an article or seeing a documentary. After talking to a few of the patients, and realising what their background had been, I became very aware of the fact that *they* were victims, victims of the situation they had grown up in. One young man I met had been brought up in a home and had never had a family of his own, and had eventually been kicked out at 16 or 18 and left to cope with difficult emotional problems on his own. He hadn't been brought up to understand the values necessary to live in the world with other people, or understand about relationships and responsibility. He had somehow shifted the responsibility and blamed everybody for the pain he was in, living his life with no home and no love and no security, and he obviously built up a huge fear and anger. That made me realise that it was not just about their victims, but about the patients being victims as well.

Meeting the people in that room, talking with them, suddenly realising they were people, normal every day people, who get up, brush their teeth, have breakfast and all the rest of it, and that they weren't born with a label saying 'I want to grow up and kill someone for no reason whatever', did very much to close the gap between the 'us and them'. You assume that you will never find yourself in a situation you could not control, or that you could not control yourself. You might get angry and wish you could throw an ashtray at someone, but something stops you, because you know that at least three-quarters of your mind is telling you not to be absolutely ridiculous, that you can't do it, that it's not done. Meeting those people closed the gap between us and them, with the realisation that it is possible suddenly to lose the three-quarters of your mind that tells you that you can't do something; and that loss of control need only last for a moment. Being out on the streets a few days later, it struck me that there must be so many people out there that get no care or attention, and maybe their moment will come, when they are going to lose that ability to control themselves. Those people will be in the situation that these patients found themselves in a couple of years ago, before they found themselves in Broadmoor.

That performance of *Romeo and Juliet* in Broadmoor was our last performance together as a cast. I felt uncomfortable and vulnerable for some time in that performance. It wasn't a feeling of physical vulnerability, because as soon as I stepped into the hospital all my preconceptions of axe-wielding murderers had begun to dispel; there was no feeling of physical danger at all. On one level however, it is such a violent play, very rude and bawdy and sexual: I became aware of myself, my character, as being very young, very sexual, a young virgin in a silky nightgown, prancing around on the stage saying things like 'Oh I want Romeo to make passionate love to me tonight, I wish it were night time now'. Becoming aware of this, I realised that I was doing this speech in front of a group of people who would not have been in a situation in which they might have a normal sexual relationship in years. Maybe even before they had come to Broadmoor they had been unable to have that kind of relationship, and maybe that was part of the whole cycle of their problems. I felt uncomfortable in that situation, feeling that I might upset or embarrass the patients, feeling perhaps like someone flaunting diamond rings in front of someone starving in the gutter.

One line in particular was difficult to say: 'But O, it presses to my memory/Like damned guilty deeds to sinners' minds'(III.2.110). Normally, when speaking that line, I would say it looking one person in the audience straight in the eye. Coming up to that line at Broadmoor, I was aware that I would probably be looking into the eyes of someone who had actually done something fairly awful. And it worried me. I wondered whether the member of the audience would take it as a personal attack, or feel as though I were picking on him or over-identifying with him. Or whether it would upset him. It went through my mind that I should lose the power of the line and just throw it away; then it occurred to me that everyone was there with the knowledge of their doctor, and that no one was going to be there whom the doctors did not think able to cope, so I played the line normally. As it happens, there was no particular reaction. I should have liked to meet the patient afterwards in a workshop situation, to discover whether that line had had an effect on him.

Juliet is a very vulnerable character. She opens herself out to the audience, alone on stage, in many soliloquies speaking directly to the audience asking for their help and advice. In many scenes she is in tears, and there is something so vulnerable about crying in public. Crying is such a private thing to do. From the age of about six onwards we crawl away in private to cry. In Broadmoor there was quite a different discomfort: there was an uncertainty about how the audience would react to Juliet's pain, because the pain of Juliet appearing on the stage must have been so insignificant in comparison with what the patients themselves had gone through.

Perhaps the most disconcerting aspect was that even after well over a hundred performances it was like the experience of a first night. On a first night you don't know how the audience will react. Of course, you know within certain boundaries what the reaction will be. The difference at Broadmoor was an anxiety that the audience would perhaps somehow view us as frauds, or even liars. As actors, we talk all the time about the extreme emotions we are experiencing. The situation in reality, of course, is that most of us have lived through such experiences. We can only imagine what it feels like to be involved in or to witness horrifying violence or death. This applies to most people in an average audience – of businessmen or school children or whatever – they also can only imagine and are therefore more likely to trust our 'truth'. The difference at Broadmoor was that we were performing the play in front of an audience which probably had been through situations as violent, as traumatic and as emotionally fraught as those in the play, and knew what those situations felt like and looked like in real life. The anxiety was that they would know instantly whether we were faking, whether we had missed the mark or were being untruthful; they were able to judge us on a much higher level of truth.

It was in a way a humbling experience, feeling that they might disclose us as frauds. It felt extraordinary to be working in front of an audience that had lived through experiences which would make most people turn grey in an instant. Speaking a lot of lines in the play, in front of that audience in Broadmoor, made you feel that you suddenly understood those lines in a clearer way than before. The verse is beautiful and so explicit, but their relevance to this particular audience made them suddenly shine even brighter.

It was a disappointment to me that we never actually went back to Broadmoor to do a workshop or follow-up. [This was because the company had disbanded. M.C.] I had hoped that through watching us on stage, translating all sorts of complicated and traumatic emotions into beautiful and eloquent language, perhaps one or two people might have come to an understanding of something that they had felt for a long time. To hear those feelings expressed in such language might then have helped them to grasp and understand the feelings. Perhaps in a workshop there would have been others who had misunderstood a line, because of the differences of Shakespeare from everday language, and the cast might have been helpful to the audience in clarifying what the language meant. So it was a disappointment in that we would like to have felt that perhaps we could have ended up helping one or two patients with our performance, with all the understanding we had gained of the play over the last year while we had been performing it. Yet still we did not feel the play was wasted or unused.

I should very much like to go back and do a workshop in Broadmoor; we felt so welcomed into the place. It was extraordinary to see how much care there was; it was wonderful and very heartening. I found it very moving; such moments as when Jenny stroked that man, and suddenly viewing a group of people as victims, and the realisation that none of that need happen if we were all different. It was moving in that way, but not depressing. No; completely the opposite.

I.2.iii

King Lear

Brian Cox
interviewed by Rob Ferris

[The session started with Brian reading passages from his notebook which referred to the Broadmoor visit.]

BC About Broadmoor the company was apprehensive, to say the least. The trip to Broadmoor had been arranged fairly early in the run, and there was a meeting in Paris to remind us that we were going. I got confused and thought they said we were going to Broadway and I said 'I haven't made any decision to go to Broadway' and they said 'But you did'. I said 'No I didn't, I did nothing of the sort. I am against the idea, I don't particularly want to go and I never agreed' and I suddenly realised that they had said Broadmoor and not Broadway! Mind you, there is probably not much difference between them in any event; except that I think the audiences at Broadmoor are slightly more intelligent than on Broadway!

By the time we had done it, it was in the middle of January; we were all exhausted and were playing a pretty heavy session. I personally find Lear, as a part, monstrous; a real monster of a part. It is partly because it is all to do with rejection. And four or five nights of rejection is enough for anybody and I find that really hard. But I think with the Broadmoor experience, especially where it came in the life of the production, it came at a low ebb. Certainly it revitalised the production considerably. In a way the audience was like an Elizabethan audience. It was an audience of people whose brains were so sharp, because their sense of the language and imagery was so sharp. There was one particular line which never got a laugh when we did it in the theatre. In Act I, Lear says:

'Be my horse ready?'

and the Fool replies:

> 'thy asses are gone about 'em,'

referring to the soldiers. So this is a play upon horses and asses and there is this constant kind of counterpoint of imagery; men being asses as well as real horses. In Broadmoor there was a huge laugh and I bet it was completely spontaneous.

I was very much influenced by the madness in *Lear* and the madness in *Titus Andronicus*, which is a play I had done previously. One of the things I came across was how Shakespeare uses madness in his plays; he uses it for extraordinary clarity and it's so clear, it's dazzling, it's bright and it's too much for the eye. And that is why I think that some of the imagery, particularly in *Lear* and in *Titus* and in *Hamlet* gave me the insight into what madness is. Always when you are doing mad people, the biggest difficulty is that they seem to be terribly, terribly clear and terribly logical. What they say seems to have a kind of frightening truth about it. In normal life we build up signals of a conversation; each conversation is codified in a way, you know ... one's behaviour, one's sense of the other person, embarrassment for the other person, caring for the other person. When Lear talks to Gloucester, he has only a single-minded vision of a kind of a corrupt world, which is so clear and so painful and has no pity at all. He is without pity for Gloucester's blindness; a sane person would immediately put on an act of saying 'Oh dear, you are blind, how do you deal with that?' or 'Oh we must help you'; Lear has no sense of that whatsoever. He has no care for Gloucester for he treats him as a seeing person; he does not see him as being blind; because blindness is a state of mind as well as anything else. I sensed the Broadmoor audience had that kind of Elizabethan clarity, a kind of space which meant that everything had an extra reverberation because it was so direct. That is why there was so much laughter, you see. Shakespeare has so much laughter in it and a wonderful kind of bold irony a lot of the time. The fool can say certain things to Lear that nobody else can. He can talk in a certain language which Lear responds to because it is direct, it is savage and it is brutal. It is immediately funny and also slightly off the wall, slightly crazy.

RF But do you think for the modern audience, the London audience that you talked about, you are kind of forced to bend or disguise this clarity and directness?

BC Well, they are not ready to take that. The Lear I did in London was a very contentious performance, because it wasn't a performance that was based on keeping everybody safe. It was challenging, and the London audiences on the whole don't deal with that particularly well.

They want to be reassured. Shakespeare can always be dressed up as wonderful poetry, or wonderful music, or something which has an aesthetic about it, though it also has hard dealings with human behaviour. But they do not like that kind of Shakespeare, they love the lyrical side, they always love the poetic. They don't realise where that poetry comes from.

RF Surprisingly for you, you found that very strange and peculiar audience from Broadmoor to be receptive to those hard dealings of Shakespeare?

BC They brought it out more than any other audience I have ever actually witnessed, except once. This was when I played Macbeth, funnily enough in India, to an audience who were coming at it very much from their culture. The whole idea of 'tomorrow and tomorrow and tomorrow' has, for an Indian, a kind of inbuilt joke about it and it immediately rings a cultural bell for them. That image is alive, but it's not the image that we necessarily intend; for them it has an additional kind of irony. An example of that is when I played the line, when Macbeth says:

> 'But wherefore could not I pronounce Amen?
> I had most need of blessing, and "Amen"
> Stuck in my throat' (II.2.30)

The Indians used to laugh at this line and I couldn't work it out. Then a fellow who ran a design school said to me 'the reason they laugh when you say that line is because they know why you cannot say Amen, and they find it very funny that you don't know! As Macbeth, you have sold out and naturally you have cut any spiritual bond going, by this killing of the King and you can't see that. To them it is a very funny notion that you, this man in the middle of it all, can't see this.'

In a way, I am more interested in an audience's reactions than I am in what we do for audiences. I want to see what they get out of it, as opposed to what we get out of it. I think it is very important to understand what an audience experiences; it does not matter whether it is an audience of mad people, or an audience of sane people. What is actually happening in that process, what is the whole act of sitting watching something about? What is actually going on in you when you watch? Because it can't be just purely about entertainment, it has to be something about expiation. It has to be something which is about taking sins away from you, which it quite clearly was at Broadmoor. When I said 'Is there any cause in nature that make these hard hearts?', one little girl sadly shook her head from side to side in a very painful manner.

RF At what stage during the performance could you feel that sensitivity of the audience?

BC You can tell that straight away. Going back to something like *Titus*, which is so much mayhem, being all about decapitation and rape; *Titus* would have been a fascinating play to do at Broadmoor for the whole experience of seeing how they deal with all that extraordinary violence that is in the play. Cultures deal with violence in their own way, you know. Playing *Titus* in England, we had lots of faintings; one afternoon we had about eight people carried out of the theatre. We actually had somebody die in Paris; a member of the audience died of a heart attack. I only found that out quite recently. There is a particular sequence where I cut the two boys' throats and I had this long speech in which I was threatening them. In England they are always very English, but in Spain the women used to be sitting forward and the men would be like that, there would be noises all the way through, they would be sort of excited. In France there was glee. There was one point when I used to make this gesture, putting a white sheet down on the ground, and there was this extraordinary glee of laughter because they knew what was about to happen; they knew I was going to cut those boys' throats. Then when we went to Denmark, there was a kind of rhythmical clapping and it mounts; but there is no emotion. The way they watched the play was just completely clinical. And it is interesting because I also played the original Hannibal Lecter. I played him as a sort of, well not quite ordinary man. I played him as a psychologist. I played him in a real one-to-one relationship, but he was actually right over the edge in another world. When I played Hannibal Lecter I had people send letters to me on toilet paper, because he used to write notes on toilet paper. It's very interesting, because it is something to do with a kind of primitive element. It's very fundamental and the act of going to the theatre is very primitive; it's very healthy. It is a celebration of the light and the dark forces. And plays, in a way, should be about that struggle between the light and the dark forces, except I want to see it with greater clarity in terms of argument.

RF Plays should be forced to address the ideas?

BC That's right, that's right. Not falling into a kind of spiritual aesthetic, esoteric or poetic trap.

RF But here in Broadmoor you were dealing with perpetrators of violence; serious violence linked with madness or mental disorder as you say.

BC Yes that's right.

RF And here they all are, these perpetrators of very serious acts of violence, which lie in the past, of course. Calmed, perhaps sedated, treated with drugs and so forth. The weight of sin and wrong-doing in that place is enormous.

BC That's right. I find it difficult to clarify that experience of going to Broadmoor. I just knew that something happened. You are dealing with so much guilt and wrong-doing, and some people have got to be less guilty than others. You go back to the question 'What drives them to do what they do?' You know, 'What is mental illness?' My mother had a massive breakdown in her fifties. She recovered well enough, but she was never the same, never ever the same. I don't understand madness and I am not sure that anybody does. I think that is the big bugbear; there is so much trial and error involved in what you do as a profession. There is so much danger in what you do, in order to discover something. So that the act of a theatrical event is dangerous, because one doesn't know. You don't know whether something in that play might suddenly set somebody off.

RF Well of course our anxiety is about that, as you say. Who does understand madness? We are the people who are supposed to be at the forefront of understanding it, and we know how much we don't know. In a sense Shakespeare understands it as well, if not better, than we do. But our anxiety about the dangerousness of putting on the event was of course at a peak before *Hamlet*. We were very hesitant. But as with *Hamlet*, so with *Lear*. It was an enormously powerful and good experience.

BC In the end, the experience seemed to be purging; there was no question of that. It is interesting if you take sports activities; they seem to arouse and can arouse violence. Football and the whole partisan nature of football seems to arouse and hit something in somebody, which becomes very violent. The theatre doesn't do that, because the theatre isn't partisan in that way. It doesn't take sides. Perhaps people in a state of mental disorder have enough clarity to realise there is something being debated there. They don't have a partisan nature or a bias towards it, they can simply be in the middle of the experience, which is difficult in a sporting activity because you are taking a side. You are immediately identifying with one team or another. It is also something to do with plays, like *Lear* and *Hamlet* particularly, because there is something about them which is essentially saying 'life is amazing, life is wonderful, life is extraordinary, life is full of the most amazing mistakes'. But, at the same time as being a celebration of life, it is also a critique of it. These things clearly go hand in hand. And perhaps the disordered mind can recognise that in some way, can actually see those things quite clearly. It is like when you test children for colour blindness with those coloured cards. You throw them down and see if they can see, in the middle of the roses, a figure 4 or 5. Perhaps the theatre is like that in a way for someone who is deranged. There is a kind of clarity about it, there is an ability to recognise the numbers within the roses. To recognise the influences of things which are of a positive nature while all this havoc is going on.

RF What interests me as a clinician, whose job it is to help these mentally disordered and dangerous patients to develop what we like to call insight into the true nature of their acts of violence, is that they often fail in our terms. And yet, paradoxically, in an artistic and theatrical sense they seem to have an enormous ability to appreciate the play and its message, with a remarkable clarity and intelligence. What strikes me is the power of the theatre, the power of the performance to get them, to approach them, to communicate with them. Often, the conventional means of going and talking rationally with them about what they have done, may go on for years without much certain benefit. Yet in a single afternoon I can feel the power of that performance to reach them, and their capacity to respond.

BC That's right. I suppose the nature of a book like this is to try and codify the experience in some way. To try and look at the evidence and see if there is a link. It has to do with the fact that something happens, like why does somebody cry, why has somebody moved? What is the theatrical act about? The theatrical act for me has always been about recognising, sitting in the dark and experiencing. In a way the theatre monitors the other half of behaviour; it is summed up by the line in *Hamlet*: 'the purpose of playing . . . was and is, to hold, as 'twere, the mirror up to nature' (III.2.20). That is what the theatre should be doing. It is precisely why the theatre is necessary in a culture, because it is necessary in terms of how we monitor where we are and what we do. In a situation like Broadmoor it monitors all too clearly what they have done, what they have been through. After the performance a consultant told me that three of her patients (who had had a hand in parental murder) came quite separately to her and said 'I did so envy the ability of Cordelia and her father to have a farewell . . . it made me think about my own situation, particularly before I murdered my parents.'

The British culture isn't very good at expressing itself, which is why we still create this theatre; we always try to express ourselves and this is why we always use the most extraordinary language and create the most extraordinary writers.

RF You say you were sceptical initially; why was that?

BC Sceptical because of the arty crafty nature of things. You see, the thing about actors is that they are whores to experience; they love a new experience, they love it. They get their rocks off on that and I think again you have to be very careful. You have just got to be circumspect in what you are doing and about what you are doing your work for, not just casting it to the wind. It was all justified, the experience was completely justified to me. The response of the audience is what I am really interested in.

RF But even given that you were most concerned about the effect on the audience, you still had reservations about the power to harm rather than help.

BC I think I was proved wrong, and I would be the first to admit it. I think it is dangerous; I felt it was a dangerous thing that one was doing, perhaps simply because Lear personally affected me. Playing Lear I found completely exhausting and knackering – mentally, emotionally, physically. Every way. I didn't enjoy playing Lear at all.

RF And did that get any easier or better as time went on?

BC No. Because you are putting yourself on the line. I remember one time in Japan when I came off stage and said to David Bradley (my understudy) 'You do it, I don't want to do it; you do it'. I always have had an ambivalent nature towards the whole business of acting anyway. My problem is that when I commit, I commit totally and I always give 200%. But as somebody very rightly said, 'You only have to give 100%'. You don't have to give 200%, it is just too much, but that is me, I can't do anything else. Lear is that part. It's a bugger, a complete monster of a role to play.

RF It's a kind of 200% part?

BC There is this old man who survives a storm, survives conditions by which most people would be killed in the first five minutes. But he isn't. He goes right through and he calls on the elements and he is being endlessly rejected, rejected, rejected and that rejection gets to you. Especially if you are, as I am, a relatively old man. All of that, the whole physical demand of the part, you know. I've still got a lot of Lear hanging around me which I haven't got rid of; a sense of physical old age, a sense of my body, all kinds of things which I find a real burden; the legacy of Lear.

RF I wonder if there was anything of Hannibal Lecter still hanging around? That is the part of someone who was very like some of the patients who were in the audience.

BC That's right. Hannibal Lecter's cleverness will not allow him to be cured, because he lives in a world of being clever. He's locked into that. That's where he gets his kicks, that's where his power comes from, and he is not going to let go of his power base. So that, in a way, he doesn't want to be cured because that is what his power base is. It gives him enormous status and credence. These are the truly mad people, the demagoguery of people who have no sense of inadequacy of any kind. I suppose you could say that Lecter was inadequate in that sense.

RF Suppose he had been in the audience; suppose as a member of the audience at *Lear*.

BC I think he would not have been affected by it, unless it was called 'King Hannibal Lecter'.

RF You felt that many of the people who were there were affected by it?

BC I think they were, and also they were people who in a way wanted to see it, needed to see it, weren't doing it out of duty.

RF Well I have to mention a patient of mine; I was talking to him only the other day and he is very interested in Shakespeare. He is a big man with schizophrenia who walks round the ward listening to cassette tapes of Shakespeare, and he didn't go. He didn't put his name down to go to either *Hamlet* or *Lear* and I asked him why. I should have asked him before, and sadly he said 'Oh I would have loved to have gone, but I talk out loud to myself when I am watching things like that' and he was afraid he would disrupt the performance.

BC That's a shame.

RF Yes it is. If I had known that beforehand I would have talked with him about that, and I would have encouraged him to go, because I don't think he would have disrupted the performance and even if he did. . .

BC It wouldn't matter, we would have accepted that. That's very interesting because those conversations should be had – 'Why didn't you go and see the play?' 'What is it that you don't need?' because that also validates the experience. It means there is something precise about these experiences.

RF If nobody wanted to go and see the play in Broadmoor, and furthermore if people who saw it weren't moved and affected by it, then we would all be stuffed, wouldn't we? The fact that they did want to go...

BC It shows the scale and the range of what goes on in that place, in terms of what each individual trauma is. There are people who are obviously the same, and there are people who are vastly different.

BC It shows the scale and the range of what goes on in that place, in terms of what each individual trauma is. There are people who are obviously the same, and there are people who are vastly different.

RF Going back to the performance itself, there is a question that Murray wanted me to ask you and he was referring, I think, to something he had read in your book [*Salem to Moscow: An Actor's Odyssey*]. You have said that at times you felt a text as well written as those of Shakespeare could carry you in the palm of its hand, whereas a badly written text would be like a load on your back. I suppose that the question would be: did you find Shakespeare's language helpful in that setting? Did it carry you in the palm of its hand?

BC Oh absolutely, it certainly does. Because, again, the thing about Shakespeare is the whole hidden dimension, the whole dimension that is very difficult to talk about. It is to do with the musicality of the text. It is to do with the rhythms, the structure of language in relation to its society and how that language carries you. You know when Lear comes on in the third act, and in his madness he talks in prose. In the early scenes, in the scenes with the daughters, he talks in verse, and there are all sorts of good reasons for it. Why verse? Why not verse?

There's a very good example in *Hamlet* in which you can see, psychologically, the basis for types of society in which the characters live. If you look at the way Act III Scene 1 is written, starting at line 56; the scene starts off with Hamlet's 'To be or not to be'; it's the most formal of speeches. It is laying out the true renaissance mind at work, the laying out of ideas of existence in a very poetic and a very structured way. It is incredibly formal and ends with a prayer. Ophelia arrives, and he asks for forgiveness; he is asking for somebody to pray for him. So much of Hamlet, I think, is based in his fears – a fear of damnation, a fear of being lost forever, a fear of losing control, so that the whole control element of Shakespeare is very important.

So Ophelia arrives and she says 'How does your Honour for this many a day'. And then there is this kind of formal dance between them, which is all to do with the world which they are inhabiting, the world of the court. The world that is tight, in which strictures are necessary to dictate its ethics and code of behaviour. It's not even Denmark, it's Elsinore. And it is the court at Elsinore. So there is a very clear way of behaving.

Hamlet, in the middle of that conversation, breaks it. He breaks by saying 'Are you honest?'; then they get into this debate which is prose, so that all the rules are being broken. She keeps trying to pull him back to the verse, pulling to the language, to the structure she understands, to the structure she can cope with, that she can actually inhabit, so that they can communicate. She is trying to find out whether he loves her or not, so she keeps trying to pull him back to the verse. Then at the end of the scene he goes through the small tirade in which he tears his mother's marriage to bits, he tears this relationship with Ophelia to bits, he tears the whole court to bits and he says 'Get thee to a nunnery', and then he says 'It has made me mad'. She then sits down and with an absolutely metronomic beat says:

> 'O, what a noble mind is here o'erthrown!
> The courtier's, soldier's, scholar's, eye, tongue, sword . . .'
>
> (III.1.152)

And you see that this girl is having a breakdown, but she is having it in terms of her own world. Not a breakdown in terms of her under-standing herself. It's a kind of complete fracturing, in which even her fracturing is actually rhythmical. That is quite frightening because, the next time we see her, there is this girl coming in singing bawdy, dirty songs and she is going into some other world. It's like Lady Macbeth; she acknowledged her madness in dreams and sleep-walking. She can't see what she has done. She's got no sense of what she has done. She has got no imagination about killing the King. Her husband has the imagination and the whole sense of it, but she hasn't. She doesn't see it, so it only comes in her dreams. It gets you, it always gets you. It gets you within your own terms of where you are. Where you think you are most safe, is actually where you are most vulnerable.

So that whole code of Shakespeare's is what's so exciting about playing him. Because that's the way the tale is told, that's the way the incantations are made. It's rhythmical and it explodes. It's like clouds going like that and suddenly they crack and there is lightning and thunder. It's elemental, and that is where Shakespeare's language takes you through. If you go into an experience like Broadmoor, the synthesis of the audience picking up on this extra energy, and you allowing yourself to go into the middle of it; this synthesis becomes a helter-skel-ter that's carrying you; you're safe, you can't get thrown off, but you feel that any minute you could and it's quite frightening.

RF Was there any difficulty for you in that setting, in that particular performance, in portraying Lear?

BC It was easier portraying it there than it was portraying it anywhere else. It was the most releasing performance that I have ever had, because it suddenly had a point to it. Because I suddenly felt that I was doing it to a bunch of people that actually understood what Lear's pain was about, whereas I don't, standing on the stage at the National

Theatre. I think that the majority of the audience there don't know what's going on because they are not in tune with themselves. They do to a certain extent, that's why they are there. Ian McKellen says that 'nice' people go to the theatre. Well they do; but sometimes they go on automatic pilot.

RF Your perception then was that the knowledge and understanding coming from the audience was actually informing your performance along the way, making it easier.

BC Making it much easier, and there was a real point to what I was doing, it was an event with a purpose. It was about expiation and it was about healing. That was what was happening – people were being involved, were recognising things, and that made the whole afternoon valid for me. Because in a way, when we had this discussion afterwards, there was no need to talk about it because the real thing was in the event. For me, that never worked, the kind of thing afterwards; it was nice, but I kept thinking and I kept saying 'well what I want to know is what they got out of it?'

RF Did you get any sense of that?

BC Well I got a few things which I quoted already. I think that's what plays do. And what the great plays do is that they show the tragedy of our lives and they show quite clearly where we go wrong. The great plays examine that. How it causes an effect; how we reap what we sow. Hamlet is more a victim than anybody; but he is more a victim of his own control; he has become so in his head that the rest of his body doesn't function properly. But Lear and Titus, interestingly enough, are men who want to retire, want to give up. But there is a bill to be paid; there are reams of bills to be paid and you have got to pay them. Shakespeare, of course, is a moralist in that way. He says you have got to pay these bills, you are not getting away with it. He rubs your nose in it. In the end he does that to Lear, but he also holds his head up and makes Lear find something which is so simple, so extraordinary. It's about death, it's about accepting your end, accepting that in my begin-ning is my end; that you reap what you sow, unless you make amends quickly and make amends in terms of yourself. Actually, it is about finding our own peace, which it must be for those tragic people at Broadmoor.

RF Their failure or inability to come to terms with themselves has put them behind the bars and kept them there?

BC There need to be instances where they can see that happening, where they can see that in a kind of non-partisan way. It must be very difficult in group sessions, if one person lets go, because even then they must feel a sense of question about that person's ability to let go in that way, a sense of envy and a sense of jealousy. But in a play form it is a part of the vocabulary of the play that we are allowed to pretend and that we are allowed to let go.

RF It seems to me that those performances are like a very powerful light that is shining quickly, and briefly, and acutely into the problem, which one can't get away from.

BC I think it is the non-partisan nature of it, I really do. In group discussions, you get the people who are going to excel at articulacy, whereas watching a play is a whole private experience and it is dealing with the individual imagination. It is like an individual search-light going on inside. A light goes on inside and starts going around and around and picking up things. For each individual this is a different kind of process.

RF But paradoxically, it is in a sense a pretence, it's a lie.

BC It is a lie, but it legitimises something. It is allowing something to happen. That is what the theatre does, anyway, it holds the mirror up to nature. I think that Hamlet's advice to the players is worth quoting again, because it is about so much of how we behave, not just in terms of theatre, but in terms of what life is about. We create a form in order to examine a form, in order to examine how we are, how we behave, what we do with one another and the kind of negotiations we go into: the blackmail, the murders, the mayhem we commit through spurious and specious reasons. Hamlet is all about trying to sort that out for himself, to try and understand what the death of his father is all about. He has to go back and sort it out, so he has to devise this sort of play where he can see the guilty person.

RF Well, he gets there in the end.

BC Yes, he gets there in the end. It is all about an event, that's where I get my proof, that's where I can see it, that's where I codify it and quantify it. (Brian then recites Hamlet's speech to the players, III.2.16) This is the really important bit:

> 'Be not too tame neither, but let your own dis-
> cretion be your tutor. Suit the action to the word,
> the word to the action, with this special observance,
> that you o'er step not the modesty of nature. For any-
> thing so o'er done is from the purpose of playing,
> whose end, both at the first and now, was and is to
> hold as t'were the mirror up to nature; to show virtue
> her feature, scorn her own image, and the very age

and body of the time his form and pressure. Now
this over-done or come tardy off, though it makes the
unskilful laugh, cannot but make the judicious
grieve, the censure of the which one must in your
allowance o'erweigh a whole theatre of others.'

RF Were there any other lines? Were there any other lines that you felt different about during the performance at Broadmoor?

BC Yes. When I said as Lear 'Oh, let me not be mad', the way this phrase reverberated around that particular room was extraordinary. I have already mentioned the line in Act I about horses and asses. That was a very funny image. There was another wonderful audience reaction, which was in the mad scene. The audience laughed in a particular way, with a particular quality to it which was quite thrilling. It was the line at the end of the speech which begins 'What! Art mad? A man may see how this world goes with no eyes . . . None does offend, none I say none.' And that was extraordinary when I said that line.

RF Just one last question. Were there any technical problems when performing in that space?

BC No, again, you see it seems to me that theatre is something that happens. It's not about sets. It's not about costumes. It's not about any of those things. They help, they add, they help make an experience, they give it that extra edge, that extra dimension. But it is the interplay between audience and player, the interplay of text and audience. The great thing about going to Broadmoor was the fact that I always wanted to perform it roughly in one setting. I believe in rough theatre, I really do. I really believe that rough theatre is the valid theatre. Lear was a rough production from the word go, and its life depended on its audience. If it was a dead audience, it was a dead performance, because we couldn't resuscitate something that wasn't there. We couldn't give life to something that wasn't there. In Broadmoor you didn't have that problem because the whole event is theatrical. To play to a bunch of psychiatric patients is a theatrical thing to do. It has its own vocabulary. Eighty people gathered with the door shut and nurses on the door, and the occasional psychologist scattered in among them. You know the ground work was already there; when the players come on they have very little to do but just inhabit the language they are dealing with. That is all they have to do, and deal with it roughly; I just played it in a track suit and did it. But they knew. They knew, because their imaginations were so acute.

RF And you reckon they have a special appreciation of the relationship between Lear and the Fool?

BC Yes, I think they did; I think they loved it. They loved that relationship because they loved the companionability of it and they loved the humour; the fact that there is this wonderful old fart and he is being knocked by this rather sharp witty man. It's all to do with authority figures you know, getting put in their places. And of course so much of that is all about authority and struggling and dealing with authority. So much of their pain comes from that.

RF They are locked in a struggle with authority and we, the staff, can't help but represent it.

BC Yes, no matter what face you put on. Whereas the actors come in in a non-biased way.

RF Non-partisan, as you say.

BC Non-partisan is very much the word.

RF Because our relationship with them is partisan, however much we don't like that.

BC That's right; that makes it doubly difficult for you.

RF Indeed.

BC It's a kind of paradox that you inhabit. A very difficult one.

From Gertrude to Regan

Clare Higgins
interviewed by Ann Barker

AB From Gertrude to Regan: we are going to talk about a personal journey for you?

CH Yes; and how taking them to Broadmoor has been part of the whole journey. When I had finished playing Gertrude having taken it to Broadmoor and came straight to rehearse Regan, the experience was so much still with me that it naturally carried on through. *King Lear* seemed to me to be full of Broadmoor echoes which was what gave me the idea that we should perhaps take that too.

Gertrude at Broadmoor is the starting point, because that changed my whole attitude to the play, the character and also, most importantly for me at the time, what audiences were giving actors, and what actors were giving audiences. It opened up a whole series of questions about audience expectations, boundaries between actors and audiences, how to break down those boundaries, and what happens when they go. They are big questions for me, like: Why am I acting? Who am I acting to? Who am I acting for? The distinction between me the actor, and they, the audience affected me on many levels, both acting levels and personal levels. It changed an enormous amount for me in many areas.

Going to Broadmoor, taking a play about madness to Broadmoor, a hospital for criminally insane people, which felt like intruding into someone else's area anyway, seemed to be a strange kind of crossing of the roads, of which I had no experience. I was very frightened about it and I did not know what to expect. Real fears were surfacing about whether they would accept me as an actress, whether they would accept me as a person. Would they take the play and what we had to offer? When we actually got there and the play started, I was in a state of fear that I don't normally feel on a first night. On a first night, you know that a well-heeled audience is coming in to watch you do a *Hamlet* that they are going to be comparing to somebody else's *Hamlet,* and there are a whole series of things that have already been set up: the show is being done for critics, it is being done for success. None of those levels were present at Broadmoor. This seemed to me to be the bottom line. I don't know how long it took for me to realise that the experience we were having was something extraordinary; but a feeling grew for me after I did my first scene, and sat down and started watching, that this was not like any audience I had ever played to: there seemed to be a whole layer of expectations that they simply did not have. And as the play progressed I realised that I was in an arena that was much freer, and it became a liberating experience.

When we got to the closet scene, which I had always felt strongly about – the relationship between Gertrude and Hamlet with its undertones of violence and sexuality, and all the unspoken things that were going on – I was still rather fearful, because I always felt vulnerable doing that scene. To be so vulnerable with those people felt to me to be a risk, a personal risk. There was a question in my mind: Shall we 'take it down', shall we minimise it? I remember going on for that scene, feeling very frightened, and deciding to take the risk. I think it was the best time Mark and I ever did that scene, because we had both decided that we would just go with it.

For me it was a kind of *catharsis* because on a personal level I broke through a barrier. I have always been looking for that point in acting where personal experience and the discipline of work meet and fuse, and it becomes a very energetic and freeing thing. And at the point where Mark took the knife out and threatened me, a lot of things clicked. When Mark had done this in rehearsal, I was not expecting it, and did not know he was going to do it. It triggered something that had actually happened to me in my life, which he could not possibly have known. In the safety of the rehearsal room, after that initial shock, we decided to use it, because you do feed your personal experience into your work. But here in Broadmoor, it seemed that all those worlds came together and fused. I thought: I'm doing this, reliving something that happened to me, within Shakespeare, within the discipline of this production, taking this risk in front of an audience of people who know about it, who may have done this, who may have had it done to them. There was a moment in the scene when something extraordinary happened on a personal level; a bolt of energy hit me in the stomach and I suddenly felt united with the energy of the people in the room. At that point I know I made a conscious decision to use this energy, to ride with it; I also knew as I have not known before or since, that I had absolute freedom yet perfect control over what was happening. And that was a very deep experience.

One line sprang out during that scene: inevitably, 'Alas, he's mad', which I perforce directed straight into the audience with full eye-contact. The freedom of saying that word to people termed 'mad', without hiding, covering up or finding kinder or prettier words, moved me a great deal. It has caused me to think about the word and its implications ever since. I experienced that scene on a very intense internal level. Other lines that struck me with new meaning were not necessarily ones I spoke myself. The lines on madness towards the end of the play: 'Hamlet denies it. Who does it then? His madness. If't be so, Hamlet is of the faction that is wrong'd; It is madness is poor Hamlet's enemy' had been cut from our production, and so it was the first time Mark had spoken them. He has since retained the lines. That was also an emotional moment. Ophelia's 'O how the wheel becomes it!' moved me to tears; it often does. But on this occasion, I had an image of a karmic wheel, with the patients bound fast on it; because in a much less devastating sense I felt I had completed a circle or cycle in my own life during the closet scene, I found myself wishing that others present could break their own circles. Later I thought about what happens to the form of a circle when it is broken and realised that it becomes a spiral, one of the most ancient symbols and methods of raising power and energy. Maybe that is how all that energy became available to me during that scene.

It was also extremely satisfying, because the audience were responding in a way that I long for audiences to respond – in a feeling way, and in a very open way. As we came towards the end of the play, I picked up feelings from that audience that I never usually pick up in the theatre. They simply seemed willing to cross the stage line, and to be part of the play: there was lot of grief in the room, and sorrow and regret, and they seemed to be pushing the play to its conclusion with us. I found it extraordinary, because I don't think many people in that room were intimate with the play, or knew how it was going to end. But they seemed to just roll with it, with us, to the end. It was a beautiful feeling; I have never felt that with an audience before – that all of us together were seeing the play through. I think it was Murray who said at the end 'We are all in one world'.

There was an extraordinary point in the play scene, which for me had never worked in the theatre. It worked in Broadmoor for the first time. Gertrude/I sat on stage being watched by therapists watching patients watching the King and Queen watching actors playing actors playing the King and Queen. There was a moment when the distinctions were so complex that they almost disappeared. 'What, frighted with false fire?' was a line I heard differently; I found myself wondering if the 'fire' was real to everyone watching, or only to the 'guilty', and if the lights demanded by Claudius in response could burn it away or only serve to illuminate it further. And how as audience, both therapists and patients were joined here as observers of this guilt and the method used to try to bring it into the light – Hamlet's rough dramatherapy which again became a mirror of what the whole event was about – *Hamlet* in Broadmoor. It was a powerful experience. And as we picked up on those moments, I think we understood the play better for the first time, on a much deeper level. We were being fed responses that we had never had before, and an understanding that we had never had before. I felt for the first time that I was in exactly the same world as the audience, an experience that I wanted to repeat. The understanding came through a combination of us and the audience; there seemed to be very few of those boundaries that I the actress accept on a nightly basis, and have always accepted ever since I started acting. All the expectations of an audience that has paid to attend were swept away. A paying audience can distance themselves in all kinds of ways, because they have paid, because they have come to the theatre and can go away again, and can either take or leave the play. This time I felt we had left the play in Broadmoor, that it stayed with those people, which is one of the reasons why I wanted to go back.

Another reason why I wanted to return, and particularly to take *King Lear*, was that Broadmoor had made me question what I, as an actor, bring on to the stage. The blinding scene in *Lear* is an example. When we played it at the National Theatre, it was violent and it was vicious because I castrated – ripped a knife up – the servant; that particular action in the National Theatre invariably had a set reaction. There would be a huge response; the audience would gasp when it happened; then there would be dead silence; and then they would laugh. It was remarkable how that response occurred every night. The effect on me as an actor, however, was that I then brought onto the stage with me every night the knowledge of what was going to happen with the audience. That in turn affected the whole situation of the blinding, how it was done, how it was structured, where the energy went, and how we led up to that moment. This is how actors are taught to work. At Broadmoor, however, when that action happened, the response was dead silence, apart from a stifled gasp, 'Jesus Christ'. All the questions emerged again, such as why do so-called 'normal' audiences respond in that way? What is the contract between me as an actor and them as an audience? I have become more aware that when I come on stage, I have already to a certain extent set up what is going to happen for them to have that reaction, because I have already heard that response. The response is, as it were, set up and learned, and of course there are boundaries; because we bring them on with us. I had never realized before how much I stop an audience from freely responding. It is as though there is almost a contract between actor and audience which runs: 'Well, I will do this, and then you can respond like that, but then you can laugh, because we all know we are in a theatre and it is just a play!' At Broadmoor, that 'contract' was completely removed; it was absent. My interest now, from that experience, is to discover as an actor what kind of expectations I am bringing on to the stage and what kind of rules I am setting for the audience.

Sometimes I get frustrated, and feel that we should hire a coach and go back and do it again in Broadmoor. It's a problem because I know that is the way audiences are, and it is my responsibility to try not come on with those own boundaries in myself, those defences. It is my responsibility to resist that temptation of saying to the audience: 'Oh look, a really interesting character has just walked on, and I want you all to know who I am immediately, I want my place on the stage, I want my place in the play, I want to tell you who I am'. One of the best things about Broadmoor was that the pressure was off to tell the audience who you were. At the moment I am struggling with that in my self. It is good because I am checking myself. I am asking myself more questions about why I am doing things on stage, whether it is because it makes me look good, because it is a favourite moment, and what does it tell the audience. I am finding out that a lot of the things I do actually stop an audience from really entering into the play.

Previously I would always make sure that I was safe. If I had a moment while I was having dialogue with another actor, and I didn't have anything to do for a while until some actor came up and talked to me, I would wonder what I could be doing, to cover myself. It would give me a feeling of panic, of having to get from this stepping stone to that stepping stone. Then I wanted to go out there and give them something; I wanted to have it all boxed up, wrapped up with a bow on the top, and say 'Here you are, do you like this?' Now, I want to say: 'Let's open the box and see what is inside'. I see my own defences mirrored in other actors, and I want a way of working that will allow those defences to vanish. It is sad to realise that we drag on an enormous bundle of stuff, build it up into a little edifice, and then present it for approval.

Actors as a group also make those kinds of decisions among them-selves: there are all kinds of defence mechanisms which start to operate as soon as actors begin to rehearse with each other. I think if we rehearsed at Broadmoor, we would not come on with those defences; we would come on with a different contract with each other. We would be in a state of energy that we are not usually in during a rehearsal. It would be wonderful for patients to be part of the rehearsal process, because their level of honesty is something I yearn for. Part of an actor's defence mechanism is that actors are trying things out when we come to rehearsal. We are frightened. It is strange to me now that we all felt so frightened about going to Broadmoor; but it was not the same kind of fear, it was gut fear. It was not the feeling of being frightened that 'The other actors are not going to think I am any good', or that 'I have to play this part in a particular way', or that 'My agent is coming in four weeks time', or that 'This critic did not like my performance last time, perhaps he will like me better this time'. None of those theatrical connotations were present. The fear was real fear, not an imposed fear about all that other stuff. And that is the kind of energy I feel I would like to work in all the time, not just in plays like and *Hamlet* and *Lear*, but also in comedies, in any kind of play, in order to reach that bottom line, to be there from day one. I would like to see where that would take us.

Outside Broadmoor, an audience assumes in an extraordinary way a corporate identity, on any given night, to the extent that actors will come off after the first scene and will immediately gauge how the audience is tonight in a very finely tuned way. The actors will then make decisions – that they have to fight this audience, or bump up the comedy, or do it faster; the response is always a given series of set reactions. There has got to be something wrong with this pattern of response; and ultimately I think it is dangerous in a very real way for the theatre, for actors, for acting, for drama, and for what drama is trying to do. Because at the moment, playing 'normal' audiences is all about going out and giving them a show. In Broadmoor it is all about the importance of experience.

Paradoxically, Broadmoor felt very safe. Once I had got through the fear and decided to risk, I felt very safe there. What I find distressing as an actor is to feel safe in the wrong way. When people can cross their legs, sit back, and tell me that they are just going to watch for a couple of hours and then go home; most of the time they have not really engaged with anything. It is rare, in my experience, for people to really give themselves to a play. That lack of involvement produces an unsafe feeling for me; I don't feel at home with that. But I do feel at home in

Broadmoor because the kind of risks I have always wanted audiences to take and to take myself are possible there. It feels safe in that way.

Before Broadmoor I used to think 'I've performed well', or 'We performed the play well this evening'. At Broadmoor those sort adjectives are irrelevant. It is simply an experience. I did not feel like making any comment such as 'It was a good show at Broadmoor'; it would have been completely inappropriate. The only thing that everyone continues to talk about was what kind of experience they had had: how they felt; what came out of it for them; what they realised from it. That is something I would love to see happening in the theatre. The usual criteria were not being applied; there was nobody standing in judgement.

It is fascinating why it felt all right to take risks in that place. When I think about it now, I realise that it was also through the medium of the play that I felt safe. The play was the discipline, the play was the container. What was beautiful was that we were all together in that container. We were free to move around within, as it were, that cauldron. We had all agreed to be there, to be in the play, but having agreed that, on many levels, emotional as well as physical, it was safe. The play was the therapist really; one always gets the feeling that the therapist is not controlling, but is moving the energy around. In that sense the therapeutic element was the play: the play was moving everyone around. It is a very secure base to have.

When we came back after *Hamlet*, we had a debriefing session, because none of us then knew where to place this experience. We were going back and playing to conventional audiences with all this new knowledge, and all this new sense of risk. We wanted to bring it back and share it with the audience, and we didn't know how. We found it very unsatisfying to be back. What we did as a group was to have a meeting, and what emerged was that we didn't feel we had any way of bringing our audience that experience, although in subtle ways it did grow into that. As it progressed and we came to the Barbican, those things did come in, and what I call the 'Broadmoor Feeling' happened a couple of times. I think the experience held us together very closely as a company. When Mark Rylance and I decided between the two of us to start taking those kinds of risks on stage, we had some memorable nights when we really allowed the audience the possibility of coming with us. There were a couple of times when they did, and we touched them, and they touched back. And that was wonderful, to have that feeling. I got feedback about those times, from people who felt it – they know when something has happened. The new experience of some emotions has given me much more confidence, and the re-focusing that the patients did for us.

I have been thinking about rehearsing at Broadmoor ever since the workshop on *Hamlet*. What was amazing was that it was billed as a workshop on *Hamlet;* what it actually became was a workshop about Ophelia. It seemed that the patients were asking to know what happened to Ophelia. Many of the perceived ideas that we have as actors come with years of history, years of theatrical expectations and theatrical history. I realised at the workshop that these people were telling me that we have forgotten about Ophelia – and that they have information that I do not have, because I am so trained. They focused on things that I did not expect, such as how does Ophelia feel? When we did Ophelia's funeral at the workshop, there was an extraordinary moment when all the patients who were to be mourners stood up. There was a very high level of emotion in the room; one of the patient actually came and spoke to Hamlet and it was very moving.

This re-focusing process had already begun for me while I was rehearsing Gertrude and was reinforced by the Broadmoor experience. When I came to *Hamlet* I had a lot of preconceived ideas about her as a rather unformed minor character on the borders of the action. Bad things happened around her and she didn't seem to have much to say. She has very few lines – less than Ophelia and not many more than Rosencrantz. Yet she takes a huge journey from the revelry of the opening court scene to lying dead on stage at the end of the play. So I asked myself how she took that journey, and I saw I had a choice – to see her as someone who doesn't have much to say, or else to see her as someone who chooses to be silent. That seemed to be the active choice. So I began to find out why she chooses not to speak. I discovered that she is in such denial at the beginning of the play – about her husband's death, her sudden re-marriage to his brother, Hamlet's grief and his behaviour – that for her to speak would be too dangerous. She lets Claudius do all the talking. Polonius, who never stops talking and who names Hamlet's madness, becomes her natural enemy; he usurps her silence and her denial. Her silence is protective. It prevents her confronting reality. During the play scene, she can continue to deny what she is seeing during the dumbshow, but when the players begin to speak, she is deeply threatened. Denial begins to crack. And as this happens, the two young people in the court are cracking too. Another mirror image – I see my silence reflected back by them, particularly Ophelia, whom I saw as an image of my younger self – forbidden to speak, controlled and manipulated by those around her. Both Hamlet and Ophelia have to go 'mad' in order to speak their truth. Hamlet in the closet scene has to murder someone in front of me to break my denial and speak the truth. When Ophelia breaks her silence through madness, I see my own choices; insanity or death. Gertrude, through her silent witnessing on and off stage, becomes a more profound character. As she sees everyone around her destroyed and corrupted, she chooses her own death, and re-claims herself. And through that journey silence became as important to me as words; I had re-focused my attention in a different way.

So when I started work on *Richard III* and *King Lear*, I came to the two plays in a way that was new for me. I felt that I was going to try and read these plays as though I was at Broadmoor, not read them like an actress getting a script, seeing how many lines you have, how many scenes you have; I wanted the re-focusing to continue, and I found interesting things happening.

In most of the productions of *Lear* I have seen, one daughter comes on with long blonde hair and a blue dress, and two daughters have dark hair and black dresses; and you think 'I already know what's going to happen'. About that time while rehearsing *Lear*, I remember going to see a play at Broadmoor that the patients were producing, and becoming riveted by a woman – a patient – on the stage. I brought this experience back with me and worked it into Regan. What emerged through Regan was that I didn't want anyone in the audience to know what was going to happen, I didn't want everyone to know who was 'bad' or 'good' or 'evil' in theatrical terms. I remember being asked what I was wearing, and replying a white dress; I was told I could not play Regan wearing a white dress. That brought home the incredible expectations that people have. Just to begin deliberately to wipe those expectations aside, and to think, now supposing I was at Broadmoor, doing the play there, what would I think, what would I bring to the play. This is invaluable, like having another eye. Gone are all the thoughts like; I've got to be a better Regan than 'so-and-so', or 'so and so did that, so I can't do that'. The other eye suggests; 'what about refocusing on that bit?'

Playing at Broadmoor is like a checking device, or perhaps more like a removal of the checks that one usually imposes; it's like having a mirror there, but a very active mirror. Normally, when we rehearse, the circle of energy is just between the actors and the director. If we could rehearse at Broadmoor, with the patients there, I think the circle of energy would be going round in another way. It would not be a closed circuit. We could open the circuit/circle, make it a spiral, bring in more energy to feed us. There was a very fair exchange of energy at Broadmoor, between audience and actors, it was very beautifully balanced. I remember almost seeing the energy during *Hamlet;* you could feel it or smell it; it was like an incredible sea that rolled and went up, shot up, and came down; it was a lovely feeling. The energy was literally palpable. I understand why the audience described it as experiencing 'raw emotion', and we could sense out there the emotion being absorbed, and fed back to us. For us the difference was that we were doing the work of acting as well. As an actor you are always divided; you are working on a lot of levels at the same time. I can understand what the audience must have felt like; they were receiving and feeding back. We were receiving and working, doing the play and receiving feedback at the same time. We were being fed with the energy to ask where, why, how much are you focusing? How much energy you are putting into something? Are you deflecting off things? Are you being truthful? If not, why not? Is it for an effect, or is it because you are scared? What is going on? We don't answer questions like that normally.

If we could rehearse at Broadmoor, it would be rehearsing with patients present, and patients taking part, using text and doing rôle plays, doing work that we would not usually do at rehearsals. I suppose the patients to a certain extent would almost be directors, or mirrors – giving instant feedback, because that is what I found they were in the end. They reflected everything right back to us, telling us whether what we were doing was true or not; true, as opposed to acceptable theatrically, which is what an audience at most theaters will tell you. And that to me is a world of difference.

Whether or not we could rehearse at Broadmoor, the whole experience has taught me a much more interesting way of working. After doing a show for a year, that terrible state sets in when you go through the play, making the same motions, getting to the same point in the evening, and then the play ends and you go off. Now what I want to do is wipe out my expectations. It is not possible to take the risks we did in Broadmoor playing in large theatres over a long period of time. But I can re-focus and re-energise my commitment to the play by using that experience, and by encouraging feedback from the audiences. Talking to groups and students is a good beginning and allows both of us to ask questions – about our expectations, and whether we need to encourage each other to take those kind of risks.

Acting is not usually about this kind of risk taking. There are actors who are prepared to risk theatrically, for instance, who are prepared to take enormous comic risks, which can be disastrous if they fail. There are actors who are prepared to build up enormous characterisations or pieces of business, and that can fail. That is theatrical. The whole issue is a crucial one for me, as I do not really want to be an actor in that sense. But actors who are prepared to take personal risk – to be an actor, a person who is acting a play, a human being, who through the medium of the play is meeting other human beings, having an experience with other human beings – that is the sort of actor I do want to be. And that is Broadmoor. Before I went to Broadmoor, I did have a lot of conventional ideas, which are reinforced all the time in the profession.

But what has captivated me is the other thing. That is where I see so many possibilities, not just for me as someone working in the theatre, but for drama in society. Drama itself has lost its rôle.

Having access to an experience like Broadmoor has turned me around; it has made me ask myself what I want to do with this experience, and to question the rôle of drama. I don't know if we ever thought of drama as having a rôle in this country, if we ever accepted drama in that way, but the possibilities for it happening have been opened for me. And so I'm basically very happy; it has opened up so many doors, and I can see so many possibilities.

Because those doors were opened for me in a place where there are so many locked ones, I want to finish by saying something to those of us on this side of the wall about what I learned from those on the other side. Broadmoor is a world I never imagined I would enter – I had a perceived idea of it as enclosed, feared, shunned, out of 'human' experience. At Stratford and the National we played our plays about madness and the farthest reaches of human behaviour, to audiences who came, saw and were free to leave – physically and emotionally. But in Broadmoor, through experience shared with the patients, nurses, actors and therapists of being in the world of *Hamlet* and later, *Lear*, I understood that we truly were in one world together. They have crossed a line that is potentially there for many of us. But for a few hours in Elsinore/Broadmoor we too crossed the line and created a new space with it, one I have never been in before, and we spiralled on a journey together with all our human feelings. I feel priviledged to have witnessed that and to be a part of this ongoing journey.

A Letter from Claudius

(Peter Wight)

27 November 1989

The past weeks away from Stratford and Shakespeare have flown by and I think I subconsciously put *Hamlet* out of my mind, having been living with it (and him!) for over a year; but I did want and always intended to put my thoughts about the day at Broadmoor down and to express more formally my continuing interest in this fascinating and fruitful meeting of the 'two worlds'.

My main preconception and expectation of what the performance in Broadmoor would be like was fairly crude, not to say melodramatic. Because there were people in Broadmoor that had a kind of notoriety and that one did know something about, even though they were not necessarily to be in the audience for the play, their proximity lent an atmosphere of slightly dangerous excitement. Many years ago I performed with a touring theatre group that specifically did plays for prisons. We put on a very slight comic review-type piece in Wormwood Scrubs and even now I still have a strong and haunting memory of the ferocious concentration from the audience. This was focused on what really was a very insubstantial entertainment and was, I suppose, just a by-product of incarceration. I know that Broadmoor is not a 'prison' but I was haunted by that audience hunger. And I didn't know what effect a play full of increasing mental anguish and madness and murder would have in what I thought would be the even more charged atmosphere of a hospital for the 'criminally insane' (which struck me as pretty much how Claudius would describe Hamlet at about Act III Scene 1). In my most lurid fantasies about the performance I thought that the play might cause a riot. In the event, of course, the reality was more sophisticated and less crude than this, but the expectations in all our minds created an atmosphere of the unknown, of slight danger that we carried with us into Broadmoor and that provided a new context for the performance, much different from the normal Stratford atmosphere.

The actual atmosphere when we did arrive struck me as subdued. I was aware of a closely disciplined, closely watched world and the audience when they filed into the hall seemed subdued (not unnaturally). Much of the initial release in doing the play that day lay in the fact of getting off the stage and onto the floor, close to and on the same level as our audience. This combined with the 'buzz' of the slightly dangerous atmosphere that I talked about before to give a huge initial boost of adrenalin to the play as we got started. The acoustics of the hall felt good and the openness and uncluttered simplicity of acting the story in such an unfettered space and in such a close and direct relationship with the audience felt wonderful. I was very aware in the first court scene of trying to tell the story as if for the first time – the space demanded this because of its simple emptiness; all that there was to tell the story and create atmosphere was the actors – an obvious truth, but one that you can lose sight of as a conscious thought in big and sophisticated theatres. The scene felt warm and relaxed and I felt very comfortable and relaxed talking to Hamlet, aware perhaps more than usual of how it was important to set out Claudius' point of view, to show that there are the other ways of looking at events apart from through Hamlet's eyes. The sense of adventure also gave the scene a new impetus and energy. On two levels we were setting out on a huge group adventure – Claudius and the court, and the whole kingdom, were setting out on the political adventure of new leadership and regime and marriage and, as a group of actors, we were setting out on the adventure of performing a play that we were very familiar with and which had bound us together, off the normal stage and for an unfamiliar audience. The two levels of adventure and unknown seemed to merge and gave the scene a depth of conviction and reality that were new. The descent from this 'confident morning' of the play (from Claudius' point of view) to a splintered fractured world, where everything, personal and political, begins to be undermined by Hamlet's disturbing and subversive behaviour, felt sharpened by my awareness again of the newness of this story to most of the audience. And of the possible resonances with their own experiences in a more first hand way than is the case with most Shakespeare audiences. I felt this especially with Claudius' speech to Polonius after they have eavesdropped on the scene between Hamlet and Ophelia:

> 'Nor what he spake, though it lack'd form a little,
> Was not like madness. There's something in his soul
> O'er which his melancholy sits on brood . . . '(III.1.165)

Claudius has recognised the anger in Hamlet that transcends any of the conventional, controlling ideas of madness in his society and he is disturbed and frightened by it; he, rightly, feels that it is a direct threat to himself and that all his status and political power will be defenceless against the rageful insights that Hamlet has into his (Claudius') black and guilty soul. Maybe some of the audience also recognised and maybe identified with the despair and anger in Hamlet and with the effect it is beginning to have on Claudius.

With these thoughts in my mind I spent the interval in a state of some anxiety and a kind of appalled yet exhilarating anticipation. In the second half, Claudius suddenly and comprehensively, traumatically, cracks open and fractures to the deepest part of his soul. All his pretences and defences are burst asunder. Dark forces within him, that in the first act he has been (briefly) struggling to suppress, pour relentlessly into the open like boiling larva from an erupting volcano. I was sure (or rather suspected) that some of the audience would know these feelings and perhaps have struggled against drowning in them as Claudius is seen to do in his soliloquy. This is also the first time in the play that Claudius actually 'goes out in front' and addresses the audience directly. The initially daunting process of doing this as an actor – especially when (as in Shakespeare's day) – there is no comforting anonymous darkness to stare into, but individual watchful faces and eyes, mirrored the inner process of Claudius' mind and soul in this scene. Every line, every moment in the soliloquy had new resonance, from the self disgusted realisation of 'O my offence is rank. It smells to heaven' through a string of suddenly new minted phrases and images – ' . . . thicker than itself with brother's blood . . . the visage of offence . . . Forgive me my foul murder . . . Offence's gilded hand . . . the wicked prize buys out the law . . . we ourselves compelled Even to the teeth and forehead of our faults to give in evidence . . . bosom black as death . . . heart with strings of steel Be soft as sinews of the new born babe' to the wretchedness and impotence of the guilty man in 'My words fly up, my thoughts remain below'.

From this point on I remember feeling that, now that all the hidden darkness of the first part of the play had been exposed, there was a much greater feeling of savage release than usual for Claudius to fulfil the role that he now has to play and to battle viciously and unscrupulously against the forces mounting against him. Again, I felt that his fight for survival, physically and psychologically, which takes the form of trying to push Hamlet away from him as though he were 'a foul disease (. . . like the hectic in my blood he rages)' was a process that possibly some of the audience would recognise more sharply than usual.

The lines of Hamlet to Laertes before the duel (which Mark spoke for the first time that day and subsequently kept in) were ringing in my mind then and for a long time afterwards:

> 'Was't Hamlet wrong'd Laertes? Never Hamlet.
> If Hamlet from himself be ta'en away,
> And when he's not himself does wrong Laertes,
> Then Hamlet does it not, Hamlet denies it.
> Who does it then? His madness. If't be so,
> Hamlet is of the faction that is wrong'd;
> His madness is Poor Hamlet's enemy.' (V.2.229)

Claudius is such a guilty man; he has committed a real and violent crime, as perhaps had some/most? of the audience. The realisation of this brought us (me and Claudius) into sharper alliance with the audience than usual and made the atmosphere sharp and heightened with mutual recognition. Yet the basic interaction of actor, character and audience remained the same. I found this fact (especially in the light of my pre-show fears) very salutary and positive and for me this was the basis of a real feeling of 'two worlds' meeting and merging, showing themselves to be not as distinct and different as we all commonly suppose. 'Guilty creatures sitting at a play . . .'; the guilt of the Broadmoor audience is, I suppose, more defined and objectified than the guilts in a Stratford audience, but the play has to work on one just as much as the other. Therefore the guilt in one person outside an institution is (or can be) as real as that in one of the Broadmoor audience. To himself, Claudius does not seem an evil man. He too was seized and driven by a kind of madness that, as with Hamlet, became his own enemy. Everyone in the play is guilty of some crime or some insensitivity or some life denying negativity. We, outside the play, actors and audience, are similarly guilty; of differing things to be sure and to differing degrees – but all guilty. The making real of this otherwise clichéd observation by the sharing of that afternoon was to me the true fruit of the two worlds meeting . . . I would love to be involved in any future similar meetings.

A Letter from Ophelia

(Rebecca Saire)

17 October 1989

As far as my own performance as Ophelia is concerned, I can remember very little of it – nothing to do with the length of time I have allowed to elapse before putting pen to paper – the memory of it was vague even as we were being presented with our wonderful medallions, which we all treasure so much.

As I said at the meeting [in Stratford. M.C.] with Rob Ferris, I had very little, if any awareness of myself as an actress. Usually a part of me stands to one side, judging myself and the audience's response to what I am doing. At Broadmoor, I found that observer's part of me sucked back in. Confronted with so much truth in respect of the people we were performing in front of, subconsciously I realised I needed 100% of my own truth to answer them. It was as if I was playing Ophelia for the first time. All emphasis, familiar or unfamiliar, with me, went unregistered.

However, in between my scenes, when I could join the group as a spectator, many lines spoken by other actors struck me as being particularly relevant to our setting and our audience. I enclose them (see below), although they seem obvious.

I found myself very aware of individual words and themes. 'Mother', 'Father', 'Death', 'Murder', 'Revenge', 'Madness', 'Frailty, thy name is woman', 'Incestuous sheets'. Like a pebble thrown into a pool, I wondered (indeed, could sometimes observe) what waves of emotion and recall were stirred by each thought or idea, especially the recurrent ones.

Apparently, some patients commented on the physical aggression I displayed against myself during the mad scene when I tore my nails across my thighs. They said how realistic it was. Interestingly enough, that was the first time I had ever done it. It happened that afternoon and is now part of my performance.

My overriding memory of the day is when we all stood applauding each other at the end of the show. And how we shook hands after the discussion groups as if taking leave of a family. It was not until a few days after I thought – I have felt so close to these people. The sort of people I used to read about in the papers and hate and condemn with all my heart because of my sense of pain and outrage for their victims. I left Broadmoor with a greater understanding. The patient I spoke with wrote in a letter afterwards that he now knew 'actors are real people'. It was a mutual discovery!

And finally, how wonderful to have such an intelligent conversation about one's performance, with such insight into the problems connected with playing Ophelia, and not once to be asked the age-old question that sends most actors running for cover – 'How do you learn your lines?'

I have heard we are coming back to Broadmoor next February. I look forward to it very much. If I can ever be of any help to you in any way at all, please let me know.

'Tis a fault to heaven,
A fault against the dead, a fault to nature'

(Claudius I.2)

'O that this too too sullied flesh would melt,
Thaw and resolve itself into a dew,
Or that the Everlasting had not fix'd
His canon 'gainst self-slaughter. O God! God!
How weary, stale, flat and unprofitable
Seem to me all the uses of this world!
Fie on't, ah fie, 'Tis an unweeded garden
That grows to seed; things rank and gross in nature
Possess it merely.'

(Hamlet I.2)

'Foul deeds will rise,
Though all the earth o'erwhelm them, to men's eyes'

(Hamlet I.2)

'To be, or not to be . . .' the whole soliloquy

(Hamlet III.1)

'O my offence is rank . . .' the whole soliloquy

(Claudius)

'So shall you hear
'Of carnal, bloody and unnatural acts'

(Horatio)

Quotations as provided in letter

Ron Daniels
(Director of *Hamlet*)

interviewed by Rob Ferris

RF Perhaps I can start by asking you to explain how the whole thing came about and how you became involved?

RD Mark Rylance mentioned it to me first, having met Murray Cox at a post-show talk, after a performance at the Royal Shakespeare Theatre. Mark passed it on to me as a means of administering it and sorting out all the organisational problems. I can hardly remember now exactly. But it was initially just one of the many business issues surrounding the life of a performance. We are often asked to give talks at the Shakespeare Institute or to meet students with 'A' level exams and there are many requests for appearances and so on. So this actually began as one of those from my point of view, not having met Murray Cox or anyone else from the hospital at the time.

RF I think that it was Mark Rylance who originally made the suggestion to Murray Cox.

RD Yes, I think so.

RF What was your reaction to the idea when you first heard it?

RD It was very much 'here is another request'; an interesting, slightly unusual idea of another way to relate, not to members of the audience exactly, but to give life to the performance in the life of this production. So it didn't strike me as being particularly extraordinary or life-changing at first. It was just another part of the administration of the life of a production. But as the day approached, the whole thing began to acquire a completely different proportion, a totally different emphasis from just going to give another talk at the Shakespeare Institute. This was partly because of the myths in one's own imagination, because of the hospital itself, and partly because of getting everybody to come on a voluntary basis. So what had begun in my mind as a piece of administration, a piece of ordinary business, began gradually to acquire a shape and an importance. So that by the time we actually got there and encountered the wall and the security system, it had already begun to assume a completely different proportion.

RF This, then, is a rather large question but, what happened on the day so far as you are concerned?

RD Well it was very strange, because here were two very different communities coming into contact with each other. Our community of performers was full of images and myths and ideas about the hospital, about the patients and the staff. We knew that it was going to be a profoundly moving experience because of the absence of freedom of the hospital community; this meant that after it was over we would have to leave and the hospital community would have to remain behind. It was very difficult not to be romantic and to keep things in precise perspective. Because there was this huge gesture of generosity made by the company saying 'well we were actually going to use our one day off after all this hard work and we are going to take the play to this group of people who do not normally have any access to theatre or even to the normal ways of the world'. So there was something that was slightly crusading about arriving there. There was something mysterious about people locked away like this, people who had done something in their lives which had not only changed their own lives but obviously those of others as well. People for whom reality had actually been transformed by one moment or several terrible moments which affected every single moment of their lives thereafter, whether criminal or insane. One could take hold of the idea that these people are very near to what being human actually is – whereas actors pretend, they continually pretend. Actors make lies of huge imaginative power. Even though they all have their own private lives and though much of those lives are bound up with disturbances, as everyone's life is, nevertheless they survive. Although often emotionally immature, or crippled, they come to terms with their lives and the difficulties in those lives. The actor's pretence may be terribly intense, at times magically all-consuming and bordering on a moment of insanity for the loss of one's personality. But here they were coming to meet people who had actually crossed the Rubicon; people who had actually given in to a surge of emotion or of pathology which I think in many ways actors are actually very close to, and can sympathise with. Far more so than your well established good citizen, for whom any form of marginalisation is *anathema*, who is interested in the straight and narrow, whose life is morally bound by very strict tenets.

To a very large extent the actor, as a part of his profession, must continually open his heart and his mind to the infinite possibilities of life, rather than finding ways which are reductive in order to lead a life which is proper and sane and correct. The actor must allow his mind to penetrate that of Macbeth, or Richard II, or Richard III, people whose personalities collapse under pressure. So here we were, coming to this place containing people to whom such things had really happened, who had actually surrendered to something beyond themselves. To arrive at such a place was a sort of frightening experience, seeing those huge walls, those bars.

RF Which were necessary to contain these people who had gone so far from that straight and narrow you have just described.

RD Yes, that's right, and who were obviously paying the price. Both in the form of their own sickness as well as perhaps in their own lack of freedom, for this moment of extreme humanity.

RF A price which the actors would have avoided paying because . . . ?

RD They don't have to pay it.

RF Because it's pretence?

RD Absolutely. And this is the great thing about theatre; that you enact and you can always say 'stop, let's start again', in the rehearsal room or at the end of a performance. So that when Macbeth has committed his atrocities he can always say 'Right, I am taking my make-up off now and then I can go home and lead a normal life.' There is always a pulling back. There is always a moment when you stop. And yet the myth of acting is, of course, that you want to identify as far as possible with your character. There is this amazing and very interesting duality between being able to both pretend and believe utterly in the pretence. This is, in itself, a contradiction. But if you believe sufficiently in the pretence then you stop pretending. But then you go home, and you go to the pub, you lead a normal life.

RF So there is a sense in which the nature of that pretence was in this performance, exposed in front of people who didn't pretend at all.

RD Yes, obviously there is very much that I remember very clearly. When we arrived there was a jittering and some nervousness among the actors which continued throughout the performance. This was in part titillation. Would certain notorious patients, mass murderers or rapists, be in the audience? It was a nervousness which was very odd and childlike of people saying to each other 'you know who' is going to be in the audience, as if they were playing with fire.

RF The whole event, the performance and the response from the audience, was an extraordinarily powerful phenomenon. I think almost everyone who was there – the patients, the staff and the performers – all agreed on that and have said so repeatedly since. Do you agree and can you say, remembering your feelings at the time of the performance and looking back now, why and in what way it was such a powerful experience?

RD I am sure each person who was there would have his or her own interpretation, but what was very clear to me was simply that the smallness of the space in which we performed was critically important. In a sense we simply had a performance like a 'run-through' situation in a small room and often those events are in themselves hugely full of impact. Often productions lose a lot of their energy when they move from this first discovery of a play in a rehearsal room, where everybody is very close to the action, where there are in fact no lights and no costumes, but only the raw emotion of the play. Often, throughout my 25 years of being a director, I have encountered the power of the run-through, only to be disappointed later on and have to strive to recapture it on stage with the costumes, with the lights and with the audience. So you already have a hugely powerful story, very full of vulnerabilities and conflict, with the intensity of the language and the harmonics of the language being played very close to you. Almost by definition, then, it was bound to be a hugely strong event.

To this you then add the fact that there was the sense of a complete unknown for the actors. It was unknown in the sense that things could have gone terribly wrong through the audience simply not being interested. We were all aware that on the whole the patients in Broadmoor are not middle-class or well educated, and probably few have passed their 'A' levels. So obviously we were aware that we were dealing with a group of people, most of whom would have had little or no experience of this level of theatre previously. And certainly not Shakespeare. We knew perfectly well that this was a three and a half hour performance with a lot of very difficult language in which the audience might simply have not been interested. We knew perfectly well that our approach to the play, dealing as honestly as it did with the genuine problem of emotional disturbance and madness, was probably going to be very near the bone. And that it could have been seen either as dishonest or as misrepresenting the very real pain of the audience. There was a feeling that our portrayal might be unbelievable in front of the real thing.

So we knew that there were many layers of uncertainty. Having been used to the performance in the theatre with costumes, sets and lights, we did not know if it would work even in terms of the mechanics of the performance. Would the audience accept the fact that people who were not in a particular scene would be standing by, watching it? There was a whole set of rather wonderful imponderables creating a sense of danger, just in terms of the performance itself. A sense of danger, at the unknown, of 'specialness', which created a focus. It created a real feeling of concentration, of mental psychic energy. As well as the sense from the audience – and I think this is terribly important – that there was a great accumulation of experience here that had to be utterly respected in terms of its appalling vulnerability. One of the overriding emotions of *Hamlet* as a play, and there are many, was simply 'There but for the grace of God go I'. The people who trooped in to see the show weren't dressed in white hospital asylum uniforms, they did not look like lunatics, they were just ordinary people. Some must have been on tranquillisers, or sedated, I suppose, but as they walked into the room they had about them an appalling ordinariness. They were just like you and me. And again the first thought was how precarious life is, how a mistake, a momentary surrender to a passion, could simply alter your life completely. So there was to me in that room a huge sense of precariousness, vulnerability, and humanity, and what was astonishing was how the production response acquired, from the first words spoken, a simplicity, a lack of pretentiousness. The actors were 'doing' much less and their performances acquired an ordinariness and humanity that was quite revelatory.

RF Are you saying that these qualities had been missing from the performance up to that time?

RD It's not that they were missing, because you can't miss that which you don't know exists! But, obviously, the extraordinary thing is that in many ways, you see, a production does have a life of its own. You struggle through the period of rehearsal and find that you dive into unfamiliar areas that are full of strain. In working out the speaking of the text or the relationship between the characters, there is always a huge amount of tentativeness and uncertainty. Gradually, during the rehearsal period you reach a consensus over what each scene is about, what each speech is about, and what its relationship is about. You lock in and begin to discover things in greater depth. Then you go into an encounter with the audience and gradually over months, through familiarity, through self-confidence, the production grows. You throw out a lot of things which are unnecessary. You discover new things and to a large extent the normal life of a production is one in which it can become simpler, truer and less fraught with anxiety. But there was something else happening in that room, which was that honesty was demanded by nobody in particular but by everybody in general; including the actors themselves. A total untrammelled honesty, through which the language required a different texture; a texture of greater simplicity, far less theatrical in one sense, and less self regarding. It was as if the life of the production was like flowing water which had been running along as a muddy stream and then suddenly flowed into an area of stillness and clarity and lucidity. You could almost sense this cleansing of the actor's minds and actions which had about them a quite remarkable sense of clarity.

RF Would you say that this became apparent almost immediately or did it grow gradually throughout the afternoon?

RD No, it was almost instantaneous, though obviously a performance is always a dialogue. What was wonderful about what happened was that the actors were not behind the scenery showing something, but were rather in a room simply sharing that event. The event, the performance itself, was a dialogue between these two different communities of performers and patients. Partly because of the way we rehearsed it and partly because of the talent of Mark Rylance and the other actors, they seemed able to enact the story of the play as if it was totally and completely new to them.

I think that what was happening was that a whole series of very complex impulses was at work. The actors were unpaid and were there because they wanted to be, rather than feeling 'This is just another evening'. For the patients in the audience it was a terribly special event, not 'Just another evening with the Royal Shakespeare Company, another piece of culture'. So both communities were coming together already with a sense that there was something more here than people just doing a job. I don't mean to imply that actors merely 'do a job' on the stage, because acting itself is a mystery in terms of the amount of psychic energy and emotional generosity that an actor brings forth. The sheer amount of emotional energy and imagination required simply to stay on stage is extraordinary, whether the actor is performing in the Barbican, the RSC, or anywhere else.

Nevertheless, there was already something special here in the act of coming, and special as well in the nature of this particular production which had been worked on with a sense of continually opening itself out to new possibilities. It wasn't a production that was hurriedly or always trying to answer questions. It was trying to ask them. It was a production that quite deliberately put itself on the line. Even the central image of a schizophrenic boy, who has trouble sleeping, who wanders around the house lost, was an image that came out of my own personal life. The play itself, of course, following its journey through trauma to a sense of self-understanding, also had a special resonance in that setting. But above all I think it was the sense of two communities actually recognising each other and combining to create this world in which hugely intense life and hugely intense art were actually enmeshing. There is a Brazilian saying to do with something that happens at the mouth of the Amazon, where the waters of the river come downstream at an incredible speed and then meet tides coming very quickly in the opposite direction. Water actually moves upwards – the opposite of a waterfall. It is a movement of water upwards and that is to me what happened in terms of the emotional experience of the day.

It was extraordinary meeting the patients afterwards, talking to them and making friends with them. Confronting the myth that they were monsters and finding instead people who were just ordinary, 'There but for the grace of God go I', people. I met one patient who said to me 'This isn't the way Shakespeare is normally done you know'. 'No, I know it's not', I said, 'but it's based on a central idea of one of my family who had schizophrenia and who killed himself at the age of 23.' This patient, this man put his arms around me and hugged me and said 'It will be all right'. He was looking after my pain and I thought what was happening here wasn't just us giving, it was us receiving as well. And I feel that gesture, that mutuality, is what is so important in the theatre. The theatre is mutuality. It is collective mutuality, rather than simply one partner saying 'I know and I present to you my knowledge' or 'I have been there and I show you the way'. It's not that. The performance in Broadmoor showed that again to me.

Then, of course, we left and went back through the gates and back to a world of normality, exhausted but having the freedom to lead our normal lives again. It was quite extraordinary, not only on a human dimension but also an artistic one, to reflect how when we are confronted by these strange and uncertain circumstances, everything just simplified, lost what was unnecessary and became one, of itself.

RF You have so well described the way in which the barriers between yourselves – or ourselves – and the patients, seemed to disappear. Because of this, the way in which the patient put his arms around you, when he heard how your interpretation of the play originated in your own life, seemed at the time an entirely natural and ordinary thing. I don't wish to romanticise or mystify it, but from my everyday perspective it is hard to over-emphasise how extraordinary, rather than ordinary, it actually is.

You are talking about what might be called a process of identification with the patients. Of coming that afternoon and feeling strongly 'There but for the grace of God go we'. But my perspective as a psychiatrist who works at Broadmoor is different, I think. Those of us whose job it is to look after and treat the same patients from day to day, month to month, and year to year, spend a lot of time examining in great detail the history of their lives and seeing the extent of deprivation and abuse and the terrible problems that have been with them, usually from childhood on. We may see how those problems followed the patients, step by step, and seem to lead up inevitably to the moment when they committed the acts that brought them here. And we might sometimes say 'There but for the grace of God go I'. More often, taking a long, detailed view of the life of such a person, seeing how marred and disordered it was from the start, we might see no similarity between our lives and theirs, and be struck by the width of the gulf between the two. So that process of standing back 'objectively' and retrospectively scrutinizing a life in great detail may enable us to set ourselves apart, because we think we can see how they began to go astray and how they got so far from the rest of us. What happened in the performance seemed in a way the reverse of all that. because the gulf between the two communities seemed to disappear, almost in a moment.

RD Yes, but you see I think there is actually a great similarity here, because an actor who is assembling a character will do precisely what you have described yourself doing with the patients. He will put together the case history of the character, so that when you are talking about Hamlet, almost any Shakespearian character, the character, usually in front of your eyes, goes on this huge emotional journey. A journey which you have just in a way described, except that Shakespeare actually picks up not at the beginnings of a life but sort of on the last slope where the collapse, the catastrophe is about to happen. Whether it is Lear discovering the sense of powerlessness and ingratitude, or whether it is Macbeth discovering that he is actually a murderer and not a king. Or whether it is Hamlet when he discovers that he is in fact hurting much more than he ever expected that he would, through these uncertainties, through his lack of moral centre, or as his moral centre collapses. But it is exactly that. You go back and you discover the case histories of the characters as you have just described for the patients. The difference is that your task is to find ways of improving the conditions that you diagnose. The aim, in many ways, is the betterment of the patient. The task of art is not quite the same. The task of the artist is to embody, to dive into the mind of a mass murderer or a lover or whoever and portray it magically, mysteriously; identifying with it in order to portray it. Not with a sense of wanting to bring about improvement, but maybe with a sense of discovering what humanity is all about. Now the actor may be able to feel that his own problems have been sublimated within larger patterns. He might feel less isolated, more 'in the world' and of the human community. In that sense, what he does may be healing for himself or even for the audience. But primarily his purpose is to understand, to embody, mysteriously to identify with, to be amoral.

RF And to portray for better or worse.

RD Precisely. To portray for better or for worse, rather than say, for instance, 'Macbeth was wrong to kill'. The actor playing Macbeth has got to go on the journey that Macbeth goes, or has got to sympathise with that journey. Even if it might lead, as with the famous Stanislavski exercise, to an actor turning to the great teacher and asking 'Do I have to kill in order to identify with killing?' The answer of course is 'No'; there are devices, there are techniques. There are imaginative games that you can play in order to identify, to discover as an actor what killing may feel like. But the purpose of that discovery is not to align yourself with, if you like, the moral forces of society. The purpose of art is to delve into and discover, behind the horrors, the ultimate humanity.

RF But once I have killed, I should in some sense identify with the act of killing, and that becomes then what the healer is about in a place such as Broadmoor. Because here we have people who have really killed. But who may in one way or another, through psychological mechanisms of a pathological kind, fail to identify with the act of killing or be unable to identify with their own act of killing, as an aspect of their mental disorder.

RD Absolutely.

RF And that is what the healing can be about. To bring them to their identification somehow and here there is some possible connection between art and healing.

RD But you see the other interesting thing, of course, is that there is a whole analysis of Durer's *Melancholia*. The woodcut in which this woman, who is obviously insane, is portrayed as having insights that are not given to the normal sane human being, an insight into the very heart of life. Or Laing's (1960) description and evaluation of the journey of the schizophrenic, as one which contains, despite its terrors, wonders and perceptions which are of great value. It is all fascinating, absolutely fascinating.

Deborah Warner
(Director of *King Lear*)

interviewed by Ann Barker

AB In retrospect, directing a Shakespeare play in Broadmoor seems a very 'normal' thing to have done?

DW When we took *King Lear* to Broadmoor, the production was highly tuned; we had played over a hundred performances. The experience would have been different for us had the piece been less mature. We have to be careful about what the experience of playing at Broadmoor really is. One of the things that is exciting about Broadmoor is the fact of playing in a very confined space, but that is not unique to Broadmoor. Eighty performances into *King Lear* we took the production to Madrid where the technicians of the theatre we were due to play in had gone on strike. The theatre was shut. It was a terrible thing to happen; to have a group of actors hanging about in a hotel day after day, waiting to see if they were going to play that night. Tempers became extremely frayed. It was like a football team having trained for the World Cup and then, at the point of play, being given the week off.

Something had to be done with all the wasted energy. So I set up a rehearsal for both shows, *Richard III* and *King Lear*, and decided that we should, since we were not legally allowed to play in front of an audience, do something for ourselves. A private experiment. And so we went onto the stage of this dark, strike-bound theatre, and re-staged both productions in the round with no rehearsal. Within a simple circle of chairs on the stage the actors ran through each play, playing to each other as audience. The result was fantastic, and some of the work in the first half of *King Lear* was the finest the actors had ever done. The production was reinvented and relationships newly defined in front of our eyes and of course we were able to channel that work back into our existing production.

My point is, had we not had that experience in Madrid we might have attributed the huge buzz which comes from changing the shape of a show to the fact of playing in Broadmoor. It is always an exciting experience when a production moves from a large space to a smaller one. There is no question that it brings out the best in everyone. Actors enjoy playing intimate spaces. Any company who has never had that experience is going to be tremendously inspired by the freshness of the result. But as a company we had already been inspired by reducing the space and so that element was not in play when we came to Broadmoor. The new dimension was that this time the experiment would be with an audience.

It is impossible to describe simply what marked the Broadmoor experience. The event was tremendously charged, tremendously exciting, tremendously alive; but what made it so different from the Madrid experience? It was, of course, the presence of an audience but, significantly, this particular audience. The actors were very aware of the audience. Many spoke afterwards of playing lines quite differently because of this. They were conscious of who they might be playing to. In a few instances, actors spoke of being thrown by the realisation that they were in a room with people whose human experience might be as great or greater than that of the character they were playing. Of course it would be impossible to describe accurately the effect of this on the acting. Suffice it to say that one was in the unusual situation of the audience being an extremely live part of the event. The members of the audience were, as they should be, active contributors to the event.

I can best describe the quality of performance that day as rather raw, rather dangerous, but new-minted and the sort of theatre that I adore. I am always sorry to lose the quality that comes with very early performances of a play – the previews or the first night. Those performances are always nervous, full of adrenaline, the actors making very early voyages, often into virgin territory, so they are very poised, very alert and very sprung.

To be any flabbier than this is, I think, not to experience theatre at its best. Broadmoor gave the edge back to our production of *Lear*. Broadmoor 'electrified' *Lear*.

I felt honoured to take the play to Broadmoor, honoured because of the wealth of human experience shared by the patients there. You are playing to people with the most astonishing personal histories. Perhaps, unusually, as astonishing as the characters in Shakespeare's plays. Murray Cox speaks about Broadmoor and its patients in the most respectful way. Through our conversations he led me to understand where our work overlaps. It has been a great inspiration to me to meet and to hear Murray and I now try to invite him along to early rehearsals to talk to the actors. We are both dealing in human emotion and at a certain level theatre workers have to do that purely imaginatively; they have only their intuition to go on. Few of us have heard people talk of homicide. Where Murray helps is by giving a commentary from a huge reservoir of clinical experience. He has living examples as big as the play one is working on. Of course he maintains clinical confidentiality at all times, never naming a patient, but his commentary brings dramatic characters and theatre life-situations alive. And although one would no more copy that in a production than a theatre designer would copy a painting, it broadens the mind. With his lateral thinking conundrums, you almost feel your brain move: there's a slight twist of the angle of the brain in the head – it's almost a physical thing!

Hearing after the performance stories of the reactions of some of the patients had a similar effect. Extraordinary to hear that two of the girls had been profoundly moved and affected by the Lear/Cordelia relationship because of their own stories. To play to those two girls alone would be enormous. The world becomes a bigger place. This makes you very critical of your own work, makes you question whether you have worked hard enough imaginatively, whether you have explored the relationships sufficiently carefully.

Broadmoor helped to re-define theatre that Sunday afternoon. The experience spoke directly of the value of the live event which is the essence of theatre. The energy of the audience at Broadmoor was equal to the energy of the performers, producing amazing combustion. Truths were defined in the instant which is what should always happen in the theatre. Performances were changing and new things happening because of the audience. Now this should be commonplace, because this is what ought to happen on a nightly basis, and indeed is what keeps me in the theatre, but I have never seen it quite so clearly or strongly. We were playing to a marvellous audience whose desire for the event was very real.

Shakespeare's language carries everything and I therefore challenge the notion that the Broadmoor audience didn't understand the language. The level of rapt attention at Broadmoor was undoubtedly connected to the level of comprehension. Shakespeare's language is accessible to all if the actors are clear in their playing. Poetry is still a part of everyday language. You have only to read Murray Cox's (1978) *Compromise with Chaos*, to see that people do speak poetically – many of the quotations from his patients are astonishingly Shakespearian. When people have a lot to express, and something has a real need to be said or a great deal of emotion is being carried, then the vocabulary or the placement of words is astonishing.

I think that, in the world of Broadmoor, the need for theatre becomes very clear. If art is there as a means of trying to understand our life or our world, then clearly it is essential that Broadmoor patients should have a chance to see human experience played out in front of them. In that respect Broadmoor is the very home for playing Shakespeare as a form of healing, both for audience and player. This, in part, is what great drama is written for. Shakespeare should go to Broadmoor.

I. 3. iii

Dominic Barber
(Director of *Measure for Measure*)

interviewed by Rob Ferris

RF We're talking about your involvement with Broadmoor, which goes
back two years, right?

DB Yes. It started when some of the nurses, from what was then the
creative department, came over and said that there was no formal arts
activity at all going on in the hospital. And they felt that the Broadhumoorists,* as a group, could do with a bit more technique, and patients
were asking for more arts activity. So it really started from there. I said
I was interested in the hospital, initially perhaps a macabre interest,
thinking Broadmoor equals raving lunatics, equals bars, equals strait-
jackets. I had done some work with special needs students and enjoyed
that, so I thought I would try it. At the first session what struck me was
that they were so normal, so friendly, outgoing, bright, helpful. Gener-
ous in the risks that they took and two years on I am still doing it. And
the good thing is that with visiting companies or with actors I know,
who have an interest in working in special needs or in hospitals, I have
encouraged them to come up with me to the hospital and join in the
workshops. So you are not only giving the patients an idea about the
different arts activities and the different practitioners, who are coming
into work with them, but you also spread the good side of Broadmoor
amongst the profession. Because before they come, they think the same
as I did. It's 'one who flew over the cuckoo's nest' and medication time.
And although I see only one side of Broadmoor, what I see is so positive.
So now I try to beat the drum and say 'Look, there are a lot of very

---

* 'The Broadhumoorists' – the patients' drama group – is the substance of an entire
chapter in *Broadmoor* by R. Partridge (1953,127–32). It is interesting to note that amateur
theatrical 'recreational therapy' was introduced in 1939 – exactly half a century before
Hamlet Day. M.C.

disturbed patients here, but they are human beings and we shouldn't ostracise them.' When I started, it was surprising how many people said 'How could you work with such patients? How could you work with prisoners?' And I said 'No, it's not a prison, it's a hospital.' And some of those people have come to see Broadhumoorists' productions. One of the severest critics at the outset is now a sort of number one fan of Broadmoor. And that's great.

RF So, as you say, the proof of the pudding is in the eating, because two years later you are still going there. So what is it that you actually do there and who do you do it with?

DB Well, basically, I teach a theatre workshop or a drama workshop with between seven and ten patients, male and female, but predominantly male. It's not dramatherapy, though it has a therapeutic quality to it, in as much as they are free to get things wrong and are free to explore crazy situations, usually comic. I feel that laughter in itself is a therapy. And getting it wrong in front of a peer group is a therapy, as much as getting it right. There are no rules and regulations. I encourage them to improvise, try things out, and enjoy it. I tend to start with a warm-up session which involves a physical loosening of the body. Then something to do with the voice, whether it's working on consonants, or vowels, or breath control. We do a lot of trust exercises, because unless the group members can trust themselves and me, or if there is a barrier, then you don't achieve as much. Quite a lot of them started off hating doing that. It involves closing your eyes and falling into somebody else's arms. Now some of them still find it a challenge, though they do it. Now I have built up the trust I think I can demand more of them. So if they say I don't want to do it, I say well just do it, just do it and try. Don't say I don't want to do it.

RF Which you probably wouldn't have said at first.

DB No. I might have thought they would have leapt on me or something. But I realised more and more how important the element of fun is – it's a sort of playground of creative ideas – they can play and they are allowed to play and what I feel they need is to increase their self-esteem. Their self-esteem is very low and they are frightened of getting things wrong. They ask me how do I do this and I say well I am not going to tell you how you do this, try it, and if you get it hopelessly wrong then I'll help you but I am not going to prescribe. I am not going to tell you this is how you act. It's got to come from you.

RF Yes.

DB And I find the men are prepared to take a lot more risks. The women tend to play very much the feminine role. They're more subservient, desperately wanting to do this, desperately wanting to get you a cup of coffee. The men, I find, are far more open.

(At this point one of Dominic's colleagues joins us.)

MS Hello, my name is Mike Snelgrove; I played Angelo in *Measure for Measure*.

RF So you went and performed at Broadmoor on a Sunday afternoon in November last year? Was that the first time that you had been to or performed in a place of that sort?

MS Absolutely the first time, yes. I live locally. We all know of Broadmoor and I knew that Dom (Barber) worked there. The image of Broadmoor is obviously one of a rather fearsome place, so to go there and do something like *Measure for Measure* was a bit frightening in a way, especially given some of the content of the play. We did wonder how that would register with the patients. First impressions going in just confirmed everything I had always thought about Broadmoor. The rather intimidating buildings, the iron bars and so on.

RF All of the trappings of security.

MS Absolutely. Personally, I have never been inside a prison of any sort. As I stood at the end of a corridor waiting for the play to start, and just looked out through an iron bar door into the courtyard, I suddenly just thought, God, you know this is what being in prison is like. I hadn't registered that before. It's just awful. Thinking outside is 'there' and I am 'here'. Liberty has gone. It gave the play and some of its themes a resonance. You say the words about being in prison, or sending people to prison, which Angelo does a lot. He sends everybody to prison. But until you stand there and look out through a barred door you don't actually appreciate what losing your liberty means. That happened just before it went on and it made me feel a bit trembly.

RF So did you have any apprehension about the audience before you began?

MS I think we all did, yes. There was lots of nervous laughter while we were getting changed and semi-pathetic jokes and trying to cheer each other up. We really didn't know what to expect and I remember being in the dressing room and people whispering 'They're coming in, they're coming in'. We didn't actually see the audience going in and it really felt like us and them.

DB And it was in the round as well!

RF So what happened as the performance began and as it developed? What sort of feeling or atmosphere did you pick up?

MS It's the old cliché. Once it started, we were so caught up in adjusting to the smaller space and the closer proximity of the people, that we hardly had time to reflect on the nature of the audience. They were an incredibly attentive audience. There was no coughing. No shuffling.

DB And at the end of the rape scene it was wonderful when she says 'I am going to tell everybody about what you have done to me' and he says 'Who's going to believe you?' Angelo says 'I am the pillar of virtue in this society and who's going to believe you?' and he strolls off and she's just left there sobbing which ends the first half. And, as Mike exited, 'Boo!' came – from just one voice. They booed him off, and I was actually pleased, because it meant it had worked. It got through to whoever it was. Nobody in the Wilde Theatre would ever do that. No way. Too civilised. Too inhibited.

RF So what was your feeling at the end, then? What was your final impression, comparing it to your initial fantasies and expectations?

MS Well, I'll tell you one thing about Broadmoor that I didn't know. I looked at the front row and there were people with arms around each other, men and women who Dom tells me have relationships, some of them even being married. I didn't know that. And that was a real shock. I wasn't expecting it. For a start, I was expecting an all-male audience and I wasn't expecting that kind of fraternising during the show. At the end of the performance we all felt absolutely exhilarated. We felt that it was an audience that had locked into the themes of the play and understood what it was trying to say. There was so much about being in prison, being incarcerated, and repressing your feelings, but letting them out in violence and anger, now and then. This had actually been understood by the audience, probably more so than by the audience in the Wilde.

How I felt as I left Broadmoor? Well, I had been talking to someone, I don't know who he was, a young chap about my age, and we had been talking about the theatre and plays and what they were going to put on in Broadmoor next and so on. It was just like sitting and talking to someone in a Lounge Bar. I had completely forgotten where we were. As I walked out I felt awful. I felt dreadful. Because I thought, there's a civilised, intelligent, educated person living a life like that. And I am going out and going back to the Wilde (Theatre) bar for a drink. It stayed with me for a long, long time. I was very, very shaken when I got back to the Wilde Theatre. And it wasn't the performance, it was the talk after. I felt really odd. I really did.

RF Was it perhaps to do with finding someone, in a sense too similar to yourself, and not a monster or a raving lunatic?

MS Absolutely, that was it.

RF Someone who could really make you feel 'There but for the grace of God, go I'?

MS That's exactly the phrase that came through my mind, yes. I felt awful that we push people like that. Whatever they have done, we shut the doors. And one just thinks that they have lost so much of what we take for granted everyday. So there were three or four of us sitting around in the bar in the Wilde Theatre afterwards and we just didn't have very much to say to each other. We were gob-smacked.

(At this point Michael Snelgrove leaves the interview and Dominic Barber continues talking about his drama classes.)

DB As I was saying, we always do a physical warm up, a bit of voice technique and breathing, a trust exercise. Then, depending upon what we are working on, it may be improvisation techniques, using the comic theme, or looking at pieces of text and looking at how you approach a text and how you get a character from the text.

RF Does the group of patients you have been working with stay the same or do they change?

DB The males tend to remain the same. The females come and go.

RF So you have been with more or less the same group all through?

DB Some have left.

RF The group or the hospital?

DB The hospital, which is great. Others have joined. There is one female patient who is my star pupil. She came incredibly introverted, mumbling. Now she is so confident. We had a journalist from the local paper, who'd heard of the work, and I talked with him at length. And he came to see a drama session, and then saw a production of the *Golden Pathway Annual*, and he talked to the patients afterwards. And dear old Mary was giving it great verbals and saying 'This is wonderful' and 'I am enjoying it' and 'I have given up music to come to these drama sessions', 'They told me that I needed speech therapy, but now I don't'. And I was thinking 'great, great!' Again, the journalist was bowled over by the whole experience and did a very good article on it.

RF So you have been able to see in the two years, in relation to her and some of the others, the therapeutic quality that you referred to?

DB Exactly, and that's an important by-product. But at the end of the day it *is* a by-product, because it is primarily recreation. It is not therapy – officially. But recreation is itself therapeutic.

RF And as you are at pains to point out, it's not dramatherapy. You are not there as a dramatherapist.

DB Exactly. We never ever role-play. We would never get into the realms of trying to relive the patient's experience or, say, taking the role of your mother or your father.

RF But you may have come to have an opinion about what role dramatherapy might have in that kind of setting?

DB Definitely. I'm wary of unlocking emotions that maybe I haven't got the right key for. Or of being unable to close the door again.

RF So it isn't that you would see it as irrelevant. On the contrary, you would see it as a potentially powerful instrument?

DB And as a specialised instrument. A very specialised area of the use of drama which I don't have expertise in.

RF But if a person who was experienced and specialised could do dramatherapy in Broadmoor it might perhaps be to great effect?

DB Definitely. Definitely. And what I want to do this year or next year is to apply for Arts Council funding or perhaps a Churchill Fellowship so that I could visit hospitals outside this country to see what they do in terms of drama. Not as dramatherapy, but as drama for its own sake.

RF And so within the hospital your work is going on.

DB Most definitely. The next stage is to try to integrate the community company here a lot more with the work that I'm doing with the patients. *Measure for Measure* was the start of that. Those who have never been inside Broadmoor can only base their opinions of it on what the press and TV say. So often this is wrong. It's always negative.

RF Yes, indeed. The garish nightmare image as portrayed by the tabloid press. So it is remarkable to hear of Mike having his opinion completely overturned.

DB Nobody came away from the *Measure for Measure* company with negative feelings about Broadmoor. Sadness perhaps. But not negative feelings. The patients made them feel so welcome and the actors were amazed at their normality.

II

Stage Directions

Introduction

It is always interesting to note how words change their meaning depending upon the context in which they are uttered, and whether they are construed as being literal or metaphorical. Such was the case as I walked with a group of actors and Broadmoor staff from the Main Gate of the Hospital towards the Central Hall. My casual question to the charge nurse at my side was 'Who is stage managing things this afternoon?' referring to a major logistic problem of ensuring that staff with keys would be available to accompany visitors who inevitably depend upon such escorts. A voice from the back of the newly-arrived theatre group confidently said 'I am!'

Of course the stage manager was doing the stage managing! How easy it is to forget that language can be concrete and is not necessarily metaphorical. This distinction is of vital importance in discerning differential implications of meaning when in dialogue with a psychotic patient who may experience 'concrete thinking'. Such a patient switched on an electric iron when trying to 'iron out' a problem which worried her. Important though this phenomenon is, it is not our direct concern here. Except to observe that many of the patients in Broadmoor, and therefore many of the audience, had at some time in the past, experienced such thought disorder that their thinking would have been 'concrete'. Such a persistent thought disorder would influence what was 'heard' and 'seen' during the performance, so that perceptual distortion would result.

This Section discusses the set and stage management, using the term in both senses. It refers to the way in which the 'stage' – or rather the staging-area – was prepared and 'managed'. In fact, Ian Bayne describes how the actual lay-out of the acting and seating area took on three different configurations, depending upon the wishes of the director and the cast. There is yet another word with an ambiguous connotation, which shows yet again how potentially confusing are words used both in the world of clinical psychology and that of the theatre. I am referring to 'The Set'. In clinical terms, we often refer to an individual's 'perceptual set' which refers to the angle from which he views things, the tint of his rose- or fog-coloured spectacles and several other metaphors which imply an idiosyncratic construction of reality. A personal way of 'seeing the world'. For our present purposes, Ian Bayne will be describing 'The Set' from a conventional dramatic perspective. Alhough it should not be forgotten that every member of the audience will tend to see the theatrical 'set' in a slightly different way, depending upon his psychological 'perceptual set'. Thus a perfectly 'innocent' chair may remind John of a pleasant summer holiday, whereas it reminds Ken of being tied to a similar chair and beaten.

This Section opens by looking at Broadmoor Hospital through a wide-angle lens. Harvey Gordon describes the hospital as a whole, before Ian Bayne gives a more detailed account of the particular location where the performances took place. Harvey Gordon also looks at the history of the hospital through a zoom-lens and takes us back to the date of its opening. Furthermore, his wide-angle lens is metaphorical in that he addresses the major philosophical clinical and legal issues which inevitably converge in any discussion of a 'special hospital' such as Broadmoor.

M.C.

The Setting – Broadmoor Hospital

Harvey Gordon

Shakespearean drama and Broadmoor Hospital have certain things in common. Both are institutions embedded in the nation's identity. Both reflect aspects of deep emotion in the way of life of its citizens. And when, in August 1989, members representing the two institutions met face to face for the first time, the history of both became fused and subsequently mutually enriched. It was an experience which has the qualities of permanency.

Broadmoor is both the substance and the title of a book by Partridge (1953). It is neither broad nor is it situated on a moor. Most people, including some health professionals, confuse it with 'Dartmoor', a prison built on Dartmoor in Devon to hold French prisoners from the Napoleonic Wars. Many also regard Broadmoor as a prison. Indeed, it is thought of as a special kind of prison, wherein are housed criminals who are mentally deranged; and who may, at any time, quite unpredictably make a homicidal lunge at someone with whom they come in contact. Visitors to the hospital, for indeed that is what Broadmoor is, are almost always surprised to find that the nature of life inside for both staff and patients is remarkably normal, albeit confined within a large perimeter wall. Stories of the tragedy of homicide can be told many times over with regard to patients admitted to Broadmoor. And when *Hamlet* was played to an audience of patients, many of whom had killed, the interaction between actors and patients was electric in its effect. The reverse of homicide is suicide, in the sense that the direction of hostility and aggression runs inwards rather than outwards. Attempts at suicide are not uncommon in the severely mentally disordered. And indeed when *Romeo and Juliet* was performed in Broadmoor in March 1990, the players and the audience were brought together as witnesses of human misery and misfortune. Offenders and victims, so clearly portrayed in these Shakespearean dramas, registered with the patients at Broadmoor in a microcosm of their lives. And they brought to focus all the whirlpool of distorted perceptions that preceded their desperate deeds. Death by any means including homicide is so final to the victim's friends and family. But so it is, in another sense, to the perpetrator who has to come to terms with what he (or she) has done.

When Broadmoor was opened in 1863 it was designated a Criminal Lunatic Asylum. It is situated only some 40 miles from Central London, in the small town of Crowthorne in Berkshire. Built on a hill, one can look down from the terrace within onto the landscape of Berkshire and Hampshire. Its origins betray the ambiguity of its function. In the 1800s, and indeed today as we approach the end of the twentieth century, the mentally disordered offender fitted poorly and without harmony into either the prison system or that of the mental hospital or asylum. Shunned by other prisoners, the mentally ill in prison behaved at times in a disturbed and disturbing way so that they were not well placed in a custodial setting. Conversely, the development in the 1800s of the county asylum system for the mentally ill did not cater well for those who were then known as criminal lunatics, particularly if they had behaved in a dangerous fashion. The Bethlem, or Bedlam as it became known, built its own wing to cater for criminal lunatics. But by the mid 1850s it became clear that a large national institution was required to relieve the prisons of their mentally ill offenders who could not easily be accommodated in county asylums by reason of public safety. A series of assaults of a homicidal nature on public dignitaries, including the Queen, may also have played some part in the process of society having to grapple with the notion of criminal acts being committed by those who were found to be insane, and thus less than fully responsible for their actions. If just punishment requires rational intent, as most would feel it should, the notion of punishment including the death penalty for those who have committed criminal acts, but who are nonetheless irrational in so doing, is a dubious if not inhumane response by a humane society.

Nevertheless, from the outset, Broadmoor, though related to and providing a service for the prison department, was not a prison but an institution of a separate nature. It looked like a prison, built in red brick with bars on the windows. Yet the Head of the institution was a doctor, not a Governor. It was staffed by attendants who were the forerunners of nurses and not prison officers. Its purpose and ethos were to provide treatment and not punishment. Broadmoor indeed was a landmark in the evolution of provision for the mentally disordered offender. It represented public acknowledgement of the need for an appropriate therapeutic, albeit secure, facility for the mentally disordered criminal of dangerous propensities. And yet in its very establishment lay the roots of subsequent public conflict. Once admitted to such an institution as Broadmoor, after a dangerous act, how could the public ever be assured that the person could not commit further heinous crimes if released to liberty? And, conversely, how reasonable would it be to detain a patient in Broadmoor indefinitely? In some cases this would mean detention long after they had recovered from their mental illness so that their dangerousness would have abated. The issue of when to discharge a patient from Broadmoor remains an active dilemma to this day. An unjustly prolonged detention of some patients, must be balanced in other cases against the risk of premature discharge. This would result in further offences by the patient which might cause serious injury or loss of life. Indeed, as was stated in a debate in Parliament a decade ago, an awesome responsibility rests upon the shoulders of the doctors at Broadmoor. The sharing of such decisions on transfer and discharge of patients by the doctors and clinical team with the Home Office is an essential reflection of a partnership. This is necessary both to offer maximum therapeutic input to patients, as well as concurrently to protect public safety.

When reflecting on the early years of Broadmoor, one can only marvel at what it must have been like to work there. It was not until the 1940s and 1950s that treatments began to become available to modify the course of some of the mental illnesses from which patients suffered. In the absence of any effective biological remedies, the safety of staff within Broadmoor could only have been brought about and maintained by their efforts in developing a professional relationship with patients based on firmness, observation and trust. Though staff have been involved in the management of violent incidents by patients, there is no record in the entire history of Broadmoor of any member of staff having been killed by a patient, although virtually all Physician Superintendents at the hospital seem at one time or another to have been assaulted by patients. It is indeed to the credit of staff that they are able to handle themselves in a manner which resolves dangerous and difficult behaviour by patients, without placing themselves at unnecessary risk. Indeed, a cardinal feature of the therapeutic objective is to attempt to evaluate and understand the nature and reason for the patient's violence. It is to be hoped that this may lead to the discovery of suitable methods to predict and prevent it.

The term criminal lunatic is no longer acceptable. Patients in Broadmoor are all detained under mental health legislation. One of the early Physician Superintendents of Broadmoor, John Baker (1902), described the patient population at the turn of the century as being made up partly of what he called criminal lunatics and partly of lunatic criminals. The criminal lunatics formed the majority, and were those whose crimes were adjudged by the courts as having been committed in the context of an unsound mind. The lunatic criminals were those who became insane during the course of their prison sentence and required transfer to Broadmoor. According to John Baker, most of the mischievous and problematic behaviour within the institution was manifested by the prison transfers, i.e. by the lunatic criminals rather than the criminal lunatics. Indeed, to this day, the hospital continues to provide for both groups and, to an extent, the same trends persist. The public is familiar with the term 'psychopath', yet its meaning is not generally known. And even to the medical and health professions its very existence remains an issue of dispute. The psychopath has a profound problem in his or her personality. Its roots probably lie in early childhood and its development results in the manifestations of persistent antisocial behaviour, including violence to others and self. Psychopaths are abnormal. Legally, they are categorized separately from the mentally ill. Whether or not the psychopath is in reality significantly different from the mentally ill is, for some, a matter of debate. Certainly, the psychopath presents a significant problem, not only for society but also for institutions such as prisons which attempt to contain them, or high security hospitals such as Broadmoor which attempt to treat them. Nonetheless, such individuals are disturbed people and they are disturbing to others. A proportion of them may respond to treatment, and may require long-term asylum. For such patients, Broadmoor has something to offer. It remains the case today, however, that patients with a deeply rooted propensity for self-seeking and antisocial behaviour pose problems in management for the staff just as great as they did over a hundred years ago. The problem, however, is a complex one. There is no doubt that the patient is best served and the public best protected by affording the psychopath treatment, rather than punishment which is likely to exacerbate rather than alleviate the condition.

Dr Patrick McGrath, the last Physician Superintendent of Broadmoor, quoting one of his predecessors, Dr Stanley Hopwood, in a television documentary about the hospital, said 'only about half the patients in Broadmoor are dangerous; the problem is knowing which half'. And yet, the assessment of dangerousness of patients is the very essence of the expertise of the Broadmoor psychiatrists and the clinical team. The track record of Broadmoor is testimony to these curious medical skills built up by individual doctors, taking account of the observations of nurses and of the results of sophisticated psychological testing and the contribution to care of all staff involved. In its existence of more than 125 years, Broadmoor has dealt with over 10,000 patients, of whom four-fifths have been men and one-fifth women. When discharged, very few have again become dangerous. When, however, such an event does occur, there is usually an understandable public outcry, with full media attention on why the patient had been let out. The public, of course, is entitled to be protected, although the world we live in is far from being free of danger. However, there is, I believe, a phenomenon of the public needing time to grieve or to recover from a dangerous act by one of its members. The rights of the patient to receive the treatment he or she requires must be balanced against the rights of the society which has been offended against. And the injured victim needs to have time to work through what has happened; as do the victim's relatives, especially if homicide has taken place. A doctor's emphasis is traditionally on his patient's needs. Yet, where the effects of his patient's illness are to endanger others, their protection must also be part of the assessment. The two matters are inter-related and indissolubly linked.

In the public mind, madness and dangerousness are often associated. Yet the majority of mentally ill people are never dangerous and most people who have acted dangerously are not mentally ill. The history of psychiatry in part turns on this conundrum. At a time when the thrust is towards the development of community care for the mentally ill, Broadmoor remains a closed facility, detaining its patients often for long periods. Whilst one sector of the public calls in the media for the indefinite incarceration of the mentally abnormal offender, another calls for the abolition of all asylums, including Broadmoor. It is suggested that it should be replaced by smaller facilities, more locally based. It is almost as if the mind of the schizophrenic is paralleled by a splitting in the mind of the body politic, where both sides are engaged in wrestling with concepts of liberty and of confinement. This duality of public perception has its roots, perhaps, in the normal assumption of rationality balanced against a repressed fear of insanity. How certain can the 'normal' person be that he or she will not one day be overcome by such mental afflictions? Was not Hamlet only a normal man who became temporarily mentally deranged as a result of psychic conflicts he was unable to resolve? Although in the 1840s the artist Richard Dadd stood on the threshold of a most promising career, and although his insanity seems never to have affected his technical ability, the illness was to render him subject to a degree of psychological disintegration which led to the killing of his father, and his admission to the Bethlem and subsequently to Broadmoor, where he died in 1881 (Allderidge 1974). Indeed, mental illness is not constrained by class boundaries, although perhaps its manifestations may be more favourably offset by financial support.

Mental health legislation designates Broadmoor as what is known as a 'Special Hospital'. It contains patients and not prisoners. It provides treatment and security rather than custody. Yet admission is confined to those who are not only mentally disordered but also dangerous to the public. So far as is possible, Broadmoor functions in a manner consistent with psychiatric hospitals in the National Health Service. However, its obligations specifically to protect the public from harm requires Broadmoor to ensure that the treatment of its patients is undertaken in a safe setting. Its intentions are well appreciated by most. Some, however, regard it as either restricting the liberty of unfortunate individuals who are the subject of clinical or political overcaution, whereas others regard it as an institution which provides conditions of luxury five star hotel quality for people who have committed serious crimes and who, it is argued, don't deserve such provision. Nevertheless, at all times it must be remembered that the humane treatment of the mentally ill offender does not negate the need for the victim and his or her family to be acknowledged, counselled and supported. It is paramount to avoid the likelihood of any further victims being endangered. The nature of the patient's dangerousness needs to be evaluated, so that when discharged he or she will refrain from such behaviour as was previously manifested. It can be modified and minimized, or even in some cases eradicated, subject to appropriate treatment and overview.

At the same time, it is not a concept to take lightly. The community will not expect patients to be precipitously discharged once dangerous acts have been committed. Broadmoor, although locked-off from the community, is nonetheless organically linked to it. It has its own internal community, but is also provided by and part of the society in which it is situated. Broadmoor is not immune from this social ambivalence. A dialectical reality pertains in regard to its interactions, both clinical and social, with its professional and social external environment. The social consciousness of the liberal society cannot adequately come to terms with the removal of liberty of those who are dangerously ill. The harshness of conscience of the authoritarian elements of the political spectrum will embrace little consideration for the provision of those afflicted by such dangerous passions. Society contains within itself its own schizophrenic dichotomy.

Throughout its history Broadmoor has admitted patients from society and discharged them, successfully for the most part, back into it. It has its own balancing mechanisms and cannot withstand for very long any extremes of operation. It is inherently a hospital which always has cared for and treated its patients and been responsible for its decisions and accountable for them. Its very function renders it an inevitable object of curiosity to the public at large. And yet its patients must be protected from outside interest where this is not legitimate, even on occasions when the patient seeks to arrange it, lest it be counter to his or her welfare. Herein lies yet a further dilemma in regard to the role of the hospital in facilitating the patient's return to a normal life, or as normal as can be allowed for; taking account of the nature of the patient's mental condition. Rehabilitation is fostered by ensuring minimal loss of contact with the community. Such loss is only to such a degree as is necessary and safe, yet sectors of the community are hostile and intrusive, so that limits must be drawn until such time as sufficient recovery has taken place.

One of the rewarding and remarkable aspects of working in Broadmoor is the knowledge that one's efforts, and those of one's colleagues, have helped a patient to improve or recover from his or her mental illness. The tragedy of the past cannot be removed, but the future can be approached with regained optimism.

Shakespearean drama as played out in constructive fantasy is real to those detained in Broadmoor. The realm of fantasy and reality blend into an indivisible unity, and this is what happened when Shakespeare came to Broadmoor. Neither the actors nor the patients knew where to locate the boundaries for the duration of the performances, staged in Broadmoor's Central Hall. Broadmoor's patients merged into the historical social analysis rendered timeless by Britain's greatest playwright. As a medical student, I remember once walking through the corridors of Vienna University Medical School and feeling as if Sigmund Freud's spirit of inspiration was still present and inextinguishable. Now, when I have occasion to enter the Central Hall in Broadmoor, I feel that Shakespeare's influence has been imbibed as an immortal part of our history and future. The alliance between Shakespearean drama and Broadmoor is indeed perceptibly magnanimous. Both worlds seemed enriched by something precious which comes but rarely and leaves an imprint which is indelible.

The Set and Stage Management

Ian Bayne

Within this large organisation is the aptly named Creative Department, which in turn takes its place in the Department of Rehabilitation. Its primary function is to organise a vast range of sporting and recreational activities for the patients. Before the introduction of the Creative Department these had been arranged jointly by the Chaplain and the Musical Director. They include football, cricket and bowls fixtures, as well as social activities such as dances, bingo and whist drives. In addition to these weekly events, an annual choral production in the Autumn and the performance of a traditional three-act farce by the patient's dramatic society, aptly named the Broadhumoorists (see p.97), takes place. It is always necessary to ensure that the needs of the patients are met, from both a participation and a spectator point of view, as well as fulfilling criteria concerning security and safety.

Those of us fortunate enough to be a part of the Creative Department in the latter part of 1989 were approached by Murray Cox, to discuss the possibility of the RSC staging *Hamlet* for our patients. This prospect provided a new and exciting opportunity to move away from the traditional entertainment just described and enable our patients to experience the thrill of a live Shakespearian performance, especially since it involved one of this country's premier theatrical companies performing in a venue itself so steeped in history.

Broadmoor has, over the years, received many visitors, amongst them the rich and the famous, who have come to entertain our patients. Never, however, in its 125 years had this hospital seen anything like this before.

Though the nurses working in this department had, through the years, developed skills in both organising and facilitating theatrical activities, most of their experience was in connection with the annual production by the Broadhumoorists. The actors and actresses are, therefore, all patients who participate in this very demanding activity. They are under the guidance of their clinical team, from whom prior approval is always sought, as well as being under the supervision of a highly experienced team of nurses from the Creative Department.

When it came to preparing for *Hamlet*, we were faced with an entirely fresh set of challenges. Our primary problem was that of creating an environment suitable for such a major production. In the early days we had no idea how much scenery and other props would be needed. However, those material considerations seemed small compared to the unknown psychological impact which the play might have upon our patients. With this in mind, the department was approached and asked to tackle three very difficult tasks.

1. Adapting to the Environment and Adapting the Environment

The first major problem was that of the venue. The Central Hall is an historic auditorium. It was built in the 1860s by convict labour, to a design devised by Joshua Jebb, who is also well known as the architect of Pentonville Prison.

This beautiful building is, however, blessed with a very small stage area. In keeping with the rest of the complex, the floor is 'punctuated' by numerous large pillars, which restrict both movement and view in both the stage and seating areas. With this in mind, it was decided to stage *Hamlet* in the round. Yet another exciting innovation for this hospital.

This created even greater problems in seating a large number of patients, because there is always the possibility – however remote – of a disruptive incident. Such an audience, so close to the stage, inevitably provoked questions about the best way of responding to any untoward events. We considered whether the close proximity of the audience might have an adverse effect on members of the cast.

The illustration shows the layout of the auditorium and the way in which the seating/acting area was modified for the four productions.

It also posed further questions about the use of weapons or potential weapons, should a patient be tempted (or even compelled by his or her illness) to try to obtain these articles. We were, of course, aware that this might be just for effect; but the risk of their use was a real one. A decision had to be reached as to whether we should allow these items to be used under the strict supervision of a member of the nursing staff, or whether we should deny the cast these props. Such a course of action would detract from the trusting bond which is created between the audience and the players. It would also diminish the visual presentation and detract from

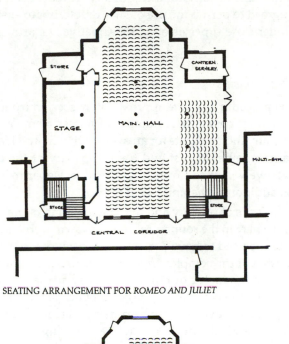

SEATING ARRANGEMENT FOR *ROMEO AND JULIET*

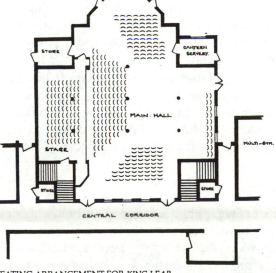

SEATING ARRANGEMENT FOR *KING LEAR*

Broadmoor Hospital – Central Hall Complex
Plans of the Auditorium

the enjoyment of the majority of the audience. After considerable discussion, it was agreed to permit the use of swords, etc. but to ensure that they were kept under close supervision of the Creative Department staff at all times.

Manpower Requirements

It was normal procedure to have approximately six staff from the Creative Department and an appropriate number of nurses from each individual unit to accompany their patients for an event in the Central Hall. However, given the large number of cast and the complexity of the event, it was decided that twelve nurses from the Creative Department would be deployed, in addition to the unit based nurses.

Besides the issue of security and the safe handling of the weapons, the performing of a play in the round presented its own problems. These were mainly due to the need to have a number of entrances to the arena. This, due to the design of the complex, required a number of external doors to be kept open throughout the duration of the play, so that players and their props could move freely about the stage and back-stage. These entrances were also required to be supervised by nursing staff at all times, to prevent the possibility of an incident or a patient attempting to abscond during the performance. In addition to these specific 'Broadmoor' issues concerning the risk of a violent incident, we also had to pay scrupulous attention to such conventional and vital matters as fire regulations.

The deployment of staff for the preparation of the venue and to oversee the cast, was achieved by allocating specific staff to particular areas/rooms. This meant that they were free to facilitate the movement of people and materials, whilst providing a safe and secure environment at all times, to do so without compromising security.

2. Preparing the Audience

The performance was publicised through the monthly newsletter, a series of posters and by word of mouth. Each patient who wished to attend the performance was asked to apply. Such applications were invited by completing a proforma which was displayed on all notice boards in patient areas. There was a total response of 108 patients (23% of the patient population), of which 105 actually attended on the day.

Their names were then forwarded to the Consultant Psychiatrist, the 'Responsible Medical Officer' (RMO). As head of the clinical team, he was asked to discuss the patient's fitness to attend. To avoid any undue distress, each clinical team was asked to make an individual assessment of each patient's physical and mental state, outlining his/her suitability to be a member of the audience. It was necessary to take into consideration the length of time of the performance, its dramatic content, the likelihood that emotions might be stirred in the patient and whether the rekindling of such emotions might have a positive or a negative effect. Such decisions inevitably involved a detailed knowledge of the patient's history and his or her present level of functioning; it could only be fully assessed by the clinical team as a whole. To the delight of the department, no patient who applied was excluded from attending the performance, though some staff accompanying their patients were given explicit instructions to monitor individual reactions during the performance.

Understandably, considerable interest was shown by all members of the clinical teams. They were both intrigued by the concept of staging such an event within Broadmoor, as well as being interested to see its impact upon their patients – both individually and collectively. This in itself caused problems from an organisational standpoint. The venue for the production was limited in capacity and the initial response from the patients was almost enough for a capacity audience. There then remained the problem of the best criteria for choosing the non-patient members of the audience.

It had been agreed that after the performance the cast, together with a small number of key personnel, would hold a workshop in which patients and other members of the audience could share their feelings, experiences and thoughts. However brief the time, it was felt that this opportunity would at least allow people on each side of the 'footlights' to meet. It was felt that this session would also act as a guide to those clinical teams who had had patients attending, whose past experiences and traumas might have been rekindled during the performance.

Two months before the performance was due to take place, Mark Rylance and Ron Daniels visited the hospital to look at the auditorium and to talk to members of the staff who would be involved in organising the event. At this point such subjects as security, the nature of the audience and the possible contingent problems that might occur were discussed.

3. Preparing the Auditorium

Prior to the day, Sunday 6 August 1989, arrangements were made for all patients' visits to take place in alternative venues, because the Central Hall complex is the usual setting for these vital encounters. It was crucial to make alternative arrangements, as a large number of friends and relatives visit our patients on a Sunday and it would be improper to either cancel or disrupt this aspect of our patients' rehabilitation. In marked contrast to prison inmates, our patients can receive daily visits if they so wish.

Arrangements were made for the Old Kitchens to be pressed into service as a makeshift dressing room. This was necessary because, for this performance, it was necessary to accommodate more actors and props than in any previous production staged during my 25 years as a nurse at this hospital. There was also the need to approve the entry of a range of vehicles to the hospital, bearing both costumes and performers, and to make provision for the safety of their cargo. For reasons that do not need to be explained, it was essential that every sword, knife and other potential weapon had to be accounted for, but so did every article – however innocent – which was brought into the hospital.

The Property Services Agency also had to be contacted to deal with a number of matters, including the preparation of stage-lighting for the performance of a play in the round, as well as having an electrician available at all times to make adjustments and oversee the whole performance. The seating arrangements had to be approved by the Fire and Health and Safety at Work representatives and a fire officer was designated to be available throughout the performance. Again, this was their first experience of staging a play in the round, unless one considers table tennis as a three-act farce!

All these preparations may seem mundane to the polished professional, but within the context of a secure psychiatric facility, with little or no experience of dealing with a major theatrical production and all that this entails, it was quite a traumatic period for all concerned.

Hamlet – 6 August 1989 – Royal Shakespeare Company

There was a buzz of excitement throughout the hospital, as the staff from the Creative Department arrived at Colchester Ward to collect the first of a small group of patients who were to assist them in preparing the arena for the day's performance. The group chatted nervously about what they had to accomplish before the arrival of the costumes and props. The hall had to be swept and polished, the dressing rooms cleared and cleaned, and the seating to be arranged.

As the group paused for a cup of coffee at about 10.30 am, there was a telephone call from the main reception area informing us of the arrival of the van containing all of the props and costumes, together with a small advance party from the cast. A nurse was dispatched to escort the vehicle and its occupants through the security network to the Central Hall complex. On arrival, the van was parked on the terrace, a large area where patients and their visitors may take a stroll. This has access to a panoramic view of the Berkshire, Hampshire and Surrey borders with – on a fine day – a distant horizon 18 miles away. The hospital is built on a steep slope, so that the lower security wall is fortuitously well out of sight of the terrace doors which open from the Central Hall.

The group entered the hall by a small side door. A discussion then ensued about the best way for the cast and props to enter and leave the arena. It was decided to make minor adjustments to the seating arrangements which would allow easier access between the arena and its points of entry. The work party then assisted, where appropriate, in the transporting of costumes and equipment to the relevant dressing rooms, again ensuring that a discrete but careful account was kept of any equipment that might be used either as a weapon, or to effect an escape.

During this period other members of the cast had been arriving and were assembling in the waiting room in the Main Reception building. These remaining members of the company were then escorted to the hall, by which time the catering department had prepared a buffet for all those who required it. Having taken light refreshment, the cast then withdrew to the dressing rooms to make their preparation for the performance.

At this point our emphasis switched to organising the movement of about 105 patients from their respective wards to the Central Hall complex in time for the performance. Patients took their seats with a small number of nurses accompanying who also acted as ushers. Within fifteen minutes the audience was assembled. Noisy with anticipation, it awaited the beginning of the performance.

After the performance, the cast and its audience mingled and gradually small groups were formed in which experiences could be shared. This achieved, the order to move the patients back to their houses was given and the company relaxed and took a well-earned break. After the movement of patients was complete, with the exception of our small band of helpers, the company's van was escorted to the rear of the hall and the task of packing the costumes and equipment into the vehicle began. This was finally accomplished and by 7.30 pm the last vehicle had left the hospital having been checked by the reception staff.

Romeo and Juliet – 18 March 1990 – Royal Shakespeare Company

The organisation of the second performance by the RSC, although filled with the same excitement and anticipation, was from an organisational standpoint very similar to that of Hamlet some seven months earlier. However, the one major change was in the preparatory work with the patients who had shown an interest in attending. A brief summary of the play was prepared and nurses from the Creative Department went to the wards and discussed it with the patients and their primary nurses. This was done either in small groups or on an individual basis if it was considered more appropriate. This pre-performance preparation was co-ordinated by Peter Whittaker, a staff-nurse seconded to this department.

Measure for Measure – 14 October 1990 – Wilde Community Theatre Company

As part of the Creative Department's initiative to improve the quality of acting of those patients who were members of the Broadhumoorist cast, we had sought the services of Dominic Barber (employed at South Hill Park, our local arts centre). He was invited to teach a range of techniques to our patients within the framework of a weekly drama group.

As part of the developing link between the hospital and the South Hill Park Arts Centre, I was pleased to arrange for the current production by the Wilde Community Theatre Company of *Measure for Measure*, to be performed in the round in our Central Hall.

Unlike the previous Shakespearian performances, the cast of this performance were either amateur or semi-professional and included the wife of a senior member of the hospital's administrative staff. The basic organisation was the same, with respect to the supervision of the cast, their props and costumes and the maintenance of security and safety. However, with the smaller numbers in the cast, we reverted to using the dressing rooms normally used by the Broadhumoorists.

The level of interest in attending this play was almost as great as for the two preceding productions by the RSC. Ninety patients attended, this being slightly over 19 percent of the total population. However, fewer members of the clinical teams attended than had been the case with the RSC performances.

King Lear – 20 January 1991 – Royal National Theatre

We were fortunate that Clare Higgins, who had played Gertrude in *Hamlet*, had been cast as Regan in *King Lear*. This meant that she had previously performed in a Shakespearian tragedy at Broadmoor and was thus well equipped to tell her colleagues 'what we did last time!'

After many initial planning meetings between Murray and myself, we arranged a meeting with the cast and their director, Deborah Warner, in the rehearsal room at the National Theatre. We eventually met prior to a performance on a wet and blustery January evening. I was able to assist Murray in preparing the cast for their visit to Broadmoor, by telling them about the probable audience they would be meeting. I took a detailed plan of the Central Hall and Clare commented on the siting of entry/exit points.

We also entered into discussions with Deborah Warner about the area in which the stage would be set. With the use of plans of the hall and Clare Higgins' first-hand knowledge, we were able to finalise most of the necessary details. At this meeting the cast lists, other technical matters and the props were agreed and I took written confirmation of these away with me. It was also decided that, due to the difficulties and cost of transporting such a large wardrobe for one performance, it would be done without costumes. I found this concept difficult to conceive at the time! Sir Ian McKellen commented ironically that his disguise as Kent might be difficult if there were no costumes!

A major refurbishment of the Central Hall complex was being undertaken during this period. This resulted in several areas being out of use, including the offices which were normally the main dressing rooms. This necessitated the use of the refurbished tribunal rooms as dressing rooms and the new multi-gym complex as a props store. Other temporary structures prevented access to the rear of the stage. However, this was to some degree overcome by the use of temporary screening placed at the rear of the hall, between the audience and the entrance.

During one of our many telephone conversations that week, the subject of providing the patients/audience with some form of programme was raised. We initially tried to write our own synopsis of the play and to photocopy the cast list, but on the day of the production, Deborah Warner presented the hospital with 100 free copies of the official programme. This gift from the National Theatre was much appreciated. Each patient was given a copy as he/she arrived for the performance.

At mid-day the company arrived and was escorted to the terrace entrance, where Murray Cox and I welcomed the party. Deborah Warner, together with some of the key members of the cast, surveyed the auditorium, requesting that we make some adjustments to the seating in the aisles, to enable a wheelchair to be manoeuvred at high speed. Some of the spotlights needed re-positioning. This achieved, the cast moved to a room at the rear of the complex where a nurse was preparing a variety of drinks and snacks. This buffet was maintained throughout the day, a service for which the cast and helpers were extremely grateful.

The company, under the direction of the Creative Department, relocated, stored and accounted for all the items on their inventory by 1 pm. By 1.25 pm the hall was once again alive with a buzz of anticipation as Murray set the scene for the play. And *King Lear* started.

Throughout the afternoon there was the scurry of players and nurses, from entrance to entrance and from stage to dressing-room, with intermissions for refreshments or the occasional press-up in the multi-gym! There was also the chance for the cast and nurses to chat about their work.

Amidst the overall feeling of organised chaos there appeared small havens of quiet and tranquillity. Players were constantly aware of their next entrance, yet they found time and presence of mind to appraise themselves of their surroundings or read the papers. At one point during the afternoon I sat astride a bench in the multi-gym discussing the hospital, its history and architecture with Peter Jefferey, David Bradley and Richard Simpson, while they tinkered with the various pieces of equipment and exercised gently. This atmosphere was, to a large degree, due to the sensitive and unobtrusive way in which the nursing staff from the Creative Department acted as advocates of the hospital. They provided informed support for our distinguished guests.

During the later stages of the performance, a male patient requested to return to his ward and was escorted there without disruption. This is a familiar occurrence at most social functions. However this apparently mundane task, if not handled with sensitivity and skill, could have marred the event.

At the end of the performance the cast received a standing ovation (and so did the audience). After Murray had thanked them, it was my privilege to present each member of the company with the hospital's 125th anniversary medal, as a token of our appreciation and to commemorate the occasion.

Afterwards, the audience was able to remain behind and share their experiences with the cast. This was in itself an organisational nightmare, with some patients and guests wishing to leave the auditorium, whilst others wanted to stay. However, charge nurse John Wooldridge and staff nurse Terry Griffiths, drawing upon their years of experience, marshalled their resources and achieved the impossible by getting all sections of the audience to their requested destinations; though it was unfortunate that some patients who had asked to remain with the actors were recalled to their wards. This is something we shall keep a particularly close eye on in any future performances, so that those patients wishing to stay will be able to do so.

At the completion of the workshop, the monumental task of clearing the hall and the many smaller rooms used during the day began. The working party of patients, together with members of the company, trudged through the hall like worker-bees returning to the hive, carrying a whole range of equipment and personal effects. That task completed, the patients said their farewells to the cast and turned their attention to cleaning and preparing the hall for the visits of their fellow patients the next day. The coach and its cargo was then escorted through the main reception area to be checked, before leaving for the return journey to London.

Once again the tea lady came to our rescue. Patients and staff enjoyed the drink and reflected upon the day, before returning to their respective wards and offices. The sense of a job well done did not seem out of place.

'Untoward Events' and Discovery Spaces

There is a happy juxtaposition of Ian Bayne's comment about 'untoward events', placed, as it is, in his discussion about the practical organisation of the set and stage management. The word 'untoward' carries a string of connotations, among them are the following: averse to; not ready or disposed for something; disinclined; intractable; unruly; perverse; hard to manage; stubborn; ungainly; awkward; unlucky; unfavourable; turning out badly; unseemly; improper and foolish. It is indeed the *mot juste* for an event which might, at least, prove a distraction to both actors and audience, or, at worst, imply some kind of danger.

In the Elizabethan theatre, there was 'an accessory stage place . . . where actors can hide, or where actors can be discovered.' Though, 'it is generally recognised that no sustained significant action takes place within this confined discovery space, but flows out onto the stage before it. . .' Slater (1982,34). Thomson (1983,50) discusses the significance of the enclosure or discovery-space and says 'We should be cautious about the idea . . . that a wide-open stage door might serve as a discovery-space. . .' But it is to Styan (1967,22) that we owe the linking of 'concealment or discovery' and the quotation from *Romeo and Juliet*. The words referring to Capulet's vault, set behind a curtain, itself set in the Broadmoor auditorium, describe a space which has much to dis-cover. The Prince says 'seal up the mouth of outrage for a while' (V.3.216).

These observations may, at first sight, appear to be diversionary. But there is such an intricate link with the dynamics of psychotherapy, in which the aim is to 'put the patient in touch with as much of his true feelings as he can bear', Malan (1979,74). In other words, he dis-covers within therapeutic space as much as he is prepared to tolerate. This trio of references in connection with the design and function of the Shakespearian theatre thus directly echoes the process of discovery and disclosure, which is an intrinsic part of psychotherapy (Cox 1978,164). There is a many-layered metaphor about the way in which that which is hidden, or covered, can become uncovered or dis-covered, so that disclosure occurs. It may also refer to the discovery of an actor on stage who had previously been hidden from view. Yet another metaphor of meeting the unexpected is the psychological significance of dramatic space becoming discovery space, when a member of the audience discovers something about himself of which he had previously been unaware. Gurr (1970,2) – whose book, incidentally, has 18 references to discoveries and discovery-space in the index – makes a comment about Hamlet which has obvious relevance to the Broadmoor audience. Having heard the 'passionate speech' about rugged Pyrrhus, Gurr comments as follows:

> And all this, as Hamlet bitterly tells himself afterwards, is monstrously for a fiction, a 'dream of passion':

> What would he do,
> Had he the motive and the cue for passion
> That I have?

> (II.2.554)

> All that is really monstrous, of course, is that Hamlet has no more motive or cue for passion than the player; he himself is as much a fiction as the player. What Shakespeare is doing in this scene is to refine on the familiar Elizabethan joke of 'tragedy played in jest', the paradox which sees murders done for entertainment, and appearances pretending to be reality. The fictitious Hamlet rails at the fiction of the player. Shakespeare's refinement is to make this paradoxical situation not a joke but an emphatic assertion of Hamlet's reality.

There may be an emphatic assertion of Hamlet's reality. But the reality of the Broadmoor audience is of a different order. It is this different order which furnishes both distance and, therefore, safety for reflective scrutiny. And if reflective scrutiny, then engagement with the self and the possibility that self-confrontation at depth might lead to disturbed feeling. This, in turn, might lead to disturbed behaviour and that this brings us full circle, because disturbed behaviour by a member of the audience could well count as an 'untoward event'.

There is a sense of dynamic interlocking and coinherence between Brook's (1972) empty space – the space set aside to receive enactment – and the healing space described by Elsass (in press) in which he compares psychotherapy and theatre. The 'tempest in my mind' rages in both.

An intricate relationship exists between self-discovery, discovery spaces and the possibility of 'untoward events', although it can be chrystallized by considering the creative tension between intrapsychic space, dramatic space and forensic therapeutic space. All three contribute to 'This Tempest in My Mind', the *collage* which follows.

M.C.

III

'This Tempest in My Mind'
A *Collage* of Comment

(*King Lear* III.4.12)

Introduction

The whole point of art is to put us in touch with things that are too far or too close for us to see in our ordinary offstage life.

(Wilshire 1982,94)

Setting the words of the title of this section in context, we read:

> 'this tempest in my mind
> Doth from my senses take all feeling else
> Save what beats there.'

Although it is a counsel of perfection, I would like this Section to be an associative free-flowing confluence of 'what beats there', in the tempestuous minds of all who shared dramatic space in Broadmoor.

> 'Tis far off,
> And rather like a dream than an assurance
> That my remembrance warrants'

(The Tempest I.2.44)

The 'far off' remembrances of those sitting 'too close' to their experiences, the dreams, the fantasies, the de-misting of memory from ordinary off-stage life are a part of what beats there. It had originally been intended to present such material as 'a stream of corporate consciousness'. It would be preferable if it emerged in a fusion – perhaps a confusion – of both conscious and unconscious comment. Some of the passages which follow are carefully structured and presented. Others are staccato, almost unformulated utterance. As far as possible this is a random, un-structured sequence and, for reasons previously given, it was felt best not to include names. Such a decision presented certain editorial difficulties. This involved a preserve of decision which could not be avoided. I hope those concerned will understand. I refer to the fact that in Section I 'Dramatis Personae', for obvious reasons, the various contributors are named. I have also included in that section letters from Peter Wight (Claudius) and Rebecca Saire (Ophelia), as their comments were so inextricably linked to the initial impact of Hamlet Day. In this Section, 'This Tempest in my Mind', letters from other actors have been processed through an editorial blender!

External Danger and Internal Dangerousness

This rubric gives us the platform for a few vital comments on the way in which the tension between psychological forces in the inner world and in the outer world can be presented and simultaneously ameliorated by dramatic enactment.

We leave the tragedies for a moment to consider three lines from *II Henry IV* which have encapsulated one of the central dynamic issues of social psychology:

> 'But I must go and meet with danger there,
> Or it will seek me in another place,
> And find me worse provided.'

(II.4.48)

These words of Northumberland do not need paraphrasing. They are crystal clear. It is important to note that his inner drive is such that he must *go* and encounter danger where it is. If he does not do so, then danger will 'seek' him somewhere else. The idea of being tracked and stalked by 'danger' which is menacing – and yet may be impersonal – can easily be transmuted into paranoid symptoms, in which phenomena not usually perceived as being dangerous will be regarded as predatory and on the move. The individual must act and encounter danger, before it finds him when and where he is least expecting it.

Setting these words alongside those of Hamlet as he begins to wrestle with Laertes, we do not find Hamlet referring to external danger – though that was certainly potentially present in Laertes' desperation and his sword.

> 'Yet have I in me something dangerous,
> Which let thy wisdom fear. Hold off thy hand.'

(V.1.262)

Hamlet had spoken for every man when he referred to:

> 'The heartache and the thousand natural shocks
> That flesh is heir to.'

(III.1.61)

He is also speaking for every man when he implies that all human beings have the potentiality for violence – all have an inherent capacity for dangerousness when external provocation is excessive or internal restraint is inadequate. There are, of course, innumerable variations on this theme. The assessment of dangerousness is an immensely complicated process. It is one of the central concerns of forensic psychiatry (see Appendix A p.253). For our present purposes, it would be entirely inna-

propriate to proceed further down this road. Nevertheless, when a man
has already done what Hamlet did to Polonius, his words

> 'Yet have I in me something dangerous,
> Which let thy wisdom fear.'

need to be taken seriously. Hamlet is to be taken at his word.

Meeting Danger with Shakespeare rather than Retreating from It

It sometimes seems that certain branches of psychology adopt a retreatist
attitude to those tragic human predicaments which occur in the 'real'
world of the market place – remembering that *predicament* comes from the
Latin, meaning 'to cry in public'. There is some truth in these allegations.
There may be more interest shown in mythology and the severed head of
Orpheus, which was still singing when it was washed up on the Lesbian
shore – than in the clinical reality of, say, the severed head of a victim in
Orpington or Aarhus or Auckland. It is not difficult to understand why
such cultural avoidance mechanisms operate. But these issues can never
be avoided in a forensic arena. All psychotherapy undertaken at Broadmoor must, sooner or later, involve the confrontation with self in which a
patient needs to move beyond Macbeth's understandable reluctance to
face what he has done:

> 'I am afraid to think what I have done;
> Look on't again I dare not.'
>
> (II.2.50)

It is one of the attributes of empathic precision to judge – as far as it is ever
humanly possible to do so – when a patient is ready to face his own music.
Or when a group-as-a-whole can endure to 'look on't again'.

One of the reasons underlying the almost unimaginable power which
the tragedies had as they were enacted in the presence of the Broadmoor
audience, is that Shakespeare enabled both actors and audience to 'go and
meet with danger there'. Shakespeare always accompanies us and stays
with us in the eye of the storm. Or in catastrophic outpourings on a
darkened heath. Or in the distracted mind of a young man aware that all
occasions informed against him. This coming alongside, yet not invading
the personal preserve of experience of another; this facilitation of intro-
spection, when looking inside is the last thing the looker feels able to do,
are evidence of the inductive power of the aesthetic imperative (Cox and
Theilgaard 1987,26). They are closely linked to the astonishing capacity
Shakespeare has for augmenting conventional clinical observation and
discernment. This is diametrically opposed to the viewpoint which holds
that poetic presentation somehow reduces precision, and necessarily

blunts perception in some areas, because it enhances them in others. These are all phenomena discussed under the heading of 'Shakespeare's Para-clinical Precision' in *Shakespeare as Prompter*.

Five quotations prepare the ground for the ferment of feeling which ensues:

> The playwright, the players, and the playgoers comprise a perfor-mance-ensemble, to which each makes a distinctive and necessary contribution. It is a partnership within which each participant has a considerable degree of autonomy. Accordingly, the theatre-event that occurs at a given performance will to a large degree vary not only with the script but with the individuals involved, whether on the stage or in the auditorium. (Hapgood 1988,1)

> . . . Each text inspires a unique rapport among the members of the performance-ensemble . . . whereas *Henry V* exhorts all concerned to put their imaginary forces to work, it is a spirit of play that animates *A Midsummer Night's Dream*, a spirit that can be so free as to be freakish. (Hapgood 1988,256)

This raises a fascinating series of questions, which time and space allow us to state, but not to answer. How did the 'unique rapport' within the performance-ensemble vary when the *Hamlet*, *Romeo and Juliet*, *Measure for Measure* and *King Lear* groups of actors came hither?

> Sometimes I would get so used to the new phraseology and level of understanding that there would come a time . . . when I would notice with horror that the poetry was fading, the image which I had loved for so many years, was somehow growing fainter, and drifting away. And I would grow ashamed of my own words which I had used to describe the image. (Kozintsev 1977,76)

> Knowledge is bathed in emotions, desires, and commitments. With-out these nurturing fluids, it withers into empty words . . . the texts were saved, but they lost their urgency! (Elsass, in press)

> All of [the incidents in *King Lear*] break upon us on a rather inchoate manner; their unfolding is as nebulous as the localities that contain them; and progression from one incident to the next is often marked by the kind of sequential discontinuity that characterizes our dreams rather than our waking moments. People and things keep taking us by surprise. (Reibetanz 1977,15)

Our sequential discontinuity of primary process feelings in free-fall, and their intermingling with formulated reflection now follows. Even that which is discontinuous has to start somewhere. What follows is 'what beats there'.

M.C.

All of a sudden it [*Hamlet*] opened doors I preferred to keep shut. And from that point I encountered the turmoil and struggle with things that in the past I've buried.

Hamlet was the most poignant of the plays, because I found myself struggling with emotions I didn't want to look at . . . He's got the skull on a stick. It made me struggle a bit. The emotion coming from Hamlet was so raw. I could feel that. He's got that rage all of a sudden. The reality is coming now. And to lighten the load is humour. The door is opened in me. I was faced with raw emotion. I struggled against it but was confronted with it again and again. Having to struggle with it again. In a different way. There was rage and confusion. All the raw emotion bubbling up. At school [Shakespeare] didn't mean anything. I wanted to do other things. [But the play] was a very strong mirror. It had the same effect on different people . . . depending on the sort of path they have walked.

It was in a time too. Duelling in the parks was generally accepted. There was carnage. Bodies all over the place . . . not altogether friendly.

We've come a long way since then . . . But I don't know? We're using cars to do the duelling now!

It was the most intimate performance I have ever been at. But it was not just a question of proximity but of improvisation. I was vaguely aware that parts of the audience were aware of other parts of the audience . . . the big group should have gone on longer.

I felt that the Broadmoor audience were far more likely to have touched the emotions and events in the play than any other audience, and that consequently the play would be far more immediate to them.

Therefore as an actor I felt a huge responsibility to demonstrate the emotion in the play truthfully. Naturally, one attempts to do this anyway, but whereas a conventional National Theatre audience may not have experienced the extremes of emotion expressed in the play, and need an actor to take them by the hand and guide them towards these feelings, I felt that the Broadmoor audience had already been there. And, somehow, it was for the actors to meet them there. Or, rather, approach something they may have already experienced . . . Although encouraged to write before the impact fades, I needed time to assess what was significant about the event and to talk to the other actors.

I found the way Hamlet greeted the ghost of his father and how he was portrayed in the play as a dead spit for the way I felt and how I have wanted to express myself. Even after all these years about the death of my father. Just to go mad and leave the world of reality behind me. The play in parts seems to express every fear and pleasure that I experienced when I committed my crime.

What I remember was that Cordelia couldn't bring herself to say that Lear was the most important thing in her life, and she was cast out for being truthful, for speaking her mind. I thought that in the past unfortunate things have happened to me for speaking my mind and saying what I felt. Is it not better sometimes to say what people want to hear? At the end she tried her best and she still died like the others.

When Hamlet was going to rape Ophelia I looked round the room to see how the rapists took it; I'm not a rapist, I killed someone.

It was a great privilege to be invited to perform at the hospital, and I think we could have carried on applauding you every bit as long as you did us! You were a simply marvellous audience, living with each beat of the performance and giving to it a unique and special quality. Live theatre is all about the interaction between the performers and the audience, but the afternoon at Broadmoor redefined that truth, as your energy and attention somehow remodelled our work. I feel most honoured to have been part of the audience.

I saw *Romeo and Juliet* here, in costume with all the bits and bobs, and I think it flowed better. I think the characters feel more in with their part if they've got their costume on; they are not so much taking notice of where they are and who we are. I got the impression that because they were in civilian clothes, it made them a bit more unprotected, if you like . . . When they're in costume, they just seem to relate better to what they were doing.

I disagree. Initially I expected to see them in costume and it was a bit of a let-down. But after a few minutes the acting was so powerful that I didn't really notice they were in civilian clothes. The acting took over.

I found the play very dramatic. More dramatic than I expected a Shakespeare play to be.

Why do you think people are talking more about the stage than the content . . . If I think about what I remember of it, I think about that Fool, dancing up and down like Max Wall: it was absolutely brilliant . . . He said afterwards that he hadn't been with an audience who could understand this part so well and he has done this part hundreds of times . . . How could he know that we understood? Because an actor of his calibre works on an understanding of the relationship between him and the audience, the rapport, all the laughing that was going on.

So much *tenderness* between persons. Kent to Lear, Lear to The Fool, Lear to Cordelia – in a place where tenderness is rare perhaps . . . The difference between The Fool and the madman; they distanced themselves from the mad Lear by laughter.

How did Ophelia know to scratch her legs like she did? All the women do things to themselves like that here; cut their wrists, scratch their faces. Men hurt other people, women hurt themselves.

Those of us at the front of the audience did pick up on The Fool's behaviour; it seemed as though he affected Lear and Lear affected him. It seemed as if the more insane Lear was getting, the more The Fool was becoming insane . . . The more he was being encouraged to act as foolishly as possible. It is difficult to explain it. None of us wants to consider ourselves a fool, but some of the silly things he was coming out with you could imagine yourself abandoning yourself, to making a load of rash foolish statements which are witty at the same time as being foolish. Well The Fool wasn't really a fool. Its a euphemism. Were they used to working with an audience that close?

For me it was very realistic, I was sitting so close, if you had wanted to, you could have got up and touched them. It seemed intimate. You could look into their eyes when they were showing an emotion. When Lear was showing rage, he was so close that you could see the spitting of his mouth. I think they also got something from us being so close, because in the brief discussion I had afterwards the actor I spoke to said they had played it all over Europe and they hadn't felt that good. The only place they had felt almost as good was in Ireland, so perhaps it says something for the small units, where they can get close. I think that not having any costumes meant that they could also improvise. I got the impressions in the little jokes between some of the actors, where there was a part that could have been seen as funny, they put in a little laugh or line of their own which added to the humour of the situation. Did you feel that or did they tell you that?

The production frightened the life out of me and it was not easy to distinguish whether or not the actors were acting or whether the action was real. King Lear was like my father, an old bigot. It was like home. All the fighting and noise.

It was easy for Cordelia, she didn't have to pay for 100 knights. By the time she had him he was only with one servant.

I found the production so powerful that I had to leave. It was like my own family – that's how they carry on. I thought I was losing my life. It is incredible to have had actors of this calibre performing in front of us.

I have not been able to take in much of the production as I was preoccupied with my own problems.

A general discussion followed about whether or not people can pretend to be mad. One patient thought that one could not pretend to be mad, whereas another thought that people could do so. This invited the reply 'You pretend to be sane' which caused much laughter in the group, apart from one member. It was very disturbing to hear Gloucester's screams when his eyes were put out.

Seeing the play was like watching something on TV. One of the actresses said that the production made her cry each time but I could not relate to that.

I wondered what appearing in such a powerful production did to the actors . . . I spoke to the actors who said it helped them in their personal lives as they could cry and shout on the stage and get their emotions out.

It is difficult to shout and cry in Broadmoor because staff assume there is 'an incident' going on . . . There have been many times when I wanted to shout. But I have usually gone to the toilet and turned this shout into a tiny squeak. [The RMO said at this point the patient demonstrated with his arms and hands to show how tiny the sound had become. Other people were generally in agreement that it would be good to have the opportunity to let some of these feelings out and the RMO suggested that dramatherapy might be useful].

Two patients expressed anger towards the RMO for trying to make them express feelings after the play when they had just wanted to thank the actors and listen to them. The only reason the RMO was forgiven was that she had been affected by the play.

I can't believe that anyone can be as bad as that . . . as when Edmund lay dying and seemed pleased that the two sisters were fighting over him.

There were two things to be frightened of – Broadmoor itself and raw Shakespeare. I knew it would change me (not my life, *me*), and it has. Thus were my sympathies enlarged. As part of the audience it was impossible not to be totally involved, although at the same time aware that the performance itself was extraordinary. Was it like this the first time this play was ever performed? I don't think it can have been, knowing about the other plays that were being written then, with their themes of revenge and madness, but also very clear sense of black and white . . . I have never been clearly aware of so many types of 'madness' in Lear, or even really noticed that the two maddest characters are the two oldest sisters. It was extraordinary to hear somebody talk afterwards about poor Tom and how much better he got when he had been with his father for a while – this was someone who said he had actually played Edgar when he was 16, at school.

The experience was far too enormous to encapsulate . . . It would be so edifying if a company of actors rehearsing a Shakespeare play might be able to hold some of their rehearsals at Broadmoor in a sort of workshop atmosphere with patients supervised by Dr Cox. The participation which we felt whilst performing *King Lear* was the kind that one rarely, if ever, elicits from the usual audience and in that participation lay the seeds of communication which I feel is the essence of any theatrical performance.

The actors were definitely inspired to play with more truth, to give a more *accurate* presentation of their characters at Broadmoor. We could cut down on rehearsal time considerably by rehearsing at Broadmoor; as all the paraphernalia of creating a character is reduced to bare and meaningful essentials with such an audience! I should love to spend a long time going into other details about the experience but have to go to Eastern Europe now.

I found it a fascinating, instructive and ultimately uplifting day. I knew that one way or another the atmosphere would be 'highly charged', but the way this manifested itself was truly extraordinary . . . I stood on stage as Oswald and felt that I was being 'scrutinized and recognized' as someone nudging at the barriers of conformity, repression and ultimately self-presentation – never more so than during my 'cowardly encounter with Kent'. The language was much more pronounced than usual, and I am sure this had to do with the heightened sense of the vagaries of human nature and *understanding* of those vagaries that must exist beneath the surface of such a place as Broadmoor . . . I came away more aware of Oswald reacting to the boundaries of his existence . . . human, in fact. If that carries through into my performance, then that is wonderful; it was certainly instructive to be reminded of the high drama of moments which, performing over a year, one can easily forget . . . On the most basic level, I will never forget how many times in the play I noted characters physically restraining each other. I was actually aware with our Broadmoor audience of the triggers which set off physical violence – it made the drama more frighteningly real. But as an experience it was immensely uplifting, because there was true understanding of human nature (holding the mirror up) going on without all the usual barriers which separate the audience from the actors and are normally taken for granted – I have to confess that I found the after-show discussion rather frustrating. This was partly because we were encouraged to sit in groups, whereas I found standing and mingling rather more promising as people would have been able to talk to who they wanted to. It was also a pity that so many of the patients had to leave. Obviously it needs time and perhaps informality to break the barriers and find a common language – the emotional stakes being so high. I wanted to ask the patients questions, but the fundamental emotional issues of the play's relevance to their experience seemed so loaded that I didn't know where to start. However, I am sure that the follow-ups with the psychotherapy will have been appropriate.

It was so brilliant that I would take my family to see it when I'm not in Broadmoor. King Lear is very well acted. What was missing was the costumes and the stuff for the stage.

The production was excellent and I enjoyed it. Edgar started off pretending to be mad and maybe he really became mad.

Broadmoor itself is very seductive, one feels very safe there – not physically safe, but mentally safe, which is probably the wrong way round! The tabloid view of 'mad, bad and dangerous to know' is a lot more comfortable, but then I don't think that one can catch the bus home from any performance of *Lear* (or any of the other tragedies) without having this undermined.

I chose to sit with the patients and their concentration was a tangible thing. Those to whom I spoke during the interval said they were totally absorbed and this was certainly obvious. One patient, shortly to be discharged, told me that he would never have dreamt of going to the theatre in the past. But since watching *Hamlet, Romeo and Juliet* and now *Lear* he can't wait to see more. I am sure there must be many more who feel the same . . . Perhaps my over-riding feeling was the pleasure in being able to witness once again the effect that a visit to Broadmoor has on 'outsiders', people to whom the very word has previously conjured up a degree of fear and apprehension, even repulsion. One visit to the hospital changes that. It is a very broadening experience and I was delighted to hear the actors confirm this and to watch the easy rapport between actors and patients.

I was flooded with different emotions throughout the play . . . from profound sadness to laughter . . . actually exclaiming 'J.H. Christ' when one of the cast was stabbed realistically in the wedding-tackle area. It was almost as if I felt it myself and felt uncomfortable for a moment.

What affected me most was the sad and violent deterioration of Lear himself . . . When Lear died I felt an overwhelming sense of loss and tears riding down my cheeks. I desperately wanted to go over and hug Lear's corpse. I felt the sense of union in death between Lear and his daughters. Also the sense of peace and wholeness in the deaths . . . Actors and actresses came here as unknown people and leave firm friends. The reason for this methinks is that we share an intimacy and oneness that can never be experienced elsewhere. Having killed and abused ourselves, we are able to understand the madness and violence and the many ranges of emotions in Shakespeare's tragedies because it is close to our heart. We don't have to use our emotions guessing what it might be like to kill, maim and feel absolute despair. Most of us have been there ourselves.

I could well understand how revealing it must have been to King Lear and the Fool – in particular – when every line must have come to them new-minted. It was undoubtedly the most understanding and responsive audience we have played to. The emotion and contact heightened by the intimacy of the setting. What was particularly interesting was the understanding of the Fool's convoluted language and humour. To the patients I spoke to he was the most logical thinker in the play . . . a most challenging, refreshing and thought provoking experience. I agree with your colleague who said that if 'Will' was around today, he would probably make more money as a psychiatrist than a playwright!

It is obvious to me that all of the cast share a special relationship. Might I say how shockingly realistic it was and how sharp the memory of their work stands in my mind . . . On two occasions now I have watched the performances brought to us and each time I have been left wondering how it is that these people can allow such personal spaces to be invaded. First I saw spitting in the face in the 'RSC workshop', then the hand laid to the pubic area 'Lear to Goneril'. Finally, the violence portrayed was in itself realistic.

But as a simple folk I can honestly say I have not been so moved by any of the plays I have seen on stage or TV. It was much like a good book, one did not want to put it down . . . It was one hell of a way to build up a sweat. And all for us. It was a very moving experience.

As someone who cannot read Shakespeare I found the performance fascinating. It was easy to follow. The clarity of the dialogue, combined with the professionalism of the acting and its close proximity, kept me riveted for the full four hours . . . I particularly enjoyed Clare Higgins who managed to portray Gertrude's emotions exceptionally well. Mark Rylance's Hamlet, especially his humour, when feigning madness was also good . . . Therapeutically it was invaluable. I found it uplifting that a group of such talented and respected actors and actresses, in their spare time, could make the effort to perform for us, a group of despised social outcasts.

There were many moments when I forgot where I was, when I wondered if it was real . . . The actors were so skilful at playing with our emotions . . . I felt like I was a puppet in their hands. It is obvious that the players sincerely appreciated this strange audience and they dealt with us humanely and with deep respect . . . They gave us all they had and we soaked it up . . . The workshops after the play could be described as the crème de la crème. I was so high emotionally with the play and I found it a great benefit to sit with a cup of tea and have a talk with some of the cast . . . I talked to one of the actors about the irony of them acting out a terrible tragedy in a place like this which deals wholly with tragedies . . . I also spoke about how some of the scenes of violence or madness must have affected many of us and how it could be used therapeutically by us . . . One of the knife scenes, for instance, reminded me of an incident when I threatened my ex-girlfriend, and it brought home to me the fear she felt . . . simply because I felt afraid watching the same. It also brought home to me how we compound our miseries through our own destructive feelings of bitterness and vengeance . . . If only we could learn not to act on impulsive urges of revenge we would so lessen the amount of tragedies in this society . . . I also learned personally how good it is to shout and scream rather than walk around holding it back and behaving unemotionally.

Hamlet, the person, could also have been my mother, brother, sister and even just a friend – and how they felt at hearing that I, their brother, had done what I had done . . . So it did have a lot of meaning . . . I hope you can understand this.

I'm still thinking about *Hamlet* five days after the performance. For me it was a journey of self-recognition through madness, and it was healthy for me to experience. Several times I saw myself in the guise of those brilliant actors and actresses. True, parts were traumatic, but somehow it was a positive calling up of my own savage memories. They could be viewed rationally from a distance, like in a play.

Too much analysis leads to paralysis, or too much paralysis leads to analysis . . . This for me was the message of the play. Although I do not know which comes first. My first spontaneous reaction to the play involved an awareness of energy and honesty. The company with no costumes or scenery had really to go for it from the opening lines. And they succeeded beyond expectation . . . Caught in the crunch of thesis and anti-thesis, he pussy-footed around, vacillated and generally shilly-shallied with disastrous consequences to his reason, his life, and the lives of those around him. His was the sin of omission, not commission. Hamlet is a tragedy of a man who could not make up his mind . . . My most memorable experience of the evening was in meeting the cast afterwards. I discovered that actors are human. They are people. It is rather analogous to parachuting. One can have some comprehension of the aerodynamics of a parachute, but it is not until one has actually made a 'jump' that one really understands parachutes. So it was not until I had talked to several of the cast did I realize that actors and actresses are human like anybody else. Quite a revelation. Shakespeare wrote something about people being actors, playing many parts. I prefer to see people myself, not as actors, but as characters in a play. Perhaps one's life is a reflection of one's personality – its strengths and weaknesses – and perhaps psychodrama leads one into insights or helps to lead one in this direction so that one acquires windows and insight into one's personal script, enabling one to have more control over one's destiny. Perhaps this is an over-simplification, but personally, I can see no harm in incorporating dramatherapy into some Broadmoor patients' treatment.

I found myself drawn into it as it touched even my cold heart and as they shouted in their dementia I was glad about their shouting. I was really glad, glad, glad, they shouted at each other from one end of the play to the other . . . Having been subject to sensory deprivation for my first six years . . . not being acquainted with physiologists' approaches I don't know what you may understand by reading trash or is it a gold nugget or with what resonant beat this letter begins to evoke 'Please read on' . . . Well my first reaction was loud and stagey, making me a little uncomfortable, but as one got over the first cringe of sincerity and then (back to I found myself drawn into it) . . . But someone must see my pain. Can you? They are turning life into steam.

It would have been a million times better if they had spoken in today's English. Hamlet was a good actor. He was supposed to be crazy and indeed he looked crazy. I know we are all crazy in here but none of us looks like that. I didn't know that there were really crazy people in the world who looked like that. Hamlet's mother got on my nerves in her pretty coat showing off her tiny breasts. She couldn't care less. There's a lot of emotion, anger, violence and sadness in the play and all the false tears and anger made the play not so good. They used a real butchery knife in the play and it lay on the floor where we were sitting for quite a while. Someone could have easily cut their throat with it or someone else's. I think I am in love with Hamlet.

I did feel very uncomfortable at some stages because of the amount of physical violence against women. Ophelia, played by Rebecca Saire, was great. This had me in tears because my sister who I love so much was a victim of this most devastating crime of which I feel largely responsible.

I've never been to anything which took me out of myself as much as this play. Absolutely bang on.

Hamlet's death was a farce. There he was lying down and supposedly dead, while his chest was going up and down, up and down. It was not his fault. The Central Hall was very hot, I blame the fencing in the last act. Shakespeare could not have taken care with this bit. And I don't think he was entirely to blame but it did take the authenticity out of it and speaking for me, spoilt the play . . . Earlier too, when Hamlet stabbed someone that was too unrealistic. However, despite these criticisms, I did enjoy myself. And so did a lot of other people, I haven't known us to be so quiet for so long. Also I noted that not many of us 'went to the loo' because we did not want to miss anything. It was a great shame that none of the girls was able to stay behind afterwards and talk to the cast.

I saw their joy and pain, and the adrenalin within them, you could feel it as you watched them.

This made me think how unaware I was about other people's feelings when committing my crimes . . . I asked one of the actors how he put his heart into the role. He said to me 'Understand the character and feel what he must have felt like.' I had to think of my victims how they felt. It was an experience I will never forget. I hope they will come again and other people can witness the event. Why not have this down on the field in a big marquee so more people can go?

It would be very good to see further productions of Shakespeare if this is possible. Though I would advise against the completely one-sided view of life by only staging tragedies.

The performance certainly engraved its mark on me. I found some scenes quite harrowing, because they were so close a link with the violence and emotion of my own offence. The performance also gave me an unsettling look into the eyes of the victim and oppressed. I think I scaled every emotion while witnessing the event unfolding before my eyes and it took me a couple of days to settle down again. So often have I seen and heard the very methodical and calculated rantings of Hamlet, the self-destruction of Ophelia and the bottled fury of the King, e.g. the kicking and hitting of the wall. I think there was a part of everybody there to be seen.

It was the fastest four hours I have ever experienced; even though I spent most of it in an intense stunned silence (as did most of the audience) broken only by Hamlet's few jokes. Anyway, as far as I am concerned, they can come back any time. Long live the Bard at Broadmoor.

You felt emotion – and the play was written 400 years ago . . . The horror you may imagine most people would feel on discovering madness in a loved relative was wonderfully portrayed by Clare Higgins who played Gertrude, the Queen, Hamlet's mother. with her reply to the question 'How is Hamlet?'. She replies 'He's m . . . a . . . d' – said so agonizingly, you must believe he is mad and that he is her son.

Electrifying, my mind expanding, door opening. Once-in-a-lifetime experience. Privilege to be there and to meet the cast afterwards. I have been to Stratford several times, but the Broadmoor performance was more powerful for me than any play I have seen. The cast seemed overwhelmed too, moved by the intensity of the audience reaction which was quite different from what they normally experience. At least one said she acted as never before. Given that particular audience and the incredible acting, the material itself at times seemed almost dangerous and frightening, but as the play worked itself through, it felt cathartic. It was therapeutic and probably more therapeutic than much 'therapy' for everyone – staff and patients alike. The actors made no distinction between staff and patients, and probably did not always know who was what. With no loss of security our patients were treated as 'people' and not as psychopaths or schizophrenics or disordered personalities or people to be feared. In a subtle way this could only help their self-esteem. Security was there, but it was more unobtrusive than normal and seems more in line with modern thinking.

Undoubtedly Mark's performance of Hamlet is and was totally spellbinding, very convincing and brilliantly portrayed . . . Yet without the remainder of the cast there would be no Hamlet. Thank you for the rare moment in time.

I believe there was some debate before hand about the wisdom of choosing a play whose themes of violence and madness might hold quite personal meaning for many of those present and might as a result prove unnecessarily upsetting. I did not receive the impression either during the discussions immediately following the performance or through later conversations with patients that this was in fact the case, indeed it could be argued that the relevance of the issues enhanced the experience for them (as it certainly did for me).

In more general terms it seems that events such as this must be of benefit to Broadmoor as a community, both by making it more open to the wider world and by enhancing the range of opportunities available to the patients.

So we could start by people saying what were their expectations, what were we feeling like as we went there, because I know I just regressed to about 12 years old. I sat on the back seat and wanted to jump up and down like a child because I was scared. As we got there I got more and more manic and I wanted to eat more and more baby food, when I saw the sign 'Broadmoor' I went terribly quiet . . . we all went very quiet.

I was apprehensive although not really wanting to admit to myself that I was frightened, because it was so unknown.

It all comes from the publicity of the name 'Broadmoor' . . . I was very frightened to be going through certain things that I imagined these people knew much more about, because they had experienced it.

We were going to do a violent play and were told by those who met us that everyone at Broadmoor was there for doing something pretty serious.

What was a frightening thing was that one would be rumbled . . . It was like auditioning. It reminded me of auditioning for the RSC. It was just terrifying.

I found it very difficult . . . The casual slaughters at the end . . . The very last speech I was saying to the audience 'Carnal, bloody and unnatural acts' and I felt I really had to come back off it and look away . . . which I have never done in the theatre, because I was becoming almost accusatory . . . somehow becoming too pressing . . . So that the text became an accusation? Not an accusation. No, it was not an accusation. I have used the wrong word. More that I was being too blatant with the text, maybe. Labouring it because I knew these people had committed these things and I felt that they were not able to be objective about the play enough . . . that the audience would become too involved in what I was saying.

I was aware of the security and for us actors being stripped of our lights and our props and our crowns – all that lovely set which we are so used to, that it is like home when we do the play. One of the few props we took was our bed, when we could have got a bed in Broadmoor. [The bed for the closet scene was a double bed. Broadmoor could not supply this. M.C.]

They wanted there to be props there, to be props and costumes and were worried about the line of division. They wanted there to be a certain separate reality.

It makes what you are doing on the stage here [Stratford] perhaps glorious or romantic. But I found in Broadmoor everything becoming so much more pertinent . . . and a lot of that romanticism came down to a much more urgent and earthier level.

There was a very electric atmosphere in telling the whole story from word one to the last line of the play. It was much more compact.

I felt there was a whole new energy between us as actors which I have never felt before. Eye contact, people's eyes were looking into eyes. I remember you Jack [Horatio], I was absolutely locked into you because you were the one thing I was sure of. And I felt so much energy in the space.

My lurid fantasies that the whole thing was going to erupt in psychological flames, and real psychosis, would take place in the interaction between a very violent play about insanity and violent insane minds I had read about in the papers. Once that did *not* happen, it went on to a lower key, rather than a crackle of static electricity. It was in a lower key than I expected it to be. You felt that strong tension, although there were a couple asleep and the nurses were all around.

I still cannot think about it without becoming choked up . . . the intensity was something I had never ever partaken of in the theatre before. You were there in a curious way out of a labour of love, you wanted to be there. There was no career. There was no job expectation. You were performing something which had about it, not only that act of generosity, but there was also a curious identification of subject matter. It reminded me of what ancient Greek theatre must have been like. We the audience and actors are completely transcended . . . suddenly that intensity was unbelievable. The identification of subject matter, of audience and actors in the room, no proscenium barrier, no job barrier, it was absolutely astonishing. What you were saying was suddenly infinitely simpler, infinitely more vulnerable and accessible.

It was very boring, I was bored stupid, I could not work out why, then I realized everyone was bored. We were bored playing to the audience because there was no truth.

No real inner necessity? That was what *was* there. I felt we were really wanted. There was a necessity there. If only theatre could always be like that.

The generosity was curious. It was very much a give and take, which is the heart of secret theatre. This is really right to the core of what the Greeks must have felt when the experience was communal. I do not think I am ever going to recover from it.

Initially, we did not know what was going to happen, and when the girl was laughing, I wondered at least if it was the start of other people laughing. It might get out of hand. No-one ever asked her to 'Shush', as in a normal theatre.

They all stood up at the end, I came off after the closet scene in a real mess and I opened the door and there was Jimmy Saville with a cigar in a pair of running shorts. And the whole day became just completely surreal for me . . . I didn't care if an elephant came round the corner with a tutu now. I was completely without any boundaries. I just completely dissolved.

It certainly was a spontaneous thing, I do not think anyone ever thought what might happen at the end. It was such a rule-breaking action . . .

I found the meeting after the performance the most rewarding part of the day. The questions they asked, 'How do you depict madness on the stage?' were so important, compared with those stupid questions like 'How do you learn the lines?'!

I kept wondering whether they were patients or psychiatrists.

It was interesting what Murray Cox said at the end. The day proved there were not two different worlds, but it was one world . . . That was the most poignant part of the afternoon when he said that.

When I drove out, the first impression I had was looking at the people in Crowthorne – the people I pass in the street – any of these could be any of those in there, and vice versa.

Any of us could be in there.

There had been such looks – turning to them at certain moments – and saying the lines that are there. And time and time again looking at them. They were so ultra-human. That was what seemed to be so different about them. There absolute openness, humanity, vulnerability. Some of them look away but most of them look back at you with such a look of . . . I don't know what it was.

Several people asked if the feelings that you feel when you act are real feelings.

There was a feeling of grief and responsibility at having done something that is abhorrent to you. And having to live with that all your life, I was quite overwhelmed. I didn't know whether it was coming from them or if I was imagining it.

The play was not only a wonderful piece of art in itself, and a wonderful document. It was also a catalyst for a dialogue between the performers and the audience. We acknowledged the same conversation. We all understood what we were talking about. I think in Broadmoor conversation was animated and very exciting. Everybody was taking an equal part and seemed to have an equal interest in it.

It reminded me a lot of touring. The intensity you get in that space, you could be doing it in a village hall somewhere. The intensity will be there because of the physical proximity.

The guy I was talking to had lost his father. And his mother had remarried three months later. He had a hard time with that. He recognized that as being the root of his particular problems. He identified so directly with that particular part of the play.

You felt it was doing something, rather than just being entertaining. Having seen 'King Lear' at the Old Vic, it was with certain reservations I volunteered to see the production in the Central Hall. But I must admit that I found the Broadmoor version more moving and a far better production. With no props or scenery, the audience concentrated more on the acting which was superb.

Sitting amongst the action, I felt that I was a part of the performance. When Lear was being wheeled out of the scene in a wheelbarrow, my foot got in the way and was promptly run over!

The scene where Lear was nearly going mad was one of the most moving pieces of acting I have seen. It was a most memorable performance and I hope we can arrange for another play soon.

It's really strange for you to bring a play about madness to Broadmoor – we are so protected from it here.

You used these things to be entertained. But you are not really entertained while you are there. Because you are living, you have to go through what they are going through, it's only when you come back that you realize.

Some things were happening. I was forced to go back and look at myself in the past. I thought I had done something similar or felt something similar and I was trying to figure out what is the feeling.

It was good to be challenged, not just as an actor but as a human being. Reflecting on the day as I left, I realized that I'd stared at people, trying to detect signs of 'madness' or hints of a violent, disturbed nature. Peoples' body language fascinated me. My final experience was one of feeling considerable guilt. This was because I couldn't tell the difference between patients and staff. As I sat there, I was confronted by the prejudices I thought I didn't have. How dare I look into someone's face and make a judgement about him? How deep-seated our behaviour patterns are, in spite of ourselves, but what a privilege it is to gain even a little understanding of them. That's what coming to Broadmoor for the day meant to me and I thank you for the opportunity.

When Hamlet came in in his pyjamas we all recognized him; we have all been there.

We all knew that the King was the evil bastard the minute he walked on stage; he's the baddie – all that asking for forgiveness did not mean anything.

I thought that Hamlet kissing his mother was just too much – I found that very shocking.

I think it was heavy going for a lot of people because it is about things they have done.

When you picked up the skull it really got to me; hit me right in the stomach; I've killed a person and I've done a lot of work on how the relatives must feel, I've played the role of the relatives; but it never crossed my mind until now that there is a corpse somewhere of the person I killed. I have never thought about the corpse before.

I didn't understand the words, but I understood the feelings.

We were not an audience but an important part of the action unfolding in front of us.

I didn't understand many of the words they were using, and I found the story hard to follow, but I understood every bit of emotion.

Many of us here in Broadmoor are able to understand Hamlet's disturbed state of mind because we have experienced such traumas.

I have heard a rumour that the RSC are to come back here again. I do hope it is true. I would dearly like to see them in action again.

The Fool is a compulsive truth-teller. His destiny is linked with Lear's. Nowhere else for him to go. As a professional, Lear is his only meal-ticket. The relationship with Lear exists on many levels; employer/employee; father/son (the son Lear never had?); son/father (a cynical pastiche of the above?); pupil/teacher. It is also bitter/sweet; love/hate; selfish/unselfish. The Fool has blinding premonition shortly before death, a vision of chaos and confusion which suddenly reveals a demonic side to his nature. Although Fool is made up on many contradictions, the one thing that rides throughout them all is his loyalty to Lear.

I liked the continuity. Most of the people who went to see *Hamlet* and then *Romeo and Juliet* also went to the *Lear* production. So there was a positive feeling among those who attended . . . like a family.

I thought Lear had loved his children.

It was disturbing to hear Gloucester's screams when his eyes were put out . . . I missed this as I was at the toilet.

A look would pass or a touch or a gesture, as if to say 'We've improvised this slightly' – especially when the daughters were buttering up Lear, to get him to part with his kingdom. And the middle daughter had to put on gross exaggerated affection for him and when she came to do it she said her lines but there was an extra touching. As if although not in costume, they were so at ease with their parts that there were these little extra impromptu add-ons to the main play. Well, perhaps some day in the future I'll see it again and see how other people act it out. And see what I remember as being there or not being there.

I felt too close. I wanted to go there as a spectator, but I didn't feel like a spectator. I wasn't aware of the drums until they actually banged them, although they were right behind me – you were also very near the army and maybe you thought someone was going to jump on you, or trip over you.

I felt the closeness of the audience affected in some ways, good or bad, the way the actors performed. We saw them, and they seemed to enjoy it. But – perhaps it was the first time they had turned up here . . . It was likely that they were fairly apprehensive . . . That's understandable.

You felt part of it – being so close – you were drawn into it. I think maybe they had to concentrate a bit more – because we were actually staring at them. I think it put more pressure on them but I think some of them enjoyed it. It was a new experience – perhaps it reminded them of training – though also I think it does affect some of them.

Were there any bits you couldn't watch? What, due to the nastiness? There was a lot of fighting with swords. It was terrible. It was a wonder they didn't get killed doing it. I was frightened of the swords, real swords, proper swords, not plastic ones or wooden ones, but real ones, steel ones . . . I was surprised at the confidence they had to use real weapons in that close environment . . . [Did you feel you were going to get a sword coming near you?] . . . I did, yes. I was really near the front row. That's why I couldn't watch . . . in case I had to leave.

Being so close you got the expressions on the faces to follow, even if you can't follow the words, which I couldn't follow a lot of, some of what was being said I couldn't follow. But being so close, I tried to figure out through the movements or the actions.

When we come to express our mental stress, people step back, or the lid is put on it straight away; but there you were, and it was emotion, raw emotion . . . and if it does happen, it is quickly put down. If somebody becomes irate and starts shouting, they are removed so that nobody else becomes affected . . . but for 15 minutes there must have been nothing but shouting and anger. And because the acting was so realistic, it was just natural anger. I could feel – certainly when some of the fight scenes were around, that there was adrenalin around and could feel my heart quicken, even though I know it is only acting and having seen *Romeo and Juliet*, I know that no-one's going to get hurt . . . but with shouting and the anger there I could feel my pulse quickening . . . it's the anger – but it's also the weapons. There were many things that could be used as weapons, but there those were; specific weapons; as you said they were real weapons, real steel, steel is a weapon. In here a sword being swung . . . is this different from a chair being swung? . . . It's got to be in some sort of way frightening . . . We usually see it suppressed but on this occasion we see it allowed to continue to happen. Here we don't see it allowed to reach a conclusion. Here we see it stopped. We are seeing what we would feel is an out of control situation . . . That's what I think people are surprised at.

What I am surprised at is Shakespeare's understanding of people having breakdowns, or suffering mental illness. Because it seemed in all the three plays I have seen here there is an element of that. The lead part appears to portray some kind of illness. I am amazed that that far back he could understand . . . or have I got this wrong? Is he differentiating emotional problems, where people get upset, and actors being more than upset, being mentally disturbed? In King Lear's part for example, it was clear that he was more than emotionally upset. He became deranged. All those centuries ago, were they aware of derangement? But did they differentiate? Did they know that this person is deranged and this person is just upset? . . . [So what was your diagnosis?] . . . King Lear was getting old, wasn't he . . . so it could have been senile dementia.

Shakespeare worked very much in tragedies . . . Is that a tragedy? Did they see that as a tragedy? . . . Would people in that age recognize what they were portraying? Would they say 'Oh he's disturbed' or 'He's jealous' . . . . They could recognize The Fool . . . that's obvious.

I think he (Lear) needed to be loved. He was suffering from some form of illness which led him to need a higher degree of comfort than perhaps he could have expected from the people around. He needed to be loved so much that he accepted the spoken word rather than looking into it, because it satisfied his immediate need to be loved. Hence, when his daughters gave him their assurances that they loved him, he then gave them everything he possessed because he believed what they were saying. But I think he must have started to realize pretty quickly that he had made a mistake and he wanted to redress the whole thing. But not being able to made him feel a deeper sense of hopelessness and he went deeper into it . . . Hamlet had it too, a sense of hopelessness. We can recognize it as mental illness, we know what it means. But then did they know; would they say he was bewitched or something else? I don't think the words 'mental illness' would have existed then.

[Was he acting or was he real?] . . . He was acting a part . . . [But was he real?] . . . He was very real. Not just his part. All the parts were.

I knew the actual fighting wasn't real. It was the emotions that were real. And distressing.

Why did that old git there, the old man, frighten me like my father used to?

I thought he [Lear] had on a pair of Broadmoor pajamas and a Broadmoor towel . . . When I saw the towel I found myself wondering for a few moments what had happened to their original costumes. And whether they had not arrived yet.

I know some people who walked out of *Hamlet*, and they didn't explain why apart from saying they couldn't handle what was happening there.

You don't have to understand all the words to understand what was happening there . . . You don't have to understand the words at all but I think the plays are good therapy. If that is how we are looking at it now, that is in therapeutic terms, rather than as a form of entertainment. And I think they should continue, because I get the feeling that people relate to things in these plays within themselves, where I don't think they would be able to relate to other people, or in the group, or even to a doctor. They are bound by defences of one kind or another. I think they delve into their own past when they see these characters acting out. And I wouldn't be surprised if this was reason why some of the patients leave because maybe it is too close to home in some way.

I kept hoping that she would suddenly revive, that she wasn't actually dead. When they had to go and try to stop the orders for her death, I remember thinking 'Is he going to get there in time to be able to save her, or perhaps they'll cut her down and she's not actually dead'. It made me feel very sad.

Every time there is a Shakespeare play on, there's sword-fighting, mad people.

Before we could go to *Hamlet* the RMO had to give consent. Some people were turned down, because it was thought it would be too disturbing.

I know the sword-fighting is staged, and I worried about them hurting themselves, but it has seemed to be the emotion that is so real. The fighting is done in the context of the play and I know the play is not real. But the emotions are . . .

We are caught in the wake of emotion. It's like watching an argument right in front of you . . . It is.

Whoever thought of it obviously knew what they were doing, fetching Shakespeare plays into here. Because it is probably the only set of plays that give actors the chance to portray human emotions to that extent: it gives them licence to go all out.

The line at the end of *Hamlet* 'Report me and my cause aright to the unsatisfied' is particularly relevant to our patients because many of them can't report their own cause aright. So Hamlet does it for them.

I liked watching it, but it took a long time. Four hours. The last hour of it I was dead bored because I never had a cup of tea . . . there were too many people queuing up. It went on and on. I missed my tea. I never had any tea. They gave me four corned-beef sandwiches when I got back.

What most struck you? The scene where he pokes his eyes out . . . I saw that very close up. I think the audience in general couldn't see that because the chair was up-turned. I think the person on the receiving end – Peter Jefferys – must have had a lot of confidence in the other actor, because the other actor didn't hold back. Peter Jefferys didn't hint in any way 'Be careful' . . . What did you see from the side? I saw the whole scene . . . We thought to ourselves, should we take that part of the play, did we do wrong? . . . No, there was no reason to. It was a very quick scene. He closed his eyes before anything happened. The other fellow jumped over and gouged his eyes out. He didn't actually do anything. He just. He didn't move anything. He didn't really go anywhere near his eyes. And then there was a whole lot of ranting and raving and screaming and shouting and then the other fellow stood up and ran off. I think he just stood up and said 'Aye–aye'. I think he just ran off, just ran off . . . He was led off wasn't he? No he ran off. No he was led on . . . . I thought he was taken off . . . I thought it was a very flimsy bandage considering he had just had his eyes taken out . . . I thought that was irrelevant, because you knew he'd had his eyes taken out . . . Why were his eyes taken out anyway? Was it a punishment of the times . . . Why the eyes? Why didn't they chop his hand off? He must have seen something. There must have been something for her to centre her anger on, the eyes. If he had said something, they should have asked for his tongue to be taken out. So did he see something? Or did he betray something by sight? Or did she think 'We'll have his eyes out' because that was the worst thing they could think of to do at that time? . . . Why not the ears, why the eyes? . . . I couldn't figure out whether the middle daughter thought that he had seen something about her. . . . It was very quick wasn't it. Maybe we have got to put it down to entertainment . . . It's gory . . . It keeps the crowd going . . . But the people who took the eyes out weren't thinking along those lines . . . they are not connected. Nobody here can see the link. [Can you see the link?] When was the play set . . . I was wondering if gouging the eyes out was the in-thing. Was it in keeping with the times? Like duckingstools and things like that . . . We might relate to it and think 'Oh that's what they did in those days' . . . In *Hamlet* they don't go anywhere near the face do they? They do something else.

I wonder if he was affected by seeing us out there, wondering 'Am I putting over a good . . . ? because he was dealing with the real thing wasn't he? The real thing was in front of him.

It was tragic, very tragic. The play is about people who turn against one another; you see the way that people work by conning others, by doing things behind their backs and how they get away with it.

Did you have a favourite character? . . . Only the bloke I saw in the wheelchair. Only the bloke in the wheelchair. I like him . . . Yes, he was very good.

But people don't have time to think and speak like that. When someone is in such a high state of emotion that he was trying to portray, you don't bother getting your words right. You just shoot straight off.

I think the experience of performing in Broadmoor will benefit the performance a bit later. I feel better in the show already and I feel better than I did last week. I think the benefits will come up later when we have assimilated it in our heads.

What's the difference between the anger that was acted in the play and the natural anger that we see in everyday life? They were acting a part, but were they really angry with the people they were angry at? They did actually show the physical contortion of the face and saliva coming out of the mouth, and frothing, and redness of the skin. The anger was portrayed, I don't know how.

It's limited. In a play. It can't go further than the play goes. Two people outside get into a real fight, whereas on stage it is only acting. The emotion is there, but you can't get the reality of real life.

I get the feeling that some actors and actresses believe themselves in the part so much, that they become the part . . . Mark Rylance actually became Hamlet . . . It's their role to make it as real as it possibly can be . . . Does it mean that the actors are basically liars? They are telling us lies. The emotion doesn't seem to be lies, to me it seems to be real . . . I don't know if I am speaking to the actress or whether I am still speaking to the part she was playing . . . I suppose she was nervous and still playing the part because of being in Broadmoor . . . They have the ability to pour themselves into more than one role when the need arises.

I can only think that the power of it comes somewhere from the pain and suffering of the patients . . . the degree of pain and suffering that those people either feel or have been associated with, I am talking about the victims there and the other thing about it is in a very real way there is some kind of sense that is hard to define and certainly hard to qualify, that the whole thing may be helping these people. Possibly helping them a very great deal in a way that is hard to explain and is going back to Greek theatre. There is something of that in the origins and conceptions of theatre in ancient times, catharsis and helping the therapy I suppose.

Murray Cox was walking around thinking about it, talking to people and mulling it (*Hamlet*) over for days and days . . . Those who had not seen the performance said 'Oh yes, that's a great idea' but they didn't really know what they were talking about . . . They didn't know what the performance was or how powerful it was. When I came to see it a few weeks before . . . it came to Broadmoor . . . I realized what Murray had been talking about and why he had been so cautious.

It was hard to know who was the patient and who was the actor,

There is a quality in the play of forgiveness, it made possible for them and us to deal with things.

I am beginning to feel a very distinctive pull between the *Hamlet* of Broadmoor and the *Hamlet* of the RSC – and for me that is becoming very difficult.

If we are going to have a workshop about the 'painful parts', they [the actors] could help us to say the words.

I've never seen a live show like that. I was *spell-bound*. That was good wasn't it? A good word that! If you get any more, I want an invite.

The thing that really struck me is how close we all are.

Closure: 'No shuffling'

We were told (p.100) that 'They were an incredibly attentive audience. There was no coughing. No shuffling.'

These words also find their place in Claudius' soliloquy:

> 'There is *no shuffling*, there the action lies
> In his true nature
>
> . . .
>
> Help Angels! Make assay.'

(Hamlet III.3.61)

The King's use of the word 'shuffling' implied trickery, evasive deception, lack of authenticity. It is doubly relevant as a description of the 'incredibly attentive audience' in which there was 'no shuffling', no restless movement; because it is also true that there was no trickery, no evasive deception, no lack of authenticity. That which is authentic is mirrored in 'such mirrors as will turn'.

'What beats there', in the tempest of the mind, is mirrored too. This chapter gives evidence of the beating in many minds and there has been no shuffling. At the height of Lear's disturbance he certainly moved with a shuffling gait. But in this chapter there has been no shuffling – no avoidance – in the responses to the presentation of the tempest in Lear's mind or Hamlet's.

M.C.

IV

Wider Horizons

Introduction

The horizons explored in this section are wider in a double sense. Yet they are inextricably linked to what happens, and what follows, when Shakespeare comes to Broadmoor.

The three chapters devoted to wider horizons each survey the scene from different vantage points. Taken together they enhance our understanding of what happens when tragedy is performed in a secure psychiatric hospital. They also provoke us into questioning various fixed assumptions which may be 'ripe for shaking'.

The first chapter, 'Performance and Projective Possibilities' by Alice Theilgaard, presents an overview of the topic and is therefore relevant to any theatrical performance. But it is also based upon the experience of being a member of a Broadmoor audience when the actors came hither. There is thus clear evidence of the primary theme which threads its way through this chapter and the rest of the book. She helps us to understand why the actors and the audience saw things as they did, so that each responds in a particular way.

The second chapter on 'The Place of Drama in Custodial Settings', has become a corporate endeavour, having almost acquired an autonomous existence. It calls for a separate introduction at the appropriate place.

The third and final chapter, 'The Nature and Scope of Dramatherapy: Theatre of Healing' by Sue Jennings recalls our attention to the opening paragraph of the book: 'It would be good if we could bring *Hamlet* to Broadmoor'. For it was beneath a dramatherapy umbrella that Mark Rylance had uttered this single sentence, which seemed to be an enactment of Brook's words 'Truth in the theatre is always on the move' (1972,157). Sue Jennings' chapter therefore fittingly brings this odyssey to a close. Indeed, if there had been no International Dramatherapy and Shakespeare Symposium at Stratford, *Hamlet* would not have come to Broadmoor. So that the Prologue 'How These Things Came About' would have been wishful thinking or delusional. On the other hand, it might have formed the basis of a speculative essay reflecting upon the nature of things which might have come about, had *Hamlet* come to Broadmoor.

There is creative exploratory energy, within the projective aspects of performance, which has applied to all those who have witnessed drama since antiquity, and applies also to the performance of tragic drama in a secure psychiatric hospital, to which these pages bear witness. The time has now come – it is the moment of opportunity – when hospitals, and similar therapeutic settings, are asking about the possibility of teaching drama and of establishing a dramatherapeutic facility for their patients.

'Mightier than an army is an idea whose time has come' (Victor Hugo) has the quality of an oracular utterance. Yet it links aspiration and the sober timing for realistic action.

Surveying Wider Horizons at the Right Time

> 'But shall we wear these glories for a day?
> Or shall they last, and we rejoice in them?'

(Richard III IV.2.5)

One of the issues over which theatre and therapy are in broad agreement is the importance of time and timing. The exact timing of an actor's entry upon the stage is as vital as the timing of a therapeutic intervention. We can never call to mind too often the important distinction so clearly evident in the two ancient Greek words for time. There is *chronos* – from which so many of our daily words, such as chronic, come – which means the moment in unfolding sequential time. There is *kairos*, which refers to *the* moment. It is the moment of peak experience, such as hearing the cry of a new baby or first seeing Ely Cathedral. Or indeed being present when 'Tis not alone my inky cloak, good mother' was heard in Broadmoor for the first time.

But what have these observations to do with the theme of 'wider horizons' and our consideration of the way in which Shakespeare comes to Broadmoor? Part of the answer is encapsulated in the lines from *Richard III*. They point to the difference between that which is transient and that which endures. Richard did not say 'But shall we wear these glories for a day ... and we rejoice in them?' Rejoicing was linked to duration ... '*Or shall they last*, and we rejoice in them?' Those present on Hamlet Day can have been in no doubt that they had participated in an exceptional 'happening'; and we have read numerous comments from the actors, the directors and the audience, which all testify to this. Nevertheless, the important question which is woven into their comments and our thoughts, is the relationship between that which is transient and that which lasts. In some ways this has been a perennial question about theatre since its earliest days. Was there merely a transient *catharsis*, or was there any permanent change in the life of the individual or the institution as a whole? Hamlet Day was a 'peak experience'. But what of the non-peak days which followed? Were these glories worn merely for a day? Or did they lead to any permanent changes in which we could rejoice? Brook's (1972,152) comments could have been tailor-made for our purposes:

> When a performance is over, what remains? Fun can be forgotten, but powerful emotion also disappears and good arguments lose their thread. When emotion and argument are harnessed to a wish from the audience to see more clearly into itself – then something in the mind burns. The event scorches on to the memory an outline, a taste, a trace, a smell – a picture . . . Is there a further possibility? We know a fleeting liberation can happen; can something also stay?

Shakespeare's Disturbing Presence

'Here they be that dare and will disturb thee.'

(*II Henry IV* IV.8.6)

Wherever Shakespeare's presence is felt, disturbance of one kind or another ensues. He stimulates. He provokes. He unsettles the *status quo*. And his coming to Broadmoor was no exception. Even the etymology of the words 'poetry' and 'drama' imply action. The former comes from the Greek *poiesis*, which implies the 'calling into existence of that which was not there before'. The latter comes directly from the Greek verb meaning 'to do'. Both poetry and drama need to be considered alongside the various meanings of the word 'play' . Shakespeare certainly gave rise to much 'doing' and many things were called into existence. We have considered four days in the life of Broadmoor Hospital when Shakespeare's plays were performed. And even though much of the enactment was tragic, there was also a sense of occasion, an awareness that a 'happening' was taking place. However serious the plays may be, there was also much laughter. Alongside the painful confrontation with self, which tragedy always provokes, there was also cathartic festive release.

Shakespeare's Unpredictable Impact

Shakespeare's coming to Broadmoor was unpredictable in several ways. Indeed this very book has not turned out as expected. In spite of the undoubtedly warm reception experienced by each group of actors, personal comments from individual patients have been relatively sparse. But, however 'interesting' it would be to know more, their reluctance to disclose what they felt when witnessing the plays, at such close quarters, must be honoured.

As I sit writing this passage, wondering how to phrase the next sentence, I am prompted by the words of caution given to Macbeth:

'Seek to know no more.'

(Macbeth IV.1.103)

Shakespeare had, therefore, invigoratingly and creatively disturbed original editorial intentions about the proportions of the various sections of
the book. Thus, Section III 'This Tempest in My Mind' is smaller than
predicted, whereas Section IV 'Wider Horizons' has itself assumed wider
proportions and a life of its own. At this moment it feels appropriate that
I am writing on behalf of all those who felt the creative, unstabilising,
energizing impact that followed Hamlet Day.

We turn now to think in depth of projective possibilities inherent in
dramatic performance. Because much of tragedy's psychological impact
is linked to projective processes.

Alice Theilgaard gives us a professional framing of that which each
member of every theatre audience will know at first-hand. She will tell us
of the psychodynamics underlying the universal experience that 'the
play's the thing' wherein the conscience, the memory, the buried past or
the fantasized future of the observer is 'caught'. The spectator's inner
world influences what is seen and heard on the stage. Karen Gaylord
describes the spectator's response to the actuality of a theatre event:

> The spectator serves as a psychological participant and empathetic
> collaborator in the maintenance and 'truth' of the fictive world
> onstage, is 'taken out of himself' and becomes for the time part of an
> ad hoc collective consciousness, ready to find meaning and signific-
> ance in the events taking place on stage.
>
> Thus the theatrical occasion involves a double consciousness for all
> concerned. The performance takes place on at least two levels of
> 'reality' simultaneously and within at least two frames. The outer
> frame always embraces both audience and performers. The inner
> frame demarcates the playing space. (1983,136)

The next chapter presents the projective dynamic interaction between the
inner psychic stage of both actor and audience, and the projectively
perceived outer stage.

M.C.

Performance and Projective Possibilities

Alice Theilgaard

'Do you see yonder cloud that's almost in shape of a camel?'

(Hamlet III.2.366)

Shakespeare's profound grasp of the human predicament is matched by his unequalled capacity to express what needs to be said. Thus the opening of virtually any theme of Shakespearian emphasis needs to draw attention to both the universality and the particularity of the topic under discussion. And so it is at the beginning of this chapter on performance and projective possibilities. Nevertheless, this consideration is set among other contributions dealing with several separate occasions on which Shakespeare came to Broadmoor. This implies that we shall need to look at both the wider topic of the projective possibility inherent in any dramatic performance and the more focused, related to these particular performances in this particular setting.

But before we embark upon our discussion we need to make a brief survey of several terms which will recur during the ensuing pages. One of the themes which pervades this book is the power of Shakespearian language. There could almost be a sense of alliterative persuasion, when all the terms begin with the letter 'P', although this must be no more than coincidence! I shall refer to perception, physiognomic perception, projection, projective identification, and phenomenology.

Holland (1964,347) in *Psychoanalysis and Shakespeare* writes:

> By projecting what is in the characters outward into external visible events and actions, a play paves the way for the audiences own act of projection. We find in the external reality of a play what is hidden

in ourselves. Drama shows virtue her own feature, scorn her own image, and the very age and body of the time his form and pressure. Watching a set of events in a play feels, for this reason, very different for reading them in a novel.

Reading this passage we have an experience of *déjà vu*, or rather, of some kind of dual understanding which takes our thoughts directly to the play-within-the-play described in *Hamlet*. Furthermore, this dramatic technique which many dramatists have used, and which Shakespeare uses in several plays, assumes augmented significance in connection with the way in which Shakespeare came to Broadmoor. There was therefore a series of levels of external reality being presented to various observers.

Perception

In our everyday life we rapidly take what we see for granted, so that we easily habituate to the objects surrounding us. We behave according to the dictates of naive realism, acting as though the physical and experiential worlds were identical, the selective aspects of perception remaining un-noticed. Indeed, the boundary between the inner and the outer world – between the image and perception – is not as sharp as textbooks sometimes imply. Perception is never an accurate reproduction of the outer world; the physical and the experiential universes are not identical. It is an active, dynamic, selective process in which projective forces play an important part. Kher (1974,69) underlines the interactional aspect of perception:

> *Perception* reveals instant relationship between the perceiver and the perceived in the act of creation . . . In the creative process, the perceived emanates from the perceiver; the objectivity of the per-ceived remains infinitely bound to the subjectivity of the perceiver. In poetics, since the perceived is rendered as a metaphor or a symbol, it is, strictly speaking, neither subject nor object, though it is under-stood as both simultaneously.

Physiognomic Perception

During childhood, perception is far more dynamic than it is as years advance. For example, a two-year-old will not experience a bicycle as lifeless. It is alive because it moves. It speaks when the bell rings. Or, when a small child, walking with his mother in the autumn forest, sees falling leaves and says 'Look the trees are crying', it is an indication of his physiognomic understanding of the world.

This quality is vividly illustrated when a schizophrenic patient, anxiously looking at a swinging door, says 'The door is devouring me.' Or again, the moon is endowed with feeling, 'It is a very troubled moon.' Kandinsky (1913) writes in his biography 'On my palette sit high, round raindrops, puckishly flirting with each other, swaying and trembling. Unexpectedly they unite and suddenly become shy threads, which disappear among the colours.'

He projects physiognomic qualities onto the surroundings. The natural world, when known physiognomically, is alive. As we get older our perception tends to fade, and our imagination is inclined to bleaken. We register phenomena automatically. They then become 'fixed' in confining, trivializing concepts, which are quickly 'filed away'. The sense of wonder is diminished. Therefore, a need arises to make the world novel, alive and meaningful, to make us alert, active participants in the perceptual process. Unbiased attention prepares us for spontaneity and lends a fresh impetus to experience. We realize that we all see the world differently, according to our personalities; we interpret it differently according to our needs, knowledge, expectation, age, life-experiences; and we all attribute different meanings to it at various times.

There is a direct link between physiognomic perception and the creative arts. Perception in this mode is universal in childhood. It is the creative artist who succeeds in maintaining this sense of wonder and aliveness in the perceived world, and who is also able to convey it to others in the theatre, the concert hall or the art gallery. As Jameson (1972,51) points out 'Art is the way of restoring conscious experience, of breaking through deadening and mechanical habits of conduct, and to allow us to be reborn to a world of existential freshness.' A theatre performance is one of the ways in which this renewal of perception may take place. And so it was on Hamlet Day (6 August 1989), when the actors came hither, and the Central Hall of Broadmoor Hospital became the setting for the perception of performance. The audience, like all audiences, was involved in its 'own act of projection' to use Holland's words again. What does projection mean in this sense?

Projection

The etymological root of projection is the Latin for 'throwing in front of oneself.' It is used as a professional psychological term indicating the process by which specific impulses, wishes, aspects of the self are imagined as being located outside the self. Thus projected ego-alien aspects of the self are often displaced into other people. Although in paranoid states, an otherwise impersonal environment can be perceived as being hostile. We recall that Macbeth felt that at one moment every noise appalled him, and Hamlet sensed that 'all occasions' informed against him. There is, however, a more particular variant of projection which is part of the normal developmental process, although it may also form the crucial part of the psychopathology of antisocial acts, such as homicide. We are referring to the process of projective identification.

Projective Identification

In this process an individual induces a feeling state in the 'other' (such as a therapist – or, as is more likely, a close relative or, even, a victim) that corresponds to the state which the 'projector' had been unable to experience or tolerate for himself. This process was first described by Klein (1946) as a primitive form of defence mechanism, which enables the individual to project undesirable parts of the self into the object and thereby control it from within. So important is this clinical concept that Ogden (1982) has devoted a whole volume to *Projective Identification and Psychotherapeutic Technique*, and elaborates the description of the phenomenon in this way:

> Projective identification is a concept that addresses the way in which feeling-states correspondong to the unconscious fantasies of one person (the projector) are engendered in and processed by another person (the recipient), that is, the way in which one person makes use of another person to experience and contain an aspect of himself. The projector has the primarily unconscious fantasy of getting rid of an unwanted or endangered part of himself (including internal objects) and of depositing that part in another person in a powerfully controlling way.

The 'recipient' of projective identification may, or may not, be aware of this equivalent of a depth-charge of feeling, which has suddenly made its presence felt. This means that unexplained awareness of anger, fear or erotic passion may prompt action which is otherwise inexplicable. In the case of psychotherapy, the therapist's training will have made him aware that he is perhaps containing, or housing, projected aspects of the experience of his patient, whereas those in social contact merely find that domestic or societal chaos may follow an apparently trivial event, which would be otherwise unremarkable. The therapist is said to 'metabolize' these projected feelings, and return them to the recipient in a form in which they can be utilized, because they are understood and seen for what they are. It needs to be stressed that projective identification may refer to 'good' feelings which may be stored in the therapist, as though he were a place of safe-keeping or a 'bank'; on the other hand, they may relate to 'bad' feelings such as murderous rage, which the projector cannot tolerate and needs to externalize. It needs to be repeated that projective identification is often a significant component in the psychopathology of the offender-patient.

Phenomenology

Shakespeare's plays penetrate the realm of the essence. He represents an artistic power which appeals to generation after generation. And this book describes the way in which both actor and audience were moved by the rigour of the absolute, when Shakespeare came to Broadmoor. Shakespearean dramas make the perception of life more meaningful. And for the phenomenologist meaning is both central and inevitable. The word 'phenomenology' comes from Greek. As its etymology implies, it seeks to articulate the phenomenon, letting it come into light, making it appear.

It is important to note that there is a degree of passivity here: it is the capacity to 'let things come to light' and allowing them to appear. The appearance of an individual, whether he is an actor representing a character in a play, or a patient narrating his story, invites the audience or the therapist to experience 'the other' in as lucid, vivid and immediate a way as possible.

This manner of approach is the antithesis of an observation of the world from a preconceived perspective, which runs the risk of introducing estrangement and overlooking meaning. There is always the risk that this may take place, when views are too firmly established and are likely to be overgrown with theory-laden ideas. Both the clinical and the dramatic world need to minimize the possibility of estrangement and the diminishment of meaning. It was, indeed, the novelty of the creative energy, epitomized in the way the actors 'came hither' to Broadmoor, which intensified and gave meaning to the experience. Furthermore, the perennial risks of institutionalization, which are always lurking in the shadows of any major institution, are minimized by the incursion of such creative energy. This inevitably reduced the sense of estrangement and lack of contact with the outside world.

To understand a phenomenon is to get close to what is being explored on its own terms, so that it is discovered through participation in the experience. This aspect of Shakespeare coming to Broadmoor was clearly evident in the various theatre workshops which took place following the performances. To give a specific example, I can cite the moment when there was a workshop centering on Ophelia's funeral. In this particular vignette, participation in the 'Ophelia' workshop diminished the possibility of estrangement, and made the chance of overlooking the meaning of experience much less likely.

Merleau-Ponty, a French philosopher and psychologist, emphasizes the importance of a descriptive approach. In *Phenomenology of Perception* (1962) he stresses that the description of experience is more than its explanation or analysis. To return to things in themselves, is to return to the world which antecedes knowledge; a world about which knowledge always speaks, and in relation to which scientific schematizing is an abstract and derived sign-language, as geography is in relation to land-scape.

However, faithful description does not exclude the indication of causal relationships, although its prime aim is to understand phenomena: to seek to understand the 'what' before the 'how' and the 'why'.

Shakespeare is a true phenomenologist. His characters are presented to us in a way which challenges our experiential capacity and our zest for empathy and insight. They make such an impact on us that we are likely to experience the surroundings charged with meaning. We see the world in a new way.

This phenomenological mode of experiencing gives us the meaning of a facial expression immediately and directly. We do not need analysis or analogical inference to reach an individual's inner state. The experience is self-validating. Yet it exists in a context.

As Macquarrie (1972,10) points out, phenomenology

offers a description in depth, causing us to notice features that we ordinarily fail to notice, removing hindrances that stand in the way of our seeing, exhibiting the essential rather than the accidental, showing interrelations that may lead to quite a different view from the one that we get when a phenomenon is considered in isolation.

The context matters, and meaning and organization go hand in hand.

The Synchronization and Shaping of Experience

The coherence of the Shakespearian canon underlines the importance of a global approach. It is the synchronization of experience of different modalities, and from different regions in the psyche, which creates an urge to engage not only in speech or acting but also to attend to their echoes. And it is the synthesizing power of Shakespeare's poetic language, reconciling dualities while preserving the integrity of their elements and the contrast between them, which prompts us. It helps us to experience a more intimate relationship with our unconscious, and to see the world in a new and unforeseen way.

Shakespeare's description of sense impressions places him as a born phenomenologist. But so do the subtle and flexible ways in which he let these images symbolize the main theme. The play alerts actors, spectators, patients and therapists and calls our attention to the inner scene. In *King Lear* much emphasis is placed on the sense of seeing. And Shakespeare's genius for transferring concrete sensations to abstract symbols is evident in many places. This carries heavy psychodynamic weight. It is not only the playing on 'sight' and 'insight' which prompts us to change from the outer to the inner world, it is also the condensed use of imagery which guides us towards the undercurrent of parallel unconscious images.

Shakespeare gives much evidence of projective dynamics. As Clemen (1951,238) points out, he can also 'condense the essence of a whole play or the gist of a central theme into a visible act in which word and gesture combine to create a symbolic impact that will linger on in the memory of the audience.'

Rose (1980) has underlined *The Power of Form*. Or, as Shakespeare expresses it, 'The forms of things unknown, the poet's pen / Turns them to shapes'. (*A Midsummer Night's Dream* V.1.14) or 'To set a form upon that indigest / Which he hath left so shapeless and so rude!' (*King John* V.7.25)

He calls for new-born shapes: 'So full of shapes is fancy / That it alone is high fantastical.' (*Twelfth Night* I.1.13)

Projection in Action: The Rorschach (Ink-blot) Test

Like Shakespeare, Hermann Rorschach, a Swiss psychiatrist living from 1884–1922, had a curiosity about form, ideas and the validity of assumptions. He wanted to experiment with psychological perception, while maintaining a stern sense of proportion.

It is said that Rorschach was inspired by a study on children's imagination in association with ink-blots – klecksographie – a study published in 1917. But I wonder if the dialogue of Hamlet and Polonius first gave him the idea:

> HAMLET: Do you see yonder cloud that's almost in shape of
>   a camel?
>
> POLONIUS: By th' mass and 'tis – like a camel indeed.
>
> HAMLET: Methinks it is like a weasel.
>
> POLONIUS: It is backed like a weasel.
>
> HAMLET: Or like a whale?
>
> POLONIUS: Very like a whale.
>
> (*Hamlet* III.2.365)

The essence of creativity lies in the capacity for rapidly changing frames of reference. This is illustrated in Hamlet's discussion with Polonius. He swiftly transforms the perception of a cloud to various other visual images. The poet uses similar dynamic shifts as he explores the edges of language. The Rorschach test with its 'accidental' ink-blots provides a unique vehicle for observing aspects of both perceptual and verbal processes. It illustrates how an individual structures the ink-blot, so that we are given an impression of the perceiver's inner world.

The Rorschach test gives numerous possibilities for pattern making. In everyday perception the surroundings are structured as clearly delineated, 'real' objects. The observer's perception is constantly oscillating from one object to another. Yet such oscillation is part of a 'perceptual hold'. The units he isolates are usually limited to certain real objects.

McCully (1987) points out that the visual connections between forms in archaic art and in contemporary perception of the Rorschach blots are not solely an archetypal way of bringing some vague inherited memories to life. The interdependence manifests itself in the nature of the psychological experience, which may be released and which is universal.

Being semi-structured, the ink-blots provide a wider range of choice than perceptual structuring of the real world. We meet the unknown in 'accidental forms'. And how we do so tells us about our way of experiencing the world. The miniature Rorschach universe, consisting of ambiguous ink-blots, does not deal in questions to which there are unequivocal answers. Neither do Shakespeare's plays. Each evokes a wide range of interpretive perspectives. The vast literature about his dramas bears witness to this. There can be no monopoly of interpretation.

Kott (in Lidz 1975,3) wrote: 'Hamlet is like a sponge. If he is not played in stylized or antiquated manner, he immediately soaks up the entire contemporary scene into himself. It is the most unique of all plays that have ever been written, just because of its porosity.'

The comparison of Hamlet to a sponge may not be the most poetic one, but the idea of porosity aptly demonstrates the capacity of the play to absorb projective material. Kaufmann (1965,139–59), writing of *Troilus and Cressida*, is impressed by Shakespeare's talents for forming ambiguous material: 'The play provides the dramatic equivalent of a colossal Rorschach inkblot test, each reader confronted by separate alternatives, identifies where he must, and thereby pragmatically indicates his own sympathetic stance within the heteronomy of its suspended judgements.'

The plot and actions are not explained. The notations of stage directions are accordingly few, giving the actors greater freedom of interpretation than in many modern plays. The fact that the Rorschach-blots are semi-structured and do not resemble anything in particular, makes them an excellent instrument for projection. Shakespeare also supports this: 'By indirections find directions out' (*Hamlet* II.1.65.).

An interesting question presents itself, though I am in no position to provide an answer. I wonder how a Rorschach Test undertaken by Mark Rylance *qua* Mark Rylance, would differ from one undertaken by Mark Rylance in rôle as Hamlet or Romeo?

Projection in Action: The Dynamics of Drama

Shakespeare's plays have escaped the prison of time and space. For example, the universe that Hamlet presents to us does not exist at any certain place or at any particular time. It is true, that Shakespeare has given *Hamlet* a geographical location – Elsinore – but there is little else to support the impression that the landscape is that of North Zealand! The few descriptive hints he gives of the surroundings of the castle, such as: 'To the dreadful summit of the cliff that beetles o'er his base into the sea' (I.IV.70) does not remind us of the setting of Kronborg.

The imprecision of the location is matched by the uncertainty of time, which is also reflected in the lack of accuracy with regard to era-related costumes of the actors; Shakespeare does not give suggestions to the designer. Throughout the play the associations to different historical periods offer themselves: Old Hamlet's and Fortinbras' 'tvekamp' (hand-to-hand fight) and the tension between Norway and Denmark remind us of Saga-time, while the description of the relationship between England and Denmark makes us think of the Vikings. Life at court has the stamp of the Renaissance epoch, while the reference to Wittenberg might give associations to the period of the post-reformation.

This lack of concreteness gives the potential for projecting the lives and shapes of the characters to something general. We recognize ourselves in them. The timelessness and spacelessness of Shakespeare's art lend a universality to his plays. And the basic, primordial themes are reflected in lives and minds everywhere, and at all times.

This uncertainty about 'facts' does not imply that Shakespeare was not a sharp observer and a fine phenomenologist, but it reflects the great potential for projection which his plays offer.

The primordiality of time is not restricted to a remote past. It is prototypical and creative. It creates what happens to-day, and is brought about through a repetition of myth which gives symbolic form and content to the timeless dynamics of life. But Shakespeare holds 'the mirror up to nature' in a way that is not unequivocal. The reflections of the mirror are

as manifold as life itself. The world of *Hamlet* is skilfully wrought to show
life viewed from so many perspectives. And therefore the question asked
by Driscoll (1983,182): 'And what is the ontological status of a character or
a play? An imitation of life? A partaker of life? Or a vision of life?' can be
answered with affirmatives, so far as Shakespeare's plays are concerned.

Projection in Action: Dynamics of Therapeutic Space

These questions dealing with the essential principles of a play address
themselves equally well to the therapeutic situation. The universal human
life is portrayed in Shakespeare's plays as it is in therapeutic space. Even
though the setting is different, both acting and therapy try 'to hold the
mirror up to nature'.

'Nature' has a mythological quality. And while Shakespeare as a
dramatist is in full command of varied and well constructed stories,
throughout his plays there is a strange vibration beyond the reach of
analysis. There is an echo from *Hamlet* here: 'thoughts which lie beyond
the reaches of our souls'. An unconscious undercurrent reflects our deepest emotions and our most magical dreams. As Lidz (1975,114) points
out, a myth can 'convey through its own type of symbolic expression much
that cannot be expressed in logical sequences – much that is valid and
meaningful precisely because it is unconscious, paradoxical, and even
contradictory in seeking to express the fundamental themes that recur
from life to life and culture to culture, themes that thus have a constancy
amid continual change.'

Literary work risks losing its aesthetic value if it debates or explains a
problem, or uses the characters as merely messengers for a political
conviction of the author. So does therapy suffer, if problems and conflicts
are 'explained' as in a logical debate. The therapist has to be attuned to
both the conscious and the unconscious processes – to the text and the
subtext – to the polyvalent content of the image. So has the actor. He needs
more than the text in order to perform. To make the next line alive and
suggestive to the fellow actors and the audience, he creates 'unspoken'
thoughts. We can learn from a genius like Shakespeare how to link
conscious and unconscious material. He taps mythical material that
stirred the interests of archaic man and that continues to hold a salient
position in the unconscious of all men.

Shakespeare is an incomparable inspiration in therapeutic work, by
reason of his deep knowledge of the mind, his poetic language (which uses
a wide range of mutually reinforcing symbols and allusions), his playing
with metaphors and paradoxes, and his oscillations between concrete and
abstract statements. He takes an image, delights in playing with it, and

compresses in one short sentence an astonishing wealth of associations. As Spurgeon (1979,149) observes, 'by some magic touch, a difference of setting, an intensification of feeling, some slight shifts of words, he recreates and entirely transforms it.'

Dramatic Space

Dramatic space is both intrapsychic, inter-personal and corporate. The Broadmoor audience was linked with all other *Hamlet* audiences. The actors were one with their present peers and predecessors. The patients were caught up in the attentive act by what they saw on the stage and its association with their previous life-experience.

Drama is one of the most important actualizations of myth. Drama is more than a relating of events, it is far more than its text. It is not even identical with the performance in the theatre. Its essence is the reciprocity – the exchange of concentrated attention between actors and audience.

Coleridge comments (Weatherhead 1967,55): 'You feel him [Shakespeare] to be a poet inasmuch as for a time he had made you one – an active creative being.' This underlines the capacity of Shakespeare to make us participate in the drama. It is the over-determination of drama which gives us ample opportunity to identify where we must, according to our desires and fears and passions.

The Language of Art

During a dramatic performance *catharsis* is often taking place. But it is an experience that resonates at many levels. We acquire knowledge of the conditions of life, and of ourselves. The projective aspects of the play allow us to interpret according to our individuality, our needs, emotions and imagination. We make our own 'gestalts' with a specific development in time and space. Even if we listen to the same words, they do not mean exactly the same to us. The knowledge gained is not that resulting from a lecture. The language of science analyses. The language of art and therapeutic language present a synthesis of different interpretations of the world. The artistic creation of Shakespeare has a magnetic pull and exerts an aesthetic imperative upon us. Coincident with something being played, said, presented in space and time, the New appears. Yet we feel that it is eternally familiar.

It is the active organizing principle, which operates below the conscious level, and the integrative power of thinking and feeling, of abstract and concrete which give the poetic metaphor its therapeutic capacity. Metaphor and play share the intermediate area of experience that lies between fantasy and reality. That space – between symbol and symbolized, mediated by an interpreting self – is the potential space, in which creativity becomes possible (Ogden 1986,213). And mutative aspects of metaphor – that is to say, the capacity to change things – is one of the assets of drama (Cox and Theilgaard 1987).

Both theatre and therapy present potential space. Each enhances creativity. Shakespeare shows a capacity for shaping characters by his startling insights into the unconscious processes and their dynamic power. He also prompts us by making us attentive to the elusive ambiguities which are a secret source of the human dilemma. He knows that people are torn by opposing motivations and prey to changing moods, as they develop under the impact of the events.

He deals with sets of polarities and sees common denominators in the conflict of illusion and fact, deception and truth, passion and reason, fancy and perception, chaos and order. And in the incessant game of shape-changing and role-playing we recognize the human story. He plays with these polarities, and the aesthetic imperative (Cox and Theilgaard 1987,200) is kindled by the dynamic tension arising from the dualities characteristic of the working mind.

The weight of sensory experience in aesthetics is reflected in the fact that 'aesthetic' is derived from the Greek word for 'sensation'. But the aesthetic experience does not only speak through the senses. It is also captured by the mind and although fundamentally it is a non-representational type of knowledge, in art it takes on shapes and forms. In this way it helps us to represent the world to ourselves.

Shakespeare alerts both the patient and the therapist to listen to deeper resonance. He invites us to consider the question: 'What seest thou else?' (*The Tempest* I.2.49.) Friedman (1953,35) writes: 'Poetry which manages to tap these (mythical) roots of the human psyche is liable to appeal deeply and permanently to all men. The reason for this profound vitality which all sense in the words of men like Dante, Goethe, or Shakespeare is simply that they traffic continually in archetypical symbols and emotions.'

It is Shakespeare's innovative imagery which exercises an aesthetic imperative on us. It stirs us by its novelty and moves us so that our memories are tapped. In this aesthetic blend of difference and sameness, change and constancy, Shakespeare helps us to be experientially absorbed and to integrate time, space and body imagery. At such aesthetic moments in the theatre the hitherto subliminal presentations and combinations of images and ideas come closer to consciousness. We rediscover the depths and limits of our inner lives, and our deep investment in the drama.

'Since things in motion sooner catch the eye'

(*Troilus and Cressida* III.3.183)

Shakespeare keeps things moving in the mind's eye.

In this chapter I have tried to show how the many facets of projection were woven into the pattern of performance and its perception at Broadmoor. It was, obviously, an immensely complex event, in which the actors saw part of their lives in the life of the audience. And vice versa.

The paradoxical setting for *Hamlet* and *King Lear*, with the audience on the stage, is entirely Shakespearean in spirit. The paradox is in the point of intersection between the imagination and the reality belonging to both the inner and the outer world. It is here that the restless movement between the different possibilities can be released. That it was utilized is evidenced by the many remarks after the plays by audience and actors alike.

The 'theatre' in Broadmoor was in fact more like an original Elizabethan theatre than many established theatres of today. As in Shakespeare's time, there was no scenery, no curtain and no barrier between the stage and the audience. The lighting was far from the computerized lighting systems in modern theatres, thus exposing the actors to the audience and *vice versa*. The actors were not 'blinded' by strong lights. And eye-contact is a vital component in psychological contact between individuals. It is perhaps particularly so between, say, an actor playing Hamlet and a patient who needed to avenge his father's death. When this took place projective identification was at stake, as it was in numerous other exchanges between the character and the inner world of the patient-observer. How powerful is the link between these thoughts and the words of Ophelia as she witnessed Hamlet's disturbance: 'The observed of all observers, quite, quite down'.

The play was not only seen, it was also heard. Even if some of the language was not understood, the emotional tone and the aesthetic beauty of the text ensured engaged contact. As a spectator – or rather as a participant – one felt that the audience was serving as an impetus for the actors to express experiences, which were in some way recognized – though not necessarily consciously identified – by the audience.

It is not easy to verbalize the experience. It was like a piece of music which created emotions rooted in the deep psychic structures, beyond the reach of words. It was a unique experience. In an untraceable way it made a profound impact on the audience and the actors.

This chapter started with a reference to 'our everyday life'. It concludes by drawing attention to the way in which drama transformed the significance of the 'everyday life' of those who took part in the performance, either as one of the audience or as one of the actors. Immense projective possibilities were present in all that followed the announcement: 'The actors are come hither.'

IV. 2

Drama in Custodial Settings

Introduction

I am aware of a particularly strong editorial imperative at this point. The original intention was to have an authoritative statement, by an appropriate expert, on the place of drama in custodial settings.

But before embarking on the place of drama in such an environment, it seems pertinent to add a more general comment about the place of creative arts Therapies, such close relatives of the performing arts therapies. Both have much to offer those detained within secure surroundings.

The advent of such an initiative evokes a welcoming response. Though, ideally, it should be received with enthusiasm tinged with caution. Such new therapeutic enterprises need to be closely linked with other more established therapeutic approaches. Furthermore, they should be monitored and the subject of audit by individuals and multidisciplinary teams with intensive and extensive forensic therapeutic experience. However relaxed, 'playful' and unstructured many 'ensembles' within such a unit may appear to be, the presence of expert, hoveringly attentive, staff provides the frame of inter-personal security which alone allows playful, exploratory freedoms to live up to their name.

Because our theme is of the setting, where drama, psychodrama and dramatherapy take place, it serves our purpose well to adapt some words from Bruscia (1990,12) who writes 'music therapy may serve as a primary or adjunctive treatment modality, depending on the client's responsiveness to music, and the other kinds of services also available'. In an attempt to further clarify the role of music therapy in various settings, and to establish qualification requirements for the kinds of clinical responsibilities involved, he has identified four levels of music therapy practice. They are:

Auxiliary level: all functional uses of music for nontherapeutic but related purposes.

Augmentative level: any practice in which music or music therapy is used to enhance the efforts of other treatment modalities, and to make supportive contributions to the client's overall treatment programme.

Intensive level: any practice in which music therapy takes a central and independent role in addressing priority goals in the client's treatment plan, and as a result, induces significant changes in the client's current situation.

Primary level: any practice in which music therapy takes an indispens-
able or singular role in meeting the main therapeutic needs of the
client, and as a result, induces pervasive changes in the clients life.
(Bruscia 1989,90)

It would be a useful exercise to replace Bruscia's words 'music therapy'
in this passage and substitute 'dramatherapy', 'art therapy', 'dance therapy' and so forth. I suggest that his four levels (auxiliary, augmentative,
intensive and primary) will help to clarify the somewhat confusing contribution which the arts can make to the lives of those in secure institutions.
On one hand it can be said that they will inevitably have a humanising,
warming-at-depth impact upon any mode of existence which runs the risk
of becoming stereotyped and repetitive. On the other hand it is not always
easy to be persuasive in the presentation of such ideas which initially
appear to run the risk of enhancing and externalising the chaotic inner
world of disturbed patients. But, rightly judged – and 'there's the rub' –
expressing inner chaos can lead to relaxed behaviour and enhanced
stability. In my view Bruscia's four levels can take such discussions
forward by offering easily recognised categories of involvement.

Returning to drama, the axis of this volume, it is evident that we need
a clear and unambiguous frame of reference for the ensuing consideration.
Because drama and therapy and the concept of custodial settings can each
point in several directions. Drama can be therapeutic in a general sense.
To write drama can be healing. To witness performance can be healing. To
participate in performance can be healing. To direct a production, or to
work behind the scenes can also be healing. Nevertheless, any or all of
these pursuits could be the occasion for manic overwork, or failure therein
might lead to a depressive reaction.

In addition to such generic types of involvement with drama there are
also specialised aspects of drama; such as psychodrama and dramatherapy.

This seems to be an appropriate place to mention the Koestler Awards
Scheme which has just celebrated its 30th Annual Competition and Exhibition. It is good to know that 'The purpose of the Koestler Awards
Scheme is to encourage and reward a wide variety of creative endeavours
from men and women held in United Kingdom Prisons and from patients
in Special Hospitals.' The chairman, David Astor, writing in the introduction to the 1991 illustrated brochure describing the scheme, says: 'From a
small exhibition of paintings has emerged a Competition of no less than
nineteen different categories of creative work. Entries come from more
than one hundred establishments and from over one thousand prisoners
and patients.' In November 1991 seminars on the performing arts, poetry

reading, drama and prose, and music were held at St Martin's-in-the-Fields, London. The enactment during the drama seminar vividly demonstrated some of the expressive and cathartic potential of one particular facet of drama in custodial settings. This took the form of a psychodrama exercise presented by young men from HM Young Offenders Institution, Huntercombe. The ensemble was augmented by one of the drama judges and one of the trustees.

The Place of the Expressive Therapies within Forensic Psychotherapy

For present purposes, the term expressive therapies covers psychodrama, dramatherapy, and expressive therapy *per se*, with its emphasis on the possibility of intermodal transfer. A moderating voice of caution needs to be sounded alongside these fresh 'expressive' initiatives, 'on offer' to forensic units, which will be described below. As Sue Jennings (p.243) cogently observes: 'overloading the dramatic framework could have disasterous results in a forensic setting'. The patient who has become a 'forensic patient' (an 'offender-patient') will have done so because of anti-social action or acting-out. He will therefore need to learn alternative modes of expression and self-esteem regulation. This creative tension inevitably augments the dialectic between forensic psychotherapy and psychodrama/dramatherapy (Cox 1992a).

A custodial setting may imply a penal setting, such as a prison or borstal institution. It can also refer to a locked ward in a conventional psychiatric hospital, a secure hospital – such as Broadmoor – or a regional secure unit. Any therapy conducted in such a setting tends to be subsumed under the heading of forensic psychotherapy (see Appendix A p.253). This has close historical links with offender-therapy.

In this section, we are looking at various enterprises in which drama – in all the senses listed above – formally takes place in a custodial setting. The fact that a particular therapeutic modality is mentioned in this section does not necessarily imply that it is appropriate in Broadmoor. It may be. It may not be. But our present concern is with wider horizons. Nevertheless, the spirit of enquiry and the search for fresh therapeutic initiatives was potentiated and liberated by Hamlet, his company and those who followed him. I am deliberately not entering the debate between the relative merits and defects of insight-orientated and cognitive behaviour-modification therapies. Not because such issues can ever be unimportant, but because this is not the place for them. Nevertheless, an affirmative statement feels called for at this juncture. It is impossible to have worked in forensic psychiatry for any length of time without being brought face to face with such phenomena as the displaced victim, or the unconscious motivation for an offence which is otherwise inexplicable. The closet scene in *Hamlet* is a tightly woven matrix of psycho-sexual tensions. It is these which give the scene its peculiar power, and make it the recipient of so many audience projections:

> 'O Hamlet, speak no more
> Thou turn'st my eyes into my very soul'

(Hamlet III.4.88)

Over the years, I have been aware of various comments from colleagues, and have read the occasional article on the topic of drama in custodial settings. But I cannot recall seeing a substantial volume, which the theme merits. I therefore thought it would be useful if this book, describing all that preceded and followed Hamlet Day, could set the whole event within the context of the wider issue of the impact of drama in custodial settings, taking custodial settings to refer to establishments which would come under the broad heading of Goffman's description of a 'Total Institution' (1961,4). *Asylums: Essays on the Social Situation of Mental Patients and Other Inmates* stands as a landmark, so that it feels appropriate to quote a paragraph on the characteristics of total institutions:

> Every institution captures something of the time and interest of its members and provides something of a world for them; in brief, every institution has encompassing tendencies. When we review the different institutions in our Western society, we find some are encompassing to a degree discontinuously greater than the ones next in line. Their encompassing or total character is symbolized by the barrier to social intercourse with the outside and to departure that is often built right into the physical plant, such as locked doors, high walls, barbed wire, cliffs, water, forests or moors. These establishments I am calling *total institutions*, and it is their general characteristics I want to explore.

I felt that it would provide a wider custodial context for our consideration of the performance of tragedy in a secure psychiatric hospital if a whole chapter could be devoted to this topic. It therefore came as a considerable surprise that a general response to my enquiries seemed to be: '. . . Very interesting . . . but you won't find much on that!' My impression was that there was some kind of overall, once removed, awareness that there *is* published material, somewhere, although it is elusive. Everyone seemed to know of one or two instances where an actor or a director had taken a play into a prison or a borstal, but no-one could name the book which everyone seemed to think must exist! And computer searches drew blanks. Perhaps we had asked the wrong questions. In any event, there seemed to be a vacuum; an authoritative book on this important theme is therefore looking for an author. Having been unable to find a fully fledged 'expert contributor' it seemed prudent to ask those with a working knowledge of this double field to write what they could, so that their various experiences could be presented in parallel. In this way we hope that some greater clarity of perception, as to what the custodial setting calls for, will emerge.

Many referred to Esslin's (1962,19) account of the actors who performed *Waiting for Godot* in San Quentin Penitentiary in 1957. In a later section, Esslin writes as follows:

> If the prisoners of San Quentin responded to *Waiting for Godot*, it was because they were confronted with *their own experience* of time. Waiting, hope and despair; because they recognised the truth about *their own human relationships* in the sadomasochistic inter-dependence of Pozzo and Lucky in the bickering hate–love of Vladimir and Estragon. (70, his italics)

Stafford-Clark (1989,144) in *Letters to George* describes how a cast of professional actors went to HMP Wormwood Scrubs 'to see a performance by the prisoners of Howard Barker's *Love of a Good Man* . . . The men said things like "rehearsing is the only time you're not in prison". They had clearly been obsessed with rehearsing, and wholehearted approval from professionals gave them huge pleasure.' The creative freedom of rehearsal, when working on the play is still 'playing', is something which is repeatedly expressed by professional and amateur actors of all levels of experience. This is the time before the play has 'crystallized' – for better or worse – and there is time and space for creative change, adaptation and testing the limits of individual freedom of the cast-as-a-whole. This phrase has so many echoes from the dynamic life of a therapeutic group, in which there is a constant oscillation between the life of each individual member and that of the group-as-a-whole.

Raymond Gordon (in Schattner and Courtney 1987,309) begins an article on 'acting therapy' in this way: 'In people who spend most of their first twenty-eight years or so in and out of prison, the dehumanisation process begins before birth . . . Prison, a microcosm of the society from which they entered, intensifies the dehumanisation process.' His final paragraph begins 'theatre training for offenders is a humanising process. The stage is more real than real life . . . On the stage . . . the actor *must* reveal and *use* all of himself.' For many years Gordon has been a leader in prison drama and he has worked with ex-offenders. He emphasised how 'theatre training begins to remove . . . unrealistic attitudes and builds a concept of future.' He then describes other intrinsic and equally vital parts of rehearsal: 'Rehearsal means repetition, practice over and over again.

Impatient, at first, at doing the same exercise more than once, the offender learns, however, that each time he repeats it, something new is discovered and he becomes a little better at what he is doing. He sees that the work process itself is both necessary and rewarding – without it he would never achieve the result he wanted.' The importance of rehearsal was again emphasised in the recent (November 1991) performance of Sondheim's opera *Sweeney Todd*. The comment of one of the prison cast watching the final mass slaughter needs no elaboration: 'I had to look away. It made me see, after all this time, how other people must have witnessed my own deed – and misunderstood it' (*The Independent Weekend* 9 November 1991,31).

Susan Bennett (1990) devotes a whole volume to *Theatre Audiences: a Theory of Production and Reception* though there is no special reference to audiences witnessing performances in custodial settings.

In reply to my enquiry on this particular topic, Susan Bennett wrote 'I'm afraid I cannot be of much help on the subject of theatre audiences in prison. The production of Beckett's *Waiting for Godot* is legendary, of course, and I always imagined I would uncover some theorizing in response at least to that experience, but I didn't. I have enclosed for your interest a recent article from the Toronto-based Canadian Theatre Journal, *Theatrum* (1990). Given Snell's experience in both England and Canada, I thought his views might have some relevance to your project' (1991). Snell's article is entitled *Behind Bars: Serving Theatre in the Prisons* (1990,11). He has set several 'news-flash' pieces within the substance of his text. One of these refers to John Bergman and the Geese Theatre Company which has begun to work in the setting of the special hospital (see p.219). Their first performance in Broadmoor was as recently as 16 September 1991 – thus following in the sustained surge of creative energy which followed Hamlet Day. Snell's final paragraph contains these words: 'But as we swirl about in this dizzying system that says so much about the larger world, we understand our own ideological context a little better'.

Bearing all this in mind, a brief glance through the pages which follow might reasonably prompt the question: 'What has all this to do with Shakespeare coming to Broadmoor?' Though further thought will make it clear that this whole issue would not have come about, had Shakespeare *not* come to Broadmoor! This is yet another example of his capacity to disturb the *status quo*. His reference to that which disturbs needs to be repeated:

'Here they be that dare and will disturb thee.'

(*II Henry IV* IV.8.6)

The place of drama in custodial settings is a topic waiting to be tackled. It seems pertinent to add that even though computer searches and personal enquiry have failed to come up with any substantial survey of this theme, if such a work does exist, the author justly deserves our apologies. Indeed, it may well be that such a much needed work is in preparation.

How This Thing Came About

Bearing in mind the surprising vacuum evident in the lack of an integrated presentation of the topic, we are greatly indebted to our colleagues who at very short notice willingly agreed to take part in this enterprise. The 'ticket' for inclusion was that the author should have experience of working with drama in custodial settings, or, as is the case with our first contributor, Oliver Taplin, could give us the expert's comments on the theme as it applies in classical Greek theatre. This gives us not only the roots of our own theatre, but even the roots of the words *theatre* and *drama* themselves. Appropriate 'CV' details about the contributors will be found on Page 267. It is to be hoped that this section will not only help to reduce the literature vacuum, but will also furnish yet more evidence of the energy Shakespeare always releases when he enters a fresh setting. Such is the case in the life of Broadmoor Hospital. This wider horizon would not have been considered had it not been suggested that 'It would be good if we could bring *Hamlet* to Broadmoor'.

M.C.

Greek Drama
in Custodial Settings

Oliver Taplin

There is not, so far as I know, any record from ancient Greece of drama being mounted for the benefit of captives. In a world with such a strong sense of who has their rights and who has lost them, such an act of radical generosity was probably unthinkable. There is, however, a remarkable example of captives performing for their captors. After the disastrous defeat of the Athenians in Sicily in 414–3 BC, the survivors were set to work in the stone-quarries of Syracuse, which also formed, in effect, an inescapable dungeon. The story, which survives both in a romanticized version in the late biographer Plutarch and in a simpler version from the Alexandrian intellectual Satyrus, tells how those who could remember the lyric choruses of Euripides were granted their freedom, especially if they taught the plays to the sons of their jailors. Whether or not the anecdote is actually true, it is plausible. It illustrates the way that in Greece cultural bonds could override political conflict; it also is a reminder of the originally Athenian achievement of drama, which went on to become an obsession for the whole Greek world.

Plato had hard things to say about drama, which he regarded as a spurious rival to philosophy as a means of access to wisdom. Nonetheless there is a strongly dramatic element in his dialogues; and two of the most celebrated, *Crito* and *Phaedo*, are set in the death cell of Socrates. Socrates gave his greatest performances in a custodial setting.

In modern times Greek drama did not really become a live force again until the late eighteenth century; and it has arguably been stronger in the second half of the twentieth than at any time since antiquity. Two plays infused with Greek drama come to mind for being set in custodial microcosms. Athol Fugard's *The Island* is set on the notorious Robbin Island in

South Africa. Two inmates work out their own version of Sophocles' *Antigone* for the Christmas entertainment; and when they eventually begin, the audience realises that it constitutes the audience on the Island.

Secondly, Timberlake Wertenbaker's powerful piece *Our Country's Good* is set at the first substantial convict colony in Australia. While the play that is actually put on is *The Recruiting Officer*, there are many references to drama in ancient Greece, and especially to its claim to have been a didactic and improving force in the ethical life of the city. Can drama really – the play asks – help people who have been reduced to the lowest degradation to find their dignity and identity?

That Secret Voice

Cicely Berry

My work in closed institutions has been totally to do with exploring text, mostly Shakespeare, to experience how language goes through us and how we react to it as we speak it. It has been spasmodic, but at times quite wonderful.

Because I have arrived at certain methods of work by way of two different strands of experience, and because that work has always been to do with relating the secret self to the forming of words, I think it would be useful to give a brief outline of this experience, and how each form of work has informed the other.

The Voice in Action

First, I will look at the work I have done with actors, as that has been my chief concern since I began teaching. As Voice Director for the Royal Shakespeare Company for the last 20 or so years, I have worked in depth with actors on most of the major productions during this time. When I began work with the Company, it was geared to 'voice production': this meant training the voice to be clear and interesting, and the speech articulated 'correctly' – i.e. acceptable to class standards. But, as I worked more and more closely on productions themselves, I became deeply aware of the physical connections between the making of the word and the emotional motive of the actor – in the terms of Stanislavski, the great Russian director, actor, teacher – the want/need of the character in the scene.

I then began to realise that the work had to be in two parts:

1. the technical facility, and

2. how this technical facility reached into, and fused with, the actor's intentions: this had far reaching consequences in that it could affect the presentation of the character.

To add to this complexity, I also realised that the perception we have of our own voice is almost totally subjective. For we arrive at our own voice through an intricate and private mixture of the following four factors:

1. what we hear – involving our early environment/accent, position in the family unit etc;

2. how we hear it – our 'ear': in other words, how we interpret sound – always a subjective response;

3. our habit of speech – involving early speech patterns plus the physical make-up of the person and his/her muscular agility;

4. how we use our voice in the light of our personality and experience, and our self-image – in other words, how we want it to behave.

I have given a full account of this in my second book *Your Voice and How to Use It Successfully* (1975,15).

All this applies to the 'ordinary' person, i.e. the person communicating from day to day. But the actor has to learn that how he/she delivers a text puts specific interpretations on the listener, and so he/she must begin to know their voices objectively, and must adjust it accordingly.

But - and this is the vital point - that adjustment may make the actor feel untruthful: and this is both unnerving and harmful to the performance. And so the actor has to match up how he/she hears his/her own voice not only with performance technique and the needs of the character, but also with the needs of the audience who must be give the right message.

So, doubly, we ask – how necessary are words, how tied up with reason and motive? For the words are there written down, and the actor has to be both taken over by them, and take them over. And this has many layers, for words have different associations for different people, and some are more confident with them than others.

Parallel with my work with actors I have run countless workshops on the language of Shakespeare in schools, mainly with 6th-formers, in community groups, and also with English teachers – these over a number of years. I think that without exception the first task was to break down some kind of received idea of how it should be spoken, in order to get near what the words could hold for them: this was not necessarily to do with how they were taught, for so often the teachers wanted the time to do work with them that opened the speaking up, but it was to do with the necessity of getting through exams. It is also to do with the fact that:

a) we treat language that is written down differently; we make it 'behave' and so straight-jacket it in some way; and

b) I believe we respect the written word more than the spoken word. In Shakespeare's day there was a strong oral tradition which is not with us now.

And so I began to realise the value of working on the physical associations of language in Shakespeare, and how that work enabled the group to:

'apprehend
More than cool reason ever comprehends'
(*A Midsummer Night's Dream* V.1.6)

If, somehow, we can release the language from its literal/academic meaning, we allow our responses to fly.

To do this work in a group it is necessary to get them to do something physical, not directly related to the text in hand, and which to begin with may seem irrelevant. The purpose of this is to free the speaker from over-concentration and so release a subconscious response. The exercise also has to fit in to the space in which we are working. My aim always has been to get them to feel something from speaking the words that enriched their understanding of them – one could hear this reaction immediately in their voices. And of course, once they had found this internal response, they could see the point of the exercise and were excited by it – and by working on language.

I remember working with a group of A level students on *Othello*: they understood it all in a hide-bound kind of way, and of course 'appreciated' it, but I could not think of how to get them 'in' to the language – to get them taken off-guard by it. We were looking at Act III Scene 3, the pivotal scene where Iago has worked so successfully on Othello's hidden doubts and jealousy that he finally believes Desdemona to be unfaithful. I got them all standing round in a circle, reading the following lines:

OTHELLO: Never, Iago. Like to the Pontic sea,
Whose icy current and compulsive course
Ne'er feels retiring ebb, but keeps due on
To the Propontic and the Hellespont,
Even so my bloody thoughts with violent pace
Shall ne'er look back, ne'er ebb to humble love,
Till that a capable and wide revenge

Swallow them up. Now, by yond marble heaven,
In the due reverence of a sacred vow
I here engage my words.

(Othello III.3.451)

We did this several times, and then quite simply I got them to link arms
firmly and then pull away from each other as hard as they could. It was
fairly chaotic, though obviously one watched to see it did not go too far:
the point was, that for a few moments they were swinging round against
each other, out of control. And one of them said; I see what he feels, he is
drowning in his feelings – always in Shakespeare the sea holds an image
of being out of control – it was a revelation. Having found that idea, we
then looked at how the verse was built, and saw that there is one long
sentence from 'Like to the Pontic sea' down to 'Swallow them up'. If you
try to do this on one breath the sense of desperation is there in the rhythm
of the words and the music of the whole passage, and this relates both to
the surge and current of the sea, and to the sense of panic when you are
out of breath.

And that seems to me what we should be after: a sense that the words
both define and release the feeling and are never separate from it. But also
when you do an exercise like that, words take on different shapes and
lengths, vowels become extended and consonants more muscular, the
movement of the words becomes one with the movement of the inner self,
and the word becomes active in every sense. It also becomes subversive –
i.e. that language does not behave quite as you expect. Now these two
strands of work have allowed me to see how text can be explored objectively, yet with a purpose to open up the individual to the possibility of
defining themselves through language. I think that the majority of people
have so little self-esteem when it comes to expressing their inner self, that
they then resort to accepted clichéd responses: and the thought crosses
one's mind as to what extent we then define ourselves through clichés.
Perhaps our greatest fear is the fear of appearing ignorant.

So, in fact, language rules: i.e. it is the people who have a facility with
language who can manipulate, and can invade and inhibit our secret voice.
There is an excellent book by Max Atkinson (1984) in which he sets out a
few simple rules of rhetoric which, if used by a politician, will win his/her
audience over and be persuasive enough to ensure success. However, he
also goes on to say that those forms of rhetoric evolved over centuries
when the oral culture was predominant: we just have to practice it. Also
the barrage of television advertising etc, telling/selling us what we should
need, what we should feel, what we should have, what we should 'go for',
all executed with wonderfully persuasive rhetoric – and some poetry –

inhibits and confuses, and makes us lose faith in our own ability to put across what we feel. We are being taken over by technological indifference to the emotional roots of language. What chance then do the less well educated have of defining themselves? But not just the under-educated; those who feel deeply, whose feelings perhaps are complex, who cannot compete/compute with those who have more facility with the language. So often the mental ability is way above the ability to express.

Having been at a point once in my life when I had an overwhelming sense of my speech being blocked so that I could not speak the words that I needed to, I realised in a very precise way the effort it takes to make words when they are felt at a particularly deep level. Obviously we do not and cannot live our lives at this level for long at a time, but how do we help people overcome some of this constraint when they need to? For when you cannot speak, what is there left but violence?

I think by using good dramatic text we can manoevre people into wanting to talk:

1. first, quite simply to see that they can get a pleasure in language, and that it is available to them: this involves some technical facility;

2. then, by using text which deals with feeling, the inner landscape, to realise that this can be put into words;

3. from this, to appreciate that feelings are quite frequently ambivalent and cannot be given concrete conclusions;

4. further, that there is a connection between what you are feeling and the body's response to what you are saying;

Now Shakespeare satisfies all these needs. I would not say it was the only text to use, but certainly I have found it quite the best in starting any work off: perhaps not the least because, if for a moment, the group has understood it, there is a great sense of achievement – such is its mystique. Also, because, there is nothing didactic there, it is open to many individual responses, and nearly everyone in the group will find something which is personal. And lastly, there is something about its musicality that touches a core of recognition of 'something other than the self'. The aim of the work should be to achieve some sort of involvement between the speaker and the words spoken – a private recognition.

Now to the practicalities. I have found that every session should start off with sensible, relaxed breathing exercises to get the breath as deep into the body as possible: this gives a sense of assurance. If you know the group, this can be done on the floor; the benefit of this is that we can feel the length and width of our body, the swing of the ribs, and any obvious tensions in the neck; also, it helps to focus on the self. Initially, however, the exercises should be done in pairs, with one sitting on a chair and the partner then feeling the movement of the ribs by putting his/her hands on the rib cage. This is good in that it gives an awareness of the whole breathing mechanism. It should then be taken into sound: an easy humming and then singing through onto vowels, which will give an understanding of how breath makes sound; what is important is that we feel our own vibrations, and, depending on the group, each other's.

To begin with in most groups there is usually a certain amount of embarrassment at this – it is curiously unnerving to listen to one's own sound, and perhaps we should ponder on this – but the embarrassment soon goes. Each one can then make sound on their own and begin to listen to their inner voice – a voice that is not trying to make an impression. The concentration of energy then becomes quite different.

One small point: it is particularly useful to work in pairs, in that the person being 'felt' has something to flex themselves against, and the person who is 'feeling' becomes more aware of his/her own body mechanism at the same time. But of course how one sets this up does depend on the group.

Having come so far, it is then right to go through some of the speech sounds, i.e. the consonants and some vowels, in order to experience their energy and shape. This starts to take us into a different view of language – into the enjoyment of its physicality. For it seems to me that the most important thing we can do is give people a voice, the sense that they have a right to speak, and that it can be enjoyed. And so my next stage is always to do with allowing the language to be subversive in some way, kicking it about – sometimes literally. And so we go on to text.

Moving into a Custodial Setting

So how can all this work in a prison or closed institution, and what are the differences? I will talk through these in a moment, but what is so striking when you begin the work, once the members of the group have got over their initial shyness at speaking text aloud, is the very raw and immediate energy that is brought to the language: they are not afraid of its extremes, nor the sense of outrage that is so often there. Are they more in touch? I started to go into HM Prison Long Lartin, the top security prison near Evesham, in about 1982. It came about because actress Sheila Hancock, who was at that time in the RSC, was invited into the prison to do some kind of show.

At that time I was working on a poetry programme called *Groupings – Gropings* in which Sheila was involved. It was a rather rich mixture of classical and modern poetry, plus bits of dialogue, a couple of Feiffer cartoons and a Bob Dylan song – a bit 'seventies', but I liked it a lot (it has been performed recently in the US with Whoopie Goldberg). As Sheila had nothing of her own that was suitable, we decided that this would be a good programme to take in; the theme was serious but had a good deal of comedy as well, and it had a small cast of only six – an ideal size. Basically, it was about how most people need to join a group, whether the group be religious, political, or a family one – we need to belong. We pursued this theme through all the stages of life, from childhood to a poem written by an elderly lady in a geriatric ward. There was some quite dense material, such as one of Donne's religious sonnets, poems of Hopkins, Yeats, Ferlinghetti – a good mixture – plus a Feiffer cartoon which started off something like this:

> 'Once I belonged to a Group that really had the Word
> I worked like hell for them
> And then another Group came along and said that they
>   had a very much better Word.
> So I left the first Group, and joined this second Group.
> I worked like hell for them etc. etc.'

And so I went on with the 'voice' joining groups and leaving them until finally, on his/her own, he/she asks someone with similar interests to join him/her and make a group. And so it posed questions about our need to belong.

By the reception we got, and the comments from the group afterwards, the programme struck a number of chords. However, what amazed us about the whole evening was the quality of the listening: the absolute attention, the hunger, which is something one does not experience normally. We were all knocked out by this attention, by the sense of energy in the listening, and by the details that were picked up and responded to in a most perceptive way.

Out of this experience I came to know the Education Department at Long Lartin quite well, in particular Gill Ganner, who ran courses in English literature and, among other things, organized talks and lectures on poetry and so forth by visiting writers, when these were possible.

I then started to go in fairly regularly for two-hour workshops. I worked nearly always on Shakespeare, though we had several sessions on Beckett and on T.S. Eliot. The sessions were arranged particularly well: Gill Ganner would prepare the group for the play we were going to look at by giving them things to read on it, and where possible, they would have seen videos round the subject. This meant that they had some kind of view of the play before I came in to work, and we could get straight down to looking at the language and to work this through on to scenes.

What never ceased to surprise me was the energy that seemed to come from the group as they walked into the room to work – like two World Cup teams – and that sense of expectancy.

My format was this: I always started with breathing exercises, exactly the same in principle as the ones I have described. However, as with any group one gears the work to the particular needs of that group, so in Long Lartin I concentrated on simple stretching and relaxing, taking deep breaths, and taking that into sound. I always did some work in pairs, so that they could feel the muscular activity of the ribs, but always did this quite briefly; for one thing the Prison Officers would get anxious, and for another it is just a very big thing for them to touch each other in that situation – and perhaps they do not want to, for there are tensions between different categories of prisoners, and so we have to leave that open. Yet I feel it is important to let it happen if possible.

I understand completely why the Prison Officers might get anxious: I think the exercises could not be readily understood, and they would appear to be perhaps too informal. We are, after all, doing things which are freeing and relaxing and which would seem to have no order; and this could release too much.

Next we would sit on the floor to go through some exercises. This is good in that not only is it unexpected, but it also takes away any kind of authority image, and I think perhaps makes one feel less threatened and more individual. For one must never forget that each one of them brings in a world that we can never know about.

In this position you can, through exercise:

i. become aware of the channel of breath from the stomach;

ii. you can lean back and feel your own weight, then sigh out and hear the breath coming through the body;

iii. you can then hum and sing out on vowels, and feel the resonance in your whole body, i.e. your chest, head and face, and, by bouncing on the floor, you feel that resonance even in your seat.

Getting this sense of ones own sound is absolutely crucial.

After a few vowel and consonant exercises to focus on the activity of language, we would start to prepare to look at the play – this sitting on chairs round the room.

I want to take as an example one particular session when we were looking at *The Winter's Tale*. We all sat round to read the beginning – the first scene and a few pages of the second scene down to Leontes' first soliloquy. We read it once round in a circle as best as we could, some more ably that others; we talked a little of the plot, and got a general idea of what was happening. I then got volunteers to read it again taking the different parts. We read it this time with the characters speaking in the middle, and the rest of the group sitting round them in a circle, and asked the group to repeat the words which they had heard spoken which were to do with love – either in the sense of affection and admiration, or, as happens later in the scene, in the sense of sexual desire. In doing this they began to choose words for themselves, and in a way to own them. They were surprised by the quality and texture there: how in the first scene Archidemus and Camillo openly compete with each other over the quality and richness of their hospitality. But they were even more surprised at the sexuality they found in these words of Hermione:

> HERMIONE: What? Have I twice said well: When was't before?
> I prithee tell me. Cram's with praise, and make's
> As fat as tame things. One good deed dying tongueless
> Slaughters a thousand waiting upon that.
> Our praises are our wages. You may ride's
> With one soft kiss a thousand furlongs ere
> With spur we heat an acre. But to th'goal:
> My last good deed was to entreat his stay.
> What was my first? It has an elder sister,
> Or I mistake you. O, would her name were Grace!
> But once before I spoke to th'purpose? When?
> Nay, let me have't; I long.
>
> (*The Winter's Tale* I.2.90)

Always the language takes us into the world of the play. There is an extremely good essay by Maynard Mack on Hamlet (1968) which elaborates on this theme.

We continued to work on the play in different ways. For instance, we took the speech of Leontes which begins 'Inch-thick, knee-deep, o'er head and ears a fork'd one – ': we worked on it all together, and then I asked them to move round the room while speaking, and changing direction on each punctuation mark in order to find the emotional movement in the language, and the sudden and violent turns of thought. We also looked at the violence in the language by repeating the words that express/contain disgust in some way, such as contempt, cuckold, sluiced, bawdy, fished, etc. etc. – the list is long. Now by doing simple things like banging your hand on the floor at these words, or kicking a chair, we become aware that the words themselves are letting us into the nature of the man, and further, they are self-feeding, for they lead him on to action. There are may ways of opening up the hidden agenda in the language, so that we realise the extent to which feelings are ambivalent and complex. And this is surely what is important: an opening up to hidden feelings through formal, articulate language.

This was a particularly good session, I remember, for near the end of it one of the group was so excited that he said something like – 'you see, they didn't need scenery in those days – it's all in the words.' And that was a revelation for them.

Now, of course, one does not only work to release the violence in the language; it is simply that if we start with that area it is unexpected, and therefore immediately awakens curiosity. It also makes a statement that one is open to these ideas.

Having found this response to the language, one can then go on to find a delicacy of feeling. a discovery of love perhaps, as in the scene between Perdita and Florizel later in the same play: Act IV Scene 4, where Florizel discovers his feelings for Perdita:

> FLORIZEL: What you do
> Still betters what is done. When you speak, sweet,
> I'd have you do it ever; when you sing,
> I'd have you buy and sell so, so give alms,
> Pray so, and, for the ord'ring your affairs,
> To sing them too; when you do dance, I wish you
> A wave o'th'sea, that you might ever do
> Nothing but that – move still, still so,
> And own no other function. Each your doing,
> So singular in each particular,
> Crowns what you are doing in the present deeds,
> That all your acts are queens.
>
> (*The Winter's Tale* IV.4.135)

The touching out of the words is very delicate: the play on the word 'do' for instance.

There are a number of exercises that we can use to find this fineness of feeling between two people. One that I have found particularly useful is to get the two people reading the characters to speak to each other from different ends of the room, and to give them the objective of trying to get to each other while they speak. Without them realising, I would then ask several members of the group to keep them apart, not by manhandling them, but simply by somehow preventing them to get close. This opens up the most wonderful sense of the need/longing contained in the words, and brings home just how difficult it is to make real contact with another person – to get inside them almost.

This exercise has produced wonderful results for me, and I have used it on many scenes, such as the beginning of *A Midsummer Night's Dream* between Theseus and Hippolyta: also between the Ghost and Hamlet – it brings a sense of urgency and longing purely through the words.

Now all these are exercises that can help take us enter into the text, and there are may more: I have written about them at length in *The Actor and His Text* (1987). They work for actors; they work for any group who want to explore text, though obviously one modifies them according to the capability of the group, and certainly you find a way of working together to get confidence before asking anyone to read on their own until they are ready.

These visits, for various reasons, stopped around 1986. However, I know they were extremely useful: there was a great deal of feedback about the sessions at the time which came back to Gill Ganner, and I myself still, in roundabout ways, get feedback about them.

In 1984 I became involved in an amazingly interesting project: Blind Summit – Dartmoor. This was started by the film-maker Paul Schoolman, whose aim was to make a film inside HM Prison Dartmoor on the story of Julius Caesar. In trying to set this project up, he arranged many workshops in Dartmoor on text, on acting, but chiefly on writing scripts. It obviously took a great deal of time and patience to set up, because here were many difficulties attached, as you will imagine, but it had very warm support from Governor May. Governor May, I know, realized the enormous value of these sessions in terms of the morale of the prison.

I did a number of workshops on Shakespeare in the prison, and for me the project culminated in a day I arranged in the RSC Swan Theatre in Stratford, when three film scripts were read by 16 members of the RSC, and by two ex-cons who had been involved in the writing workshops.

These three scripts: *Nonce, The Stone Hotel* and *Julius Caesar,* were extremely powerful pieces of writing. The audience numbered around 120 who nearly all stayed for the very valuable discussion at the end. Among those from the prison service who attended were: Governor May, Governor Timms from Maidstone and Mr S.C. Handley who was deputising for Judge Tumin. There was also one Deputy Governor and a number of Prison Officers.

The discussion afterwards was chaired by the film producer Rex Bloomstein, and was really excellent in that it dealt with English attitudes to crime and punishment: an on how we should be preparing prisoners for life outside. Several members of the audience said that the day had altered their whole perspective on the prison system, and wanted to know how they could positively contribute to improving it. It seems to me crucial that this kind of work continues in order to prepare prisoners better for their re-entry into society.

I like to think that finding 'that secret voice' is part of this process.

Psychodrama in a Custodial Setting
A Cautious Exploration

Eva Røine

This brief account is perhaps best presented by following the course my professional life has taken. Looking back over the past twenty years, there seemed to be many paths leading to a main road. This, for me, is work in therapy based on the methods of the theatre. As a very young drama student in the 1950s, I was greatly fascinated by the psychology of crime. I spent many a day in the Central Criminal Court, instead of going to acting classes. Years later, I sat on the press bench, covering the trial of the last woman to be hanged in England. Then, many years later, when I had qualified as a clinical psychologist, my first post – one which I held for eight years – was in the psychiatric clinic at Ullevål Hospital in Oslo. At that time, it was under police administration. Many patients admitted to the acute crisis ward came from the Hospital for Criminal Offences, having attempted to commit suicide. I developed an increasing interest in the way in which the psychology of crime presented a challenge, both to dynamic understanding and therapy.

Following my initial training as an actress, the various strands of my academic background, combining clinical psychology, criminology and the history of the theatre, led to a Magistergrade (equivalent to a PhD) in the University of Oslo. This, in turn, led to a four months' scholarship from the Norwegian-American Association, to be spent in America. This award was primarily due to an article I had written about a theatre guest-performance in Copenhagen by Daytop Village, a therapeutic community in New York. The play, called *The Snake Pit*, had been developed by drug addicts using methods based on drama therapy. The scholarship allowed me to visit Daytop Village, so that I was able to study at first-hand the effects of drama therapy as training, both for emotional release and stimulation of creativity. I participated in the daily routine. And, as I had several years of training with drama students in Oslo, from a more conventional point of view, I soon found it very exciting to work with dramatisations from a therapeutic aspect.

During my first week in New York, someone took me to the Moreno Academy of Psychodrama. From that night, I knew how I wanted to spend my future. Virtually every evening, I was able to study different styles of directing; from Jim Sachs' introverted way of leading the protagonist, to Hannah Weiner's temperamental and highly original style. Hannah took me on as her assistant, and I learned the first basic steps. Towards the end of my stay, Dr J.L. Moreno – the creator of psychodrama – cordially invited me to the famous Beacon, the training centre for psychodrama. This, for me, was the Navel of the World! I therefore had the pleasure of meeting Dr Moreno personally (he died three years later, in 1974). My meeting with him took on an added significance because, at the time, I was the only student at Beacon who spoke German. And, as he liked to speak in his native tongue, we had long talks about his work. We discussed his visions of the immense possibilities inherent in creativity and spontaneity to help those on the wrong side of the law. He had been the first psychiatrist to work with group psychotherapy inside prisons (Sing Sing). He is also credited as being the first to use the term Group Psychotherapy. At Beacon, I also met Zirka Toeman Moreno, his wife, who was thirty years his junior. She is a highly gifted psychodramatist who was of great help and inspiration in establishing The Norwegian Institute of Psychodrama in 1986.

In 1976, the Chief Psychiatrist of the police ward in Oslo asked me to join his staff. He must have been a little worried, however, because on my first day he called me in to his office and told me about the general policy of Reality Confrontation: 'It is very important with psychotic patients.' He implied that when patients spoke of hearing voices and seeing strange things, I had to reply that this was 'not my reality.' 'Then this is no job for me,' I said, adding 'because in psychodrama our interest is such that we often ask "What do you hear? What do you see?" Only then is it possible to enter the patient's world.' After this he smiled and said 'Do as you like then.' So this was the opening of the first permanent therapeutic theatre with a stage, lighting outfit and video cameras. All these facilities were supplied by the authorities, though the stage itself was built by the patients. This theatre still exists today and I still have the key. Unfortunately, there are too few trained psychodramatists to meet the demand for this kind of work. But, from February 1992, we hope that the first ten students from the advanced training course will qualify. The Norwegian Psychodrama Institute is now training approximately 60 students and of these, 28 have embarked upon advanced training. The educational standards of the Institute are in keeping with those developed by the Nordic Board and the Psychodrama Institute of Europe.

Going from the ward to the theatre, we had to pass through locked doors and walk down a steep staircase to the cellars. It was dark and frightening and had a faint smell of something indescribable! Usually, it was my lot to go first and there were times when I had fantasies of being killed on the way down. We were working with patients who had committed homicide, in addition to other patients with a conventional spectrum of psychiatric disturbances. Some of the patients in prison were directly referred to the psychodrama theatre. One man came with two police escorts, who sat outside the theatre while the drama was taking place. This young man was dangerous, a highly intelligent person who wanted to study while he served his sentence for brutal manslaughter. But, as he had shown no remorse or willingness to try to understand the motivation for his crime, the prison authorities did not want to give him any extra privileges. He was a real tough one. His first line to me was: 'I demand that you do your damndest.'

'How much can you take?' I asked. He looked at me and said: 'Everything.'

This was a big challenge. I used the strongest weapon in psychodrama, namely, role-reversal. I asked him to lie down on the floor, to close his eyes and to go into the body of the man he had killed. This strange therapy session did not last very long. Moreno's potent way of using Surplus Reality worked, catching repressed feelings of guilt, anger, grief and longing for security and love. An interesting aspect of his history was revealed during the course of the therapy. Namely, that as a boy of five, he had been abused by his father on exactly the same spot as the killing had taken place many years later.

Another patient, a woman of 38, referred for psychodrama, had been in the habit of stabbing people in the street. These actions always happened at random and, one night, she killed a man. In this case, role reversal also proved most effective. One day we managed to enact the scene where the man was stabbed to death. By this time she had started to show emotions, having previously worked on her relationship with her father. She had been an incest victim, and had lived part of her life as a prostitute. We felt that she presented a very difficult case for rehabilitation. But there was something unique about her personality and we did not want to give up. The day she role reversed with the dead man, she cried. She told us that she had read the newspapers at the time of the trial and knew that her victim had recently been married and that his wife was expecting a baby. She could not remember the last time she had cried. When she left hospital, she returned to prison to finish her sentence. Her fierce behaviour was greatly reduced.

Most of the psychodramatic work with offender-patients and other psychotic patients was done as a *monodrama*. This means that there were no groups, only two assistants to play auxiliary roles, these usually being a junior doctor and a nurse. With patients suffering from extreme anxiety, we played the dramas with a *vicarious protagonist*; this is with the patient watching the drama played out with somebody else in the main role. Some patients preferred to play all the roles in the drama themselves. This is known as *autodrama*. It is now seven years since I left the hospital, and I miss these strange and profound performances. As one of my colleagues said: 'What is Strindberg compared to life?' At times, such drama is almost unbearable. So many destinies. So much pain. And yet so many transformations towards new creative levels of hope. And therefore so deeply rooted in life.

Recommended Reading

Fox, J. (1987) *The Essential Moreno*. New York: Springer Publications.

Holmes, P. and Karp, M. (eds) (1991) *Psychodrama – Inspiration and Technique*. London: Tavistock.

Marineau, R. (1989) *Jacob Levy Moreno 1889–1974* London: Tavistock.

Moreno, J. L. (1973) *Theatre of Spontaneity*. New York: Beacon House Press.

Moreno, J. L. (1978) *Who Shall Survive*. New York: Beacon House Press.

Moreno, Z. T. (1965) Psychodramatic Rules, Techniques and Adjunctive Methods. *Group Psychotherapy and Psychodrama*, 18, 73–83.

Moreno, Z. T. (1975) The Significance of Doubling and Role Reversal for Cosmic Man. *Group Psychotherapy and Psychodrama*, 28, 55–59.

Røine, E. (1978) *Group Psychotherapy as Experimental Theatre*. Oslo: Aschehoug. English translation in preparation.

IV. 2. iv

Creating a Character in a Locked Facility

Melinda Meyer

Introduction

This article discusses the way in which expressive therapy has been used with two different target groups; namely, offender-patients who receive treatment in a locked facility, and refugees whose experience of being the victims of organized crime has prompted them to seek out-patient treatment. The majority of the latter have been tortured in prison. Strictly speaking, they endeavour to re-create a character which had been lost or taken from them in a locked facility. Psychologically, their inner worlds have developed some characteristics of locked facilities – as a protective defence.

The terms used in the title need to be defined at the outset. By 'creating a character' I am adopting a psychodramatic term used by Moreno (1972,157): 'Roles do not emerge from the self, but the self may emerge from roles.' He maintained that the self emerges from role-playing, rather than being its origin. In this article I will use 'character' and 'role' synonymously. As Pitzele (in Holmes and Karp 1991,15) observes, 'Moreno seems to be saying that we might well regard ourselves as a collective of roles, as if we were a kind of theatre company, containing within ourselves many possible actors.' This echoes much of Stanislavski (1980), a pillar in psychodrama's supporting literature. If the self lacks important characters for full social functioning in daily life, e.g. the nurturer, the worker, the partner etc., he or she will only be able to function in a limited capacity. By creating and becoming the missing character(s), given the possibility to integrate it (them) as part of the self, the chance of living in a 'larger world' is enhanced.

By 'a locked facility' I mean an institution where offender-patients are locked up because they are a risk to themselves, others close to them or the wider range of 'others' who constitute society. They have been deprived of their freedom for differing time spans, depending upon the severity of their offences and diagnostic or prognostic uncertainty.

The material presented here comes primarily from work undertaken in my present position at The Psychosocial Centre for Refugees, University of Oslo; and also from Centerpoint, Boston, USA, an institution for juvenile delinquent boys who were sentenced on account of severe crimes and subsequently offered treatment as an option to being detailed in gaol. Other sources are Ward 16, Ullevål Hospital, Oslo, which is a locked facility for clients who are being assessed and/or treated for severe mental illnesses, and Ullvin, Oslo, an open institution for chronic drug addicts. In this unit many are receiving treatment during their sentence for crimes committed in the support of their addiction. I am currently working with torture victims, and the majority of my work is with refugees who have been traumatised (many having been tortured in prison) and with them I conduct both individual and group psychotherapy which involves the use of the expressive arts.

The focus of my research is to endeavour to assess how the arts applied as a method in psychotherapy can stimulate an individual's creative capacity. Those who have been traumatised very often sense that they have lost their creativity; so that helping the client to recover and re-energize his creativity is a vital part of the therapeutic process. One of my basic assumptions is that each human being needs to be in contact with his creative ability if he is going to be able to survive.

Working with the creative arts, within a relatively conservative system, is either viewed as a conventional 'everyday' activity, rather than a therapeutic method or, at the other extreme, as a potentially 'dangerous' psychotherapeutic technique. Many psychiatrists and psychologists believe that the method will lead to acting-out behaviour. In fact, it is precisely the opposite which usually transpires when such methods are used by trained and experienced expressive therapists. Such a population of clients needs to work within a clearly demarcated structure, and professional expressive therapists should have special skills in this area of expertise. Another vital condition necessary for the optimal use of the creative arts as a therapeutic method within locked facilities, or indeed within any institution, is that the milieu is receptive and encourages such an approach. It is essential that there is support, interdisciplinary cooperation, knowledge and space – both architecturally and in terms of time and conceptualisation – in which to explore these new therapeutic approaches. If such an environment does not exist, these methods are contra-indicated.

I will now describe various characteristics of the client-population with whom I have been working, and indicate some of the essentials of the expressive therapies (the creative arts) and psychodrama. This will be followed by two vignettes which illustrate how these methods have been applied.

Children of War

What do juvenile delinquents have in common with torture victims?

The criminals I worked with at Centerpoint and Ullvin were battered children, victims of war in their families and on the street. The clients I am currently working with have, on the whole, been children of war before they were imprisoned and tortured. Being abused by the parents has the same effect on a child as torture has on the torture victim. There is no way to fight or escape the situation. The one who abuses is the one who comforts. These children and adults end up with crushed egos, low self esteem, and shame. Their relationships with others are full of mistrust, denial, guardedness and fear.

Children who have grown up either in families or in societies where there has been violence and abuse often end up with 'a crushed ego'. They have never been safe enough to be children, they have not been able to play; instead they have been taught how to engage in 'games'. The difference between a play and a game is that, when playing, time and space disappear; it is the process which engages, while in games the goal is superior – usually, the goal is to win. Reality for these children is that they always have had to be on guard in learning the game of survival, instead of trusting the environment and engaging in themselves and developing an inner world full of fantasy, energy and self-consciousness. Life is unpredictable. The one who kisses is in the next moment the one who abuses. A common expression 'jail-bird' can be interpreted as a bird who can no longer survive without the cage. Freedom can only be tolerated for short moments. It is safer inside the cage than it is outside. A child who has never learnt how to play, or has forgotten how to do so, is like a bird who has never learnt how to fly.

When observing an addict, it appears that he seeks to be contained in everything he does. Every time he puts the needle in his body it is as if other forces take over and 'hold' him. Drug addiction often leads to breaking and entering 'houses'. Then it is the 'house' that holds him. He literally ends up in a container, a cell in a state of detention, later to be transferred for shorter or longer periods of time for treatment. This is the cycle which is repeated over and over again. Why do they never stop, except in death?

When I was working at Centerpoint, I had a very violent boy in therapy. He had no furniture in his room. Twice a week I had him in individual therapy. We had an aeroplane we were building in each session, while we were talking. In this period he made no major assault on anyone. One day, one of the guards came to crush his plane, with the result that my patient totally lost control and punched one of the staff. As a result, he was carried by seven staff members to his room.

For many of these clients, feelings are experienced as impossible to contain. The expression often is 'I can't stand it.' What is it that they cannot stand? Is it what is happening outside them, or is it what is turning and tossing inside them? Probably the latter. These children are dropped children. Their egos are weak and their boundaries are floating in relationship to others.

Feelings end up as something that either destroy self or others. We can imagine a mother's arms as the outer wall of a container which make it possible for the child to get to know what is going on inside him because the arms create this safe environment. If the child has not had the experience of being held by these arms he will become afraid of the strong forces within. There will be too much, and the child will numb himself.

In *The Untouched Key* Miller (1991,41) discusses the childhood dynamics of several well-known people. One of the characters she discusses is Buster Keaton:

> In spite of remembering what happened to him, Buster Keaton undoubtedly repressed the trauma of being abused and degraded. That is why he had to repeat the trauma countless times without ever feeling it, for the early lesson that his feelings were forbidden and were to be ignored, retained its hold on him. I have observed young people in the cafés and bars of a small city who also must have learnt this lesson. They stare dully into space, cigarette in hand, sipping a glass of something alcoholic if they can afford it, and biting their fingernails. Alcohol, cigarettes, nail-biting – all serve the same purpose: to prevent feelings from coming to the surface at any cost. As children these people never learnt to experience their feelings, to feel comfortable with them, to understand them. They fear feelings like the plague and yet can't live entirely without them, so they pretend to themselves that getting high on drugs in a disco can make up for all they have lost. But it doesn't work . . . they begin to steal, to destroy property, and to ignore the feelings and rights of others. They don't

know that all this was once done to them. For there is no way for mistreated children to defend their rights.

Expressive Therapy Applied to the 'Children of War'

Expressive therapy is a combination of movement, art, writing, music, drama, and poetry, verbal and non-verbal communication methods. Its objective is to strengthen inner consciousness, the ability to express one-self, creativity and insight. It includes an integrating process in which intuitive capability is linked to logical thinking. It is a holistic approach, incorporating non-verbal forms of expression as an essential part of the human being's total communication, including the expression through and of the body.

In expressive therapy the point of reference is all that is normally done during a day; all the daily rituals. We focus on these, and try to make them more conscious. Ritual can also function as a container, something that is predictable, something that provides safety. They can give the human being something to rely on and lead to a sense of safety. Rituals may be divided into four phases: preparation or warming-up, action, closure and a reflection phase. All individuals have their own rhythm. Some need a long warm-up before they can go into action and some people go into action without preparation. This is also a cultural variable. If one or more of these phases are excluded, the consequences are that the individual loses 'balance'. The clients I am focusing on in this article have all lost their balance. They all exclude one or more of these phases.

It is, therefore, important for the group to re-establish this balance by including all phases and focusing on their importance in the rituals of daily life.

Psychodrama

Psychodrama, one of the expressive therapies, is an action method of group psychotherapy developed by Jacob Levy Moreno. In 1921 he developed the Theatre of Spontaneity in Vienna. This is where his interest in the use of drama and social interaction as methods of psychotherapy emerged. He emigrated to the USA in 1925 and continued to develop the method there at his private hospital in Beacon, New York, in 1936. Psychodrama means 'soul action', and it is an active participating method.

The five main instruments of a psychodrama are the director, the protagonist, auxiliary egos (group members or co-therapists), the scene, and the audience. The protagonist (client) is the one who leads the drama and the therapist is the director. Psychodrama is based on the theory of spontaneity and creativity. Creativity is the child and spontaneity is the energy which it is necessary to bring it out in the world.

In this article I will only address two psychodramatic techniques: role reversal and mirroring.

Role-reversal has several uses in the psychodramatic process. It enables other group members to get a more complete picture of the protagonist's perception of important people in his or her life through the dramatization of these individuals; it enables the protagonist to experience the world from the viewpoint of the other, and in this position to receive the impact of himself (now played by the auxiliary ego, a member of the group or co-therapist who play significant individuals from the protagonist's life, thus helping the enactment of the drama) as experienced by the world. This experience can be very powerful, salutary and therapeutic. Role-reversal may also be used to encourage the protagonist to develop self-control, should a protagonist be experiencing intense and violent feelings towards 'the other'. Role-reversal immediately puts the protagonist into an alternative role, a technique that encourages self-control and also gives him the experience of himself viewed more objectively. Role-reversal is a way of transcending the habitual limitations of egocentricity (Blatner and Blatner 1988).

Mirroring is a technique that gives the protagonist the possibility of looking at himself objectively and in relationship to others. The protagonist in the drama is in this case replaced by a member of the group and can thus stand aside and watch the drama unfold.

What makes expressive therapy different from the more traditional and verbal approaches of psychotherapy?

In expressive therapy the client is given the opportunity of acting out his thoughts and feelings in active communicative action. Because each individual has his own cultural background, his own set of rules and his own frame of reference for understanding the world, it is difficult for a psychotherapeutic group to understand each others' reality solely through verbal communication. When the participants are able to express their feelings through a drawing or to show what they are feeling through movement or role-reversal, it gives the group another dimension for understanding what the individual is really trying to express. Working through creative arts gives the group the possibility of engaging in the here and now, i.e. in the same reality. I have found this very important in my work with criminal and cross-cultural groups of refugees. Many of my patients have reported that they have never been able to play, so that using creative methods in psychotherapy gives them a feeling of playing and playfulness. Psychotherapy is then seen as play and not only hard work with pain and distress.

In verbal therapy a word can become a container for feelings, but it is not conserved before it is written down. All the arts can serve as an extension of the ego. The agenda book for most people has this containing function. If the book is lost, chaotic feelings will emerge. While working through deep emotions with people who have a weak sense of self and poor boundaries, the arts can provide the containing structure.

In more traditional forms of psychotherapy, it is the therapist who performs as the container of feelings. Indeed, transference and its successful resolution depends on this. In contrast, the expressive therapist is often active himself and the art performs as the projection for feelings.The therapist will participate in drawing, in dance and/or simultaneously take the director's role, but he performs also as a guide, going in and out of the action, thus helping the clients to master whatever they are doing. In expressive therapy we focus very much on story telling, and when the individual tells a story about his life, the participants become the listeners to each others' stories. This may be an asset when one is working with a cross-cultural population where psychotherapy is often an unfamiliar tradition. People who are illiterate, coming from the mountains of Kurdistan or other war-ridden areas, have no idea what is implied in 'going to a therapist'. But I have found that most people understand the meaning of telling their stories and the importance of having listeners and witnesses. The group can function as a container for the individual's feelings, so that the members feel held, maybe by people who, for the first time in their adult life, have been able to trust. Having witnesses to one's story can often take the 'bad energy' out of it, so that it no longer functions as an enemy in one's life. Perhaps it can even be transformed into an asset, by focusing on the knowledge of the story's importance, rather than on the damage the story has done in itself. By stimulating the creative ability in each individual, we are giving that person the tool to recreate his own life.

Intermodal Transfer

Expressive therapy does not focus on one modality, it encompasses all the senses of the human being. With the help of the creative process, we are able to stimulate visual, auditory, kinaesthetic, smell, and taste modalities. We can start with a dance, expressing what the individual in the group feels. From the dance, rhythm and music emerge, and from the music we can proceed to draw a picture of the dance, and finally gestalt the picture and move into sociodrama or psychodrama. Each modality has the capability of helping both individual and social life. This is what expressive therapists call intermodal transfer. Table 1 demonstrates this.

Table 1

Commun-ication Modality	Lends itself favourably to	can be 'stretched'		What 'Stretch may make conscious'
		to:	by eg:	
Painting Drawing Poetry/ Prose	Individual-ization	Social-ization	Collective painting etc...	'Find my space in the group'
Music	Social-ization	Individ-ualization	Solo structures etc...	'How can we relate as a group?'
Dance Theatre	Coalition Group inter-action {	Individ-ualization	Centering in mime.. etc...	'Who am I in the a group?'
		Social-ization	Structured with rhythm sound lang-uage etc...	'Who are we as a group?'

(Source: Knill, 1978, 33)

Expressive Therapy in Practice

I will now describe two cases which exemplify these issues. One is from a locked facility with juvenile delinquent boys, the other from my present work at the University of Oslo.

First, the case of the juvenile delinquents. The group consisted of eight patients, aged 16 to 21, and was mandatory. They would meet once a week for two hours. The group members had all committed serious crimes. They carried the diagnoses of schizophrenia or extremely primitive borderline disorders. One or two milieu-therapists would always be present, in addition to a co-therapist and myself. The former always knew what had taken place in the group, so that they could follow up the participants in the milieu after the group.

The patients understood that many of the therapists were suspicious of this kind of therapy, and if the group should result in anything near acting-out behaviour, that would mean the end of the group. Even though the group was mandatory, the participants quickly became appreciative of the group and did not want to lose it. During the one and a half years I ran the group, there was no acting out behaviour, either during or immediately after which could be directly related to the group session. It took about six months to weave the group together and to familiarize it with the different expressive modalities. They all learned how to use the video camera. The group was ego supportive – working on drawing out positive qualities in each member, who created a character that he would wish to become when he left the institution. One wanted to become a restaurant owner; he started drawing the character, discussed the responsibilities with the group, what kind of restaurant it would be and how the owner would behave. Then he 'became' the restaurant owner; the restaurant was created and, as the owner, he moved and interacted with others. The whole process was videoed, which added tremendously to the power of the psychodrama process; he was able to 'play back' the role-playing, look at it objectively, and criticize it. He was able to be his own guide, and at the same time receive comments from the other group members.

We worked with each character in this way. Psychodrama techniques were applied when there were group conflicts. In such cases, they could reverse roles, learning something about the projections they invested in each other. When issues arose such as: 'I will never manage, I'm not good enough and will never be, I'm bad and everything I make is bad', the mirroring technique was helpful. They could reverse roles with one another in the group. They could thus 'talk to themselves' about the negative 'voices' and through insight learn how to cope. The group wrote a group story which included all the characters. The story was played and videotaped. The process of creating something together was, in itself, therapeutic. They had to co-operate, delay gratification, and commit themselves. But it was also important for the group to work towards a product; the videotape, representing something to show – literally – for all the energy they had invested in themselves and in each other. Without this 'evidence', no-one would have believed us if we had told the rest of the staff what we had done.

The group ended by producing a videotaped drama which was viewed at the annual academic reception at the end of the inmates' school year. As a result of this production, an expressive therapy position was established in the institution.

The second example comes from the Psychosocial Center, based on my work with a group of eight refugees in an outpatient setting in which all the participants are voluntary. The group consists of four women and four men. Their countries of origin are Kurdistan (Iraq), Eritrea, Chile, Argentina, Turkey, Vietnam, and Kossovo (Yugoslavia). All the participants suffer from post-traumatic stress disorders; lack of concentration, agitation, insomnia, low self-esteem, memory deficit and lack of trust in other human beings.

My co-therapist is a psychiatrist who has specialized in body-oriented psychotherapy and had advanced training in expressive therapy.

During the first six weeks we focused on working on identity through the arts. Here I will describe sessions seven and eight. We endeavoured to change the focus from 'Who am I in the group?' to 'Who are we as a group?' The structure we used was drawing a group picture on one large piece of paper. The theme was *trust*. Instead of drawing a group picture, all had started by drawing their own individual picture. After some time my co-therapist began to draw on everybody's picture by expanding his own. A woman in the group at first got very angry, but she had difficulty expressing the anger. Afterwards she began to excuse herself. She curled up and looked as if she was expecting some sort of punishment. The group and the leaders supported her in having the right to establish boundaries, and for the first time she realised how she was taking responsibility for other peoples' feelings and interpreting her own as bad. Other members of the group were able to share that they had the same experience. The next session we looked at the picture again, with the participation of those who had been present in the previous session.

The group agreed to make a new picture with the same theme. After everyone had finished drawing, the group created a story about the picture:

> Once upon a time there was a princess who was exploring the different worlds that existed, and was trying to decide which one she wanted to be in. But it was a very difficult decision. One world was very light and full of positiveness, laughter and peace. Another was very dark. It was so dark that she could not see the different elements this world could offer. As she kept on searching, she came to a world of nature, full of trees, lakes and mountains. But she could see no human beings. The next world she discovered was a world full of bushes and colours; her eyes fell upon two big eyes which were staring at her in fear. She found a tree with one big apple left on it and wanted to pick the apple and offer it to the staring eyes. The tree was relieved that someone picked the last apple, so that it could continue to grow. The princess decided that she had to live in all the worlds, but she had one concern: how was she going to prevent the dark world taking over and covering all the worlds?

The group spent a long time trying to find a resolution, and everyone was given the opportunity to use the paints again. The dark world was changed into a placenta, and the bridge into an umbilical cord linked to the light world, which in turn was transformed into a womb with a foetus inside. And the princess became pregnant.

The group as a whole liked this picture. The group ended up talking about fairy tales in their land of origin. The Kurd shared with us that he did not tell his children fairy tales. Now, the only concern of his was the war in Kurdistan. This led the discussion to the importance of giving the next generation a history, and not only the darkness that exists today.

The effect of these methods with refugees is currently a subject of research, and it is hoped that the findings will be published when completed.

Summary

The expressive therapies can function as a container for feelings, which would otherwise be too frightening to express. The different modalities of expressive therapies can represent the third object, through which the client and the therapist can work. The third object is the receiver of both the therapist's and the clients' projections. Because of the rage which 'children of war' often carry inside them, the therapist has to be very aware of the negative projections which he temporarily needs to contain. The arts can serve as the recipient of projections, and allow the therapist greater freedom to help the client understand what is happening within and around him.

Adults, who have never had the opportunity of being a child, have the chance to re-live unlived childhood experience, such as drawing, drama and dance, paradoxical though it sounds. Thus enhancing their creativity and spontaneity, and so giving hope that each individual may become able to take part in creating 'a new life' for himself.

Geese Theatre Company

Saul Hewish

Geese Theatre Company of Great Britain is the country's only full-time professional theatre company working exclusively within the prison and probation services. Set up in 1987, the Company is a franchise of the highly regarded Geese Theatre Company US, founded by British-born theatre director, John Bergman in 1980. Since beginning work in this country Geese have worked in over one hundred prisons and young offender institutions in the United Kingdom and Ireland, as well as working extensively for over 25 probation services. Now recognised by many as leaders in the use of theatre as a rehabilitative tool with offenders, the company is increasingly called upon to share its skills with staff working within the criminal justice system.

One of the company's principle aims is crime prevention. In practice this means working with identified offenders to promote responsible living and prevent recidivism. Geese Company, where possible, work together with other disciplines to provide the most effective help possible for those in prison. It is not possible to force people to change, but it is vital that support and treatment is available to those individuals who do wish to stop returning to prison time and time again. Geese Company try to offer a range of activities. These vary from stimulating thought about change to providing drama techniques to help bring about that change.

The work of the company falls roughly into five areas: performance, workshop, residency, long-term programmes and staff-training. Presently, the company has a number of productions in its repertoire. Two of these performances are audience interactive, structured improvisations using half-mask that examine issues of coping with release from an institution (*Lifting The Weight*) and the maintenance of family relationships whilst in prison (*Plague Game*). They are designed to allow the audience to examine new strategies and find new solutions to old problems.

Are You Positive? is a HIV and AIDS information play designed specially for offenders, and *The Violent Illusion* is a trilogy currently in development. *The Violent Illusion*, once completed, will be offered as a three or four day residential package designed to be used with small audiences of violent and/or sexually abusive offenders who are engaged in a treatment programme of some description. The trilogy focuses on family interaction and, put very simply, Part One is 'The Problem', Part Two 'Potential Solutions' and Part Three 'The Test'.

The different areas of Geese's work are designed to complement each other. Performances are followed by workshops where issues are examined using role play and other drama techniques. During a residency the company will work with a group of inmates over three or five days to produce a group devised performance concentrating on a specific issue. Whilst this work is of great value to inmates and staff alike, it is often difficult, due to a lack of time, resources and follow-up to do anything other than begin the process of thought about change.

Geese Theatre Company's theoretical line is to use theatre as a dynamic means of stimulating change within the individual; to challenge offenders to examine their own behaviour and to act out new approaches to change. This approach can be fully implemented in longer-term programme work, which represents the most exciting development for the company.

It has long been acknowledged, by criminal psychologists and other criminal justice professionals, that many offenders in prison and on probation have destructive patterns of behaviour which have common characteristics. This can be manifested by offenders in a number of ways; deficiencies in problem-solving skills; a disregard of pro-social moral values; a lack of tolerance of constraints, (for example family, work, authority); a manipulation of others and a tendency to see him or herself as a victim of society who is treated unjustly when things go wrong. Thus a very specific therapeutic approach is required if these anti-social personality traits are to be overcome.

> Changes are not brought about by insight, but by a painstaking re-education of the offender in such concepts as trust and interdependence. In correction therapy for offenders insight follows challenge and re-education. (Yochelson & Samenow 1976)

Theatre and drama can provide an invaluable tool to the criminal justice professional in helping to confront offending behaviour in an easily understood and experiential manner. It has the ability to make both easily accessible and deeply resonant pictures out of often difficult emotional and intellectual information and constructs, and can often provide the vital key to opening up channels of communication that may otherwise remain closed. Theatre works on both an affective and cognitive level, and can help provide an overview of an offender's thoughts and feelings. From dramatic portrayal of past experiences to improvisations based on plans for the future an offender has the opportunity to 'rehearse for life'. Throughout this process an individual will become more self aware, identify common problems and test out alternative solutions.

Geese Theatre Company's long term programmes use a combination of cognitive-behavioural and drama-based techniques. The programmes are currently being used in the Probation Service as direct alternatives to custody. Throughout a programme a company member will train staff and work with offenders. It uses theatre to: challenge anti-social beliefs and attitudes; discover regular patterns of thought, feeling and behaviour; promote self awareness and the concept of self-change; and test the ability of individuals to practice cognitive intervention and solve problems in a more pro-social manner. Programmes have been adapted to be used as part of wider treatment programmes for both violent and sex-offenders.

To date the company have developed the bulk of their programmes in a probation setting. However, it is hoped that recent Home Office initiatives to introduce treatment programmes for serious sex offenders in prison will open the door to much further work in custodial settings. The major advantage of this over probation-based programmes will be the space and resources for much longer, more intensive treatment.

Theatre in all forms, be it a one hour performance or as the foundation for a pre-release course, has an extremely important role to play in custodial settings. Theatre's great strength is that it can be used as an accessible and immediate tool in any setting to examine new approaches to old problems. Paul Heritage, lecturer in drama at Manchester University, is currently researching and writing a book about Geese Theatre Company. The book will provide an in-depth examination of the Company's work and explore some of the practical issues involved in the use of drama in prison.

Following Hamlet Day, a staff study day was organized at Broadmoor on 16 September 1991, to explore the opportunity and need for creative arts' therapies. Geese ran a workshop and aroused considerable interest. They will soon (27 February 1992) be working with Broadmoor patients. The wheels are turning. M.C.

Awakening the Voice Inside
Dramatherapy and Theatre Initiatives in Prison

Jessica Saunders

I am a dramatherapist working at HM Prison Holloway, England's largest prison for women. My work here involves facilitating open drama and movement sessions for women on the hospital wing in the prison's day centre, running a closed dramatherapy group for women on a new drug rehabilitation unit opening in January 1992, and running courses using drama and movement with a closed membership entitled 'Drama and Ourselves'. This recently devised course is shortly to begin and I will refer to it later in this chapter.

The Interface Between Theatre and Therapy

My other role is that of performer and a year ago I set up a theatre company with a colleague, Jay Vaughan, called 'The Theatre of Reflection'. Drawing on our extensive experience within the theatre, and our clinical practice as dramatherapists, our aim was to utilise our diverse skills to create powerful pieces of theatre and through this to explore the interface between theatre and therapy. The culmination of this year was the company's first production *The Tragedy of Ophelia*. This explored the events of Shakespeare's *Hamlet* as seen and experienced through Ophelia's eyes. It had been my intention after the production had ended to write up my experience of playing Ophelia, exploring the notion of role taking and playing, within the rehearsal and performance process, as a research piece into the relationship between theatre and dramatherapy. A few nights ago I received a telephone call from Murray Cox asking me whether I would write a piece for this book about playing Ophelia and the links between this experience and my work at Holloway Prison. Time was short. It seems important for the reader to know that, had I not had such constraints placed upon me, I might have taken some time in coming to this point of writing, as the play had only ended recently. Since that time, my mind has wandered back to what proved to be an extremely intense experience both personally and as a performer. Only to find that the moment I begin to ponder on it, I hurriedly move away from it again. It is as if the memory of it holds such potency that I find it hard to focus on it, my reflective capacity as audience to stand back and witness my performance as Ophelia is still in the very early stages of development – it is a slow separation process.

This is also a process I have observed in the women at Holloway, particularly those who have committed serious crimes. They often have difficulty in focusing on the reasons for their imprisonment, the returning to the event and thereby the re-living of that experience. The reasons for which they are within the confines of prison walls hover suspended in time, like a powerful dream feeling both real and yet unreal. They need to be translated, to be given a language; the crimes themselves are symptoms of a greater malaise. So, too, with my experience of playing Ophelia. The final product was a culmination of many different processes and levels of investment.

I feel the need to explore what propelled me into taking on this role and what the play meant to me on a personal level, and to find a voice for this process. One vehicle for this is through the written word. This piece is only the very beginning of that unravelling and exploration, coming as it does in the wake of the play. This will necessarily be a condensed account of what I hope to explore in greater depth and to publish at a later date.

Why Ophelia?

I had always been fascinated by the character of Ophelia and this was brought to the fore at the International Dramatherapy and Shakespeare Symposium, May 1989, when one of the core texts and RSC productions we focused on was *Hamlet*. I found myself gripped by Ophelia's story and the apparently sudden onset of her madness. Why, I asked myself, does this happen to her? What are the events of her life that cause this to happen and what is she trying to communicate to those around her through her madness? Madness, acts of violence to self and others, drug and alcohol abuse (frequently partners with crime), are destructive manifestations of voices crying out to be heard through the chaos. Playing Ophelia caused me to listen to that voice and to look at labels and their meanings – what do we mean by 'madness', what is mad and in whose terms are people mad? With Ophelia, I began to feel and experience her as most real, most sane as the madness came to the fore. Her true self and her voice seemed to emerge during this process. But she had no form of containment for it, no external witness in the form of a positive parental figure, or internalised witness, to hold her as she let go of her false self; the role into which she had been cast within the court that becomes her prison. This act, this sense of unveiling, peeling away the mask and releasing the voice within, because there is no sense of holding, ultimately and tragically, leads to her own destruction.

It is impossible within this limited space to work systematically through our production and my process; yet ultimately it needs to be done, both dramatically and personally. There are, however, two particular themes from the piece that are evoking a response from me now: that of reflections and boundaries.

I spoke of the court in which Ophelia lives as her prison. The set for our production was very simple. The stage was raised with a pillar standing on each corner and the audience placed on three sides. The dolls, suspended from the rafters representing the significant characters in Ophelia's life, became representational to me as a performer of the part-selves that she has split off and projected onto her play objects. Towards the back of the stage hung a black gauze from the ceiling to the floor and the area behind this was Ophelia's closet, her private world, also symbolising her internal world. As the play progresses, we see that her inner chaos cannot be contained within this physical and psychic space and it begins to spill over into the courtly world and the main thrust of the stage. The boundaries of her world, the pillars and the gauze, i.e. the court, and the objects that have journeyed with her as friends, the dolls, no longer offer her containment and companionship. They become restrictive and repressive forces upon her and objects of her anger, hatred, suspicion and fear. The boundaries and objects have become so imbued with meaning that Ophelia experiences a shift in the control. The dolls, once playthings, begin to control her; the boundaries, once stone pillars and the walls of the court, have taken on characters from her own drama and she starts to experience them as invasive and oppressive.

What of my process through this? Once behind the gauze which also framed the sides and back of the stage, creating the effect of a box, I could no longer see out. It was a very strange experience, I knew that the members of the audience were out there and that they could see me through the gauze, but I could not see them. They seemed beyond the boundary of my existence. It was a most lonely place, holding echoes of a prison cell in its isolation and it seemed also to reflect Ophelia's isolation and loneliness within the world she inhabited, increasing her sense of being watched and observed. The set and objects began through the performance to take on such intensity and meaning for me as a performer during the two week run, that there were moments when I felt as if I were in a different reality from that of the audience. The drama was a living, breathing and experienced event. But once it had ended each night, and particularly so after the last night, I frequently found myself questioning my sense of reality – coming out of the performance was like waking up after a dream. I knew I had been on a journey into what felt like another time and place. And, try as I might to de-role from this process as a performer, I was aware that some part of me was still in the drama, whilst also experiencing the memory of it as strangely distant, beyond my reach. I couldn't touch it, but it had touched on something in me very personal and deep. It seems as if I had cut off from the feeling and over-distanced myself from the lived experience of playing Ophelia because of its potency, thereby making the memory of it difficult to focus on, to grasp hold of, as I described above. The boundaries placed upon me in writing this have afforded me the opportunity to begin re-tracing my steps. And the boundaries of the performance I now begin to see gave access, not only to Ophelia's voice within Shakespeare's *Hamlet*, but also to a voice inside myself.

This is the paradox of becoming an other; by taking on a role it can enable the true self of the performer to emerge, the reflection of the self in the role calling forth the voice within.

There is a particular moment from the play that highlights this aspect for me. At the end of the Nunnery scene in *Hamlet*, we see Ophelia questioning what has happened to Hamlet's mind and lamenting her own plight. In our production this took place behind the gauze and so for me as performer it had an added intensity. On the first line of the speech:

'O, what a noble mind is here o'erthrown!'

(*Hamlet* III.1.152)

in role as Ophelia I am looking at my own reflection in a hand mirror – the mirrored image reflects back to her what she is saying about Hamlet. She ends the speech by saying,

'O woe is me
T'have seen what I have seen, see what I see.'

(*Hamlet* III.1.162)

As she utters the words, so again she looks at the mirror and sees herself. Confined within the gauze space I, as performer, knew that I also saw myself and that it was a moment both deeply personal and private. Yet it was shared with an audience who witnessed it in the public arena of the theatre space. Ophelia's words had enabled me to find a voice for feeling and experiences within myself.

The culmination of this seemed to come at the end of the play when we moved into what Jay and I called the reflection process. This is a process in which Ophelia moves from her death behind the gauze out onto the main stage to survey the arena of her life, to reflect on her journey and the choice she has made through her death. This reflection process was a way of acknowledging that this was Ophelia's story, her tragedy. But also to look at it on a larger scale, to bring it right into the here and now, linking into our clinical work as dramatherapists. Her life can be seen as a reflection of the lives of many women I have worked with, who are in-patients and imprisoned, searching for a voice, whose language has become manifest through mental illness and criminal acts. In this closing sequence Ophelia speaks the first ten lines of Hamlet's speech:

'To be, or not to be, that is the question'

(*Hamlet* III. 1.56)

In this speech as Ophelia I focused on her conflict between Life and Death. On a personal level it spoke to me not only of this, but also about the choice of whether 'to be' in a creative and full way part of this life, or whether to be but a walking shadow of myself. Yes, the play was and is both a private and public experience, a drama that has the potential to be used for growth and learning for those involved in its birth and for those who witnessed its life.

Taking Drama Inside

What of this experience do I take into Holloway? The parallels that I could make between the structure of our play with its pillars as boundaries encapsulating Ophelia's spirit, and that of a prison and the encapsulation of women's spirit, are many; but cannot be explored here. However, one point I will share that has emerged for me during this experience of playing Ophelia and my work at Holloway. The boundaries of the theatre and the prison can create the possibility of venturing into unknown ways of being. That which sets limits can also create a sense of freedom, freedom to find one's self through a role. There are women for whom prison, with all its restrictions, affords an opportunity to stop and look at the patterns in their lives. Women talk to me about the experience of being in prison and how it strips them of their false selves and enables them to be 'real'. Like Ophelia and her mirrored image, they can see themselves reflected in the women around them, there can be no pretence. Some women actively seek the confines of the prison as a container for their chaotic and destructive impulses and acts, a place of safety away from the danger of the worlds they inhabit. The play, because of the personal resonances it held for me as a performer, felt like a dangerous place to be at times – 'it must be contained' I heard myself saying to Jay. Perhaps that is what Ophelia was screaming out through her madness, 'someone take note of this chaos, fear and hurt and contain it'. Alas for Ophelia, it fell on deaf ears, as it does with many of the women at Holloway. However, there are some who, despite this, wish to survey the arenas of *their* lives, who want to challenge the boundaries of the prison walls that they have sought refuge in and the meaning this holds for them. It seems that drama with its reflective capacity and its boundaries offering containment, might also offer the possibility for these women, some of whom are so entrenched in their roles as prisoners, captives, to explore other ways of being. And, through this, to touch a part of themselves, a truth, a new and different reality, the voice inside called forth to claim its rightful place upon the stage, both in the dramatherapy group and in life. It demands to be heard. Let us as audience open our ears to what it has to tell us. All should be entitled to tell their story.

The course I devised for Holloway 'Drama and Ourselves' has several aims. One is to give the women an opportunity of being in a closed group and to experience building relationships in a safe environment. It is also hoped that through this, with the aid of written journals and the use of video, both used as monitoring and reflecting processes, the members will be able to observe the development of both the group and themselves within it. They will then create their own piece of theatre, drawing on their personal lives and using this life experience creatively through the drama.

Reflection

As Ophelia, when I turned from the graveside of my father, where I had laid out my dolls towards the end of the play, I saw my own shadow reflected on the gauze in front of me. Huge, dark and awesome it stood challenging me. I moved towards it and as Ophelia I put it behind me, turning from it into the arms of death. As the performer I know that playing Ophelia has caused me, and continues to cause me, to look my own shadow right in they eye. We humans have a choice it seems. We can get to know the shadow or we can attempt to run away from it, in the hope that it won't swallow us up. Drama causes us to look at our own shadows reflected in the roles we embody and those around us. At drama school I remember being told that no matter how much I might despise a character I was playing, I had to learn to love it – so too with the shadow self. This I have learnt in playing Ophelia and that the process of role playing in drama can be a very creative act. This I take with me into Holloway, I ask the women to bring themselves and I hope that together, through the drama, we can learn and grow and find a language for the feeling and a voice for the heart.

Drama offers the possibility of nurturing the witness within, of awakening the voice inside.

These views are personal and do not necessarily reflect those of the Home Office and the Prison Department.

Further Reflections

By way of closure to this section, we need to be reminded that the whole *corpus* was carried along in the wake of the enthusiasm which followed *Hamlet*. Previously, it could be said that there was an attitude of scepticism to what dramatherapy, and allied arts initiatives might be able to offer the forensic patient in Broadmoor Hospital. The various days when Shakespeare came to Broadmoor changed this. They set in motion a series of workshops and led to a special study day on 16 September 1991, when the place of the creative arts therapies in special hospitals was the key theme. Once again, there was a general feeling that the time had come. There also seems to be a healthy awareness that all such therapeutic initiatives need to be integrated at every level with established clinical expertise. In a setting such as Broadmoor, no therapeutic enterprise can go it alone. But there is a climate of cautious welcome to the possibility of seriously considering what creative arts therapies can provide. This is, in part, because of the manifest caution of the creative arts advanced party who show no signs of over-playing their hands. They are keen to learn from established long-term therapeutic experience at Broadmoor of the risks and opportunities that the creative arts initiatives bring with them.

It is in this light that it is not unreasonable to express therapeutic optimism and encouragement, as there is definite evidence of the therapeutic potential of drama in custodial settings.

M.C.

IV.3

The Nature and Scope
of Dramatherapy
Theatre of Healing

Sue Jennings

'What's Hecuba to him, or he to her,
That he should weep for her?'

(*Hamlet* II.2.553)

Dramatherapy is the specific application of theatre structures and drama processes with a declared intention that it is therapy.[1]

Introduction

The two words, 'drama' and 'therapy', were first put together by Slade (1954), and from that time there has been a slow development in the theory, practice and application and the training and recognition of practitioners. Dramatherapy is considered to be one of the arts therapies[2] which are now practised in the UK, USA and some parts of the Continent. Recently there have been several moves to formalize dramatherapy and set up state registration (about which I shall comment later in this chapter); these contemporary developments can obscure the fact that what we now call dramatherapy has a very ancient history. Although it may be viewed as new in a society that emphasizes science and technology rather than artistry, in fact we are re-discovering ancient truths in the power of the drama that have been eclipsed during recent history.

However, before defining the aims of this chapter, it must be stated that both the chapter and its author work within certain constraints. First, there is some anomaly that a chapter on dramatherapy should be included in a book about Shakespeare at Broadmoor, when neither dramatherapy (nor any other arts therapy) is practised there. Nevertheless, there is a certain paradox in the fact that dramatherapy was the catalyst which led to the Shakespeare and Broadmoor initiative through the first International Dramatherapy and Shakespeare Symposium.[3] Second, I can write only as someone with a lifetime's experience of Shakespeare and dramatherapy, and not as someone with extensive forensic expertise. These limitations dictate the aims of this chapter, which will endeavour to:

1. Discuss the roots of dramatherapy and its contemporary practice, including both technique and theory.

2. Describe the central rôle that Shakespeare's plays have in dramatherapy practice.

3. Reflect on the dramatherapeutic potential that could be realized in a forensic setting.

There is the playhouse now, there must you sit.

(*Henry V* II.Chorus.36)

Drama, ritual, theatre, performance, seance, ceremonial, enactment, rôle-play – whichever word we are to use – have all been part of ancient healing practice, dating back into our history and pre-history. There is even evidence from the ancient cave paintings (for example, Drury 1989) of dramatic rituals being performed in masks. However, it does not therefore follow that there is an evolutionary unbroken line of development from the mists of time until the present day. All we can say with some degree of certainty is that healing theatre has always existed in some form or other.

Dramatic rituals are about consciousness-raising – about empowerment. People need empowerment against the wrath of the gods, or to alleviate the dangerous malady (which may have been caused by the wrath of the gods), or to procreate or to be a successful cultivator or business person. People are also empowered into appropriate social, domestic and political rôles and relationships. We could say that, through acting, people are empowered to act.

Dramatic rituals also touch and set in motion deep internal processes in individuals and groups. Altered states of consciousness and degrees of unconsciousness, such as trance states, allow people into the nebulous area that is not under individual ego control. It is formless and undifferentiated and is in the realm of the creative process, rather like a journey underground. We could say that, through participating in external dramas we are able to be in touch with our internal dramas.

Some Vignettes

'I am sitting in a tiny chapel in a suburb of Rio de Janeiro; it is packed for a Makumba ritual. The black servant of the Spanish doctor who brought me here tells me that it is a very powerful seance. The woman priestess has special powers, especially for women patients. After the drumming, the dancing and the trancing, the priestess asks all patients to come forward for healing and she gives us home-rolled cigarettes. We are instructed to smoke half the cigarette and place the other half in our bras.'

'I am standing on the catwalk of The Round House Theatre, to watch The Red Buddha Theatre with Stomu Yamashta. His musicians create several atmospheres. We are transported to the devastation after Hiroshima. There is a bleak mountain where an old lady is left to be taken by the death spirits; then we see a chain gang of prisoners being beaten by towering, hooded guards. A prisoner escapes and hides in the audience. The guards search roughly for the fugitive with powerful beam torches, and the audience protect the prisoner.'

'I am sitting in a bamboo hut with thirty other Temiar men, women and children. There are ritual decorations hanging from the roof and ritual objects – cigarettes and leaf fans – lying next to the dampened-down fire. The native healer or shaman dances slowly round his patient – a young boy who has complained of sharp stomach pains. He makes loud sucking noises through his clenched fist on the boy's stomach and shows the audience an angry looking thorn.'

'I am "in character" as a villager attending Ophelia's funeral in the Hamlet workshop run by Ron Daniels and Mark Rylance at Broadmoor. When Hamlet speaks to the actor playing Laertes at the graveside, a patient steps forward in character as a second Laertes[4] and says to Hamlet, "I really am very sorry, Hamlet, very sorry", and he accompanies Hamlet and Horatio from the scene, having been asked to keep an eye on Hamlet.'

'I am sitting out of the glaring sun near a whitewashed school in the Galilee. Children are just coming out with their multi-coloured bags and packs. One young girl says to those around her, "Let's play at schools – I am going to be the teacher." Her friends comply and set up a classroom. The girl playing the teacher says she is going to teach her class English and asks for my help with some words; however her performance of a teacher both gave her status with her peers but also "re-worked" the experiences of the school day.'

These examples are brief vignettes from my experience of healing or therapeutic theatre, or where a theatre structure has had an impact on me as observer-participant/active-part-participant/or active-full-participant. In all these examples there is a designated space-set-apart, within which there is a transition from everyday reality into dramatic or theatrical reality. Dramatic distance has been established from everyday experience which enables a move from the actual to the symbolic, from the concrete to the metaphoric. It is because we can move from everyday reality into dramatic or theatrical reality that transformation of our experience becomes possible. Whether it is the experience of an individual or of a group,[5] or both, there is transformation within the fictive drama.

'Stay illusion'

(*Hamlet* I.1.130)

> Our ability to recognize illusion depends upon the extent to which we accept some method of apprehending it. Such a statement sounds self-evident, yet what is called for is basically paradoxical: the accept-ance of what empirically is not. This is the skill of make-believe; in science it is the very nature of hypothesizing. Pretending, whether it be something about ourselves or about the outside world, is basic to our apprehension of change. (Napier 1986,3)

The human capacity not only to accept but also to create what is not actually there through fictive drama, lies at the very core of our under-standing of dramatherapy. It is the most fundamental principle of the efficacy of dramatherapy, whether it is being applied in a preventative or a curative context.

> Thus, the recognition of illusion is the single pre-requisite for under-standing something that seems self-contradictory – in other words, for recognizing paradox – and the recognition of change is possible only with this understanding: that something may appear to be something else. (ibid)

Rather than viewing drama as less than relevant because 'it is only acting' or 'it is only playing' or 'it is not real', we can begin to see how relevant it is *because* it is acting, playing and unreal. Let us now see how this underpins dramatherapy theory.

Towards a Theoretical Model

We may well look back upon the twentieth century as the age of psycho-analysis. Certainly in relation to art and, in this writing, specifically drama and theatre, psychoanalysis has been a dominant influence in explaining and interpreting not only dramatic rituals, plays and characters but also the social groups or individual actors who portray them.[6] Non-techno-logical societies and actors alike are considered regressive or narcissistic or exhibitionist, certainly immature and childlike. In some psychoanalytic writing (Bettelheim 1955, for example), there is an equation between children and non-technological peoples, who are thought to be simple, less developed, less 'civilized' and therefore less moral/ethical than their western counterparts (and how often does society see actors in these terms!). Alternatively we may project a kind of idealized image into a non-western society or indeed into actors, who somehow represent a longing for a seemingly more natural, more real mode of existence.

Typical in this context is the romanticization of the Senoi Temiar of Malaysia about whom there is extensive literature which describes them as a 'dream people' (for an excellent critique, see Domhoff 1985) who hold family dream clinics during or after breakfast. Despite ethnographic reports[7] which can find no evidence of these dream clinics, the myth is still perpetuated, particularly in the USA amongst psychotherapists and growth movements. Somehow a fiction has been created that continues to be believed (rather than a fiction which we know to be a fiction). This fiction has something of a double paradox: the dream, for the most part, is our own personal internalized drama, played out on our own stage (all dreams have dramatic form). On waking, we know the dream isn't 'real', although, like drama, it is about real issues; it is our own personal fiction, an internal theatre that all of us experience. However, another fiction is created about the personal fictions of a tribal people, which makes them into an ideal people, capturing an innocence that western civilization longs for. Western civilization demonstrates its own innocence by continuing to believe its own fiction, rather than knowing it is fiction.

Similarly, we collude with the media to create fictive personae for actors, and are able to project onto actors – both on the stage and in the street – a rarefied existence that we both envy and reject. The subject of society's perception of the actor is developed more fully below.

Thus non-western societies – especially their belief-systems and rituals – as well as actors and members of the theatrical professions serve as useful projective phenomena for our hopes and fantasies. There is nothing wrong with this in itself, except when it gets in the way of our understanding of healing ritual and theatre art.

Dramatherapists, like theatre and drama theorists, struggle to understand the processes of theatre art. Although there are dramatherapists who make use of a group analytic model of dramatherapy, as well as the use of enactment within conventional psychotherapy, this is not, as I have discussed elsewhere (see Jennings 1987), dramatherapy in its own right (or rite?). Mitchell also supports this idea when he says that there is too much emphasis in dramatherapy theory and practice on established schools of psychotherapy and that 'drama' has been the appendage (Mitchell 1992).

> Dramatherapists need to remind themselves constantly that they are first and foremost creative artists within the theatre and drama art forms which includes actor, director, scenic designer and writer, and

that the art form is a constant renewal of creativity for the therapist as well as the client. (Jennings 1990)

I believe it is an important task for dramatherapists to identify a conceptual system that employs the inherent healing factors of theatre or drama as the *primary* therapeutic process in dramatherapy. (Mitchell 1992)

Although other models for dramatherapy have been applied with care, e.g. psychoanalysis (Irwin 1985), development (Johnson 1982), Jungian archetypal psychology and object relations (Parker-Lewis 1989), they are, in fact, derivative and tangential to the primary source of the field, that of drama. (Landy 1991)

I am in agreement with Landy and Mitchell in differentiating psychotherapeutic processes that are facilitated by drama or that are explained through psychological theory and dramatherapeutic process. I would emphasize what Landy calls 'the primary source' (op cit) which I (Jennings 1990) and Mitchell describe as the *primary process* of dramatherapy found in theatre art (though it must be noted that Landy refers only to the drama, whereas, from my view, it must include theatre as well).[8]

Mitchell has developed the *para-theatre model* of dramatherapy, which he describes as forming an artistic inquiry towards health and towards spiritual values, rather than primarily focusing on a client's psychopathological or negative behaviour. Influenced by the work of Grotowski, Brook, and the late Ryszard Cieslak, para-theatre aims to develop the primary dramatic processes inherent in human beings, and Mitchell sees it as ultimately allowing clients to devise their own healing rituals:

The group begins to explore varying activities that they suggest which, through the *doing*, will bring answers to their needs, or reveal the next stage in their work – a re-defined proposal. I have found three general categories into which the activities proposed appear to fall. These are: i. shared physical challenge, including tactile and sensory improvisation or games; ii. propositions that generate information about one another at a cognitive verbal level, where life stories and personal difficulties are shared, or through varying forms of creative media, factual information is pooled; iii. the sharing of emotional issues; disclosures concerning the reason they are in the group, leading to a proposition which will act as a rite of passage, thereby re-shaping the affective material and integrating it in a new and constructive way. (Mitchell op cit)

By contrast, Landy's model is based on *rôle theory*, and emphasizes the learning or re-learning of rôles, rôle expansion and rôle repertoire (see also Grainger 1990). Landy says:

> It seems to me that the concept of rôle opens up a conceptual framework that is essential in explaining why and how drama therapists work. In understanding the rôle concept and the rôle method, drama therapists might then have a clear sense of purpose and meaning in a relatively new field that has yet to fully discover its uniquely dramatic roots. (ibid)

However, although Landy reiterates that the concept of rôle is primarily a dramatic one, rôle is usually perceived as being the prerogative of clinical and social psychologists. rôle is associated with behaviour and the rôles we play in everyday life, rather than deriving from the rôles we play on the theatrical stage. As one psychologist said to me very recently, 'What on earth has rôle play to do with drama?'

For Landy, the dramatic paradox lies in the possibility of being both in rôle and out of rôle at the same time, of being in two realities simultaneously of the 'me and not me'. He suggests that this is the essence of Hamlet's dilemma, 'to be or not to be'. While I would totally endorse Landy's belief in a theatre art basis for dramatherapy, and his initial work on a taxonomy of rôles is impressive, it is not sufficient to embrace all the possibilities inherent in a theatre of healing. However, as one major theoretical stance that should be available to and understood by all dramatherapists, it is a breakthrough in current thinking.

By contrast to these para-theatre and rôle approaches to dramatherapy, I want to describe the *shamanic theory* of dramatherapy which complements the other models. The traditional shaman occurs in many cultures as a native healer and is usually distinguished for his or her use of trance in healing seances. In the trance there is usually a change of rôle either for shaman and/or patient and there is *symbolic* enactment of the malady and its roots. There is an altered state of consciousness that takes place in the dramatic seance:

> Shamanism is a visionary tradition, an ancient practice of utilizing altered states of consciousness to contact the gods and spirits of the natural world. (Drury op cit)

Just as academic opinion has been divided about art and artists, there has long been divided opinion, at times very hostile, between clinicians and anthropologists. One major focus of this divided thought is in the writings about shamanism. It is suggested that shaman are neurotic, psychotic, exhibit schizophrenic symptoms, and even that their malaise reflects the malaise of their culture (Devereaux 1956). An equally impressive body of work disputes the 'madness' of shaman and the assumptions about their psychological pathology. Levi Strauss (1968) suggests there is a complementarity between psychoanalysts and shaman in relation to the defined healing rôle they have in societies.

It is not within the scope of this chapter to explore further the 'shamanic' debate concerning normality, which is well documented (see Lewis 1971 for detailed documentation) by several authors. I want to move beyond our often distorted perceptions of shamanic practices where they are seen as bizarre ritual practices, and consider their basis as ritual theatre. The word 'trance' is often disturbing; for many people it conjures up an image of unconsciousness or loss of control. However, I want to suggest that we move in and out of trance states without realizing it, especially when we become absorbed by something. For example, we can realize we have travelled 50 miles and not been aware of the landscape; we can feel ten minutes have gone by and in fact several hours have passed; the book we are reading can so absorb us that we are not aware that we are feeling very cold until the telephone rings and brings us out of our *preoccupation*. One form of this light trance state is day-dreaming. Waking trance is a state that most of us enter in our day-to-day lives.

Johnstone (1981) describes reports from actors who report 'split' states of consciousness, such as Fanny Kemble who said:

> The curious part of acting, to me, is the sort of double process which the mind carries on at once, the combined operation of one's faculties, so to speak, in diametrically opposite directions; for instance, in that very last scene of Mrs Beverley, while I was half dead with crying in the midst of *real* grief, created by an entirely *unreal* cause, I perceived that my tears were falling like rain all over my silk dress, and spoiling it; and I calculated and measured most accurately the space that my father would require to fall in, and moved myself and my train accordingly in the midst of the anguish I was to feign, and absolutely did endure. (Archer 1888)

When actors talk of allowing themselves to enter a character or allowing a character to enter them, it sounds a very similar process to the shaman and the native healers who talk about being possessed by spirits or about their soul going on journeys.

Clare Higgins was trying to articulate to me the effect of visiting Broadmoor on her acting, and said that actors and theatre companies get caught up in making the experience safe for an audience, so that, for example, there will be an alerting of an audience before the actual blinding scene in *King Lear*. She felt that her first Broadmoor visit had freed her as a person and as an actor (as Gertrude in *Hamlet*), and that her second performance, as Regan in *King Lear*, has freed her *as a character*.

CH I felt that they would understand, that they would receive this character, and that was very freeing – that was a real step forward from the last time too. So, I felt much freer – I felt more *real*. I didn't feel I had to display or show or act as such, just *be* the character in the lines. What Broadmoor gave me was *being the character. Now, I've yet to find a way through* to daring to be in front of a so-called normal audience . . .[9]

Higgins describes very well the shift between 'acting' a character and 'being' a character, and that paradoxically, by being the character, she felt more real. Some actors claim never to enter a character, but put on the right voice and gesture rather like putting on the right costume, but there are few who do not admit to some internal shift in consciousness.

The actors in a theatre performance invite us to enter their world – not their personal world, but the 'world' they have created onstage – and to do this we have to suspend our disbelief. For the 'two hour traffick' of the play, we allow ourselves to believe what is taking place, while we know at a logical level that it is not true – i.e. the actor who is shot is not really dead but will perform again tomorrow night. However, we must note that a not uncommon theatrical expression for a performance or production that 'does not work', is that it has died: 'I went out there tonight and died' and audiences and critics are seen as having the power to 'kill off' an actor or a production.

Nevertheless, in most performances where we are invited into this world, we have to let go of much of our conscious control, knowing that however frightening the play may be, we will survive the experience. We survive it because of the theatre structure; the way a play is organized, right down to the rituals necessary for getting into a play and the rituals for getting out again (have you noticed how you can never leave a theatre in a hurry?). We are assisted in the transition back to everyday reality by the actors lining up for our appreciation: they are out of character, but still in costume, and go through a very formalized ritual which, to a certain extent, is controlled by the audience. We are regaining our autonomy and expressing our elation – joy, adulation, politeness, tolerance – through that very primitive ritual movement, the hand-clap. It is sometimes accompanied by ritual sounds of individual appreciation which only rarely become group sounds. All this, before manoeuvring our way out of the theatre and into some part of our everyday reality. We have impressions of the play as a whole and individual performances within it. We process, check things out, and later even have different impressions from those we had immediately after seeing the performance.

Unless the play is really very bad or we do not wish to be there or are more concerned about our performance as a member of the audience (here

I would include the man who answered his mobile-phone in the middle
of the National Theatre's *King Lear*), we have, for the duration of the play,
entered the 'world' of the performance. Just as we are influenced by the
play as a whole and individual performances within it, the actors are
influenced by the audience as a whole and individual responses within
it.[10]

It has become a *shared world*, in which there are lesser or greater degrees
of trance both for actors and audience, and the whole is contained within
the dramatic framework and theatrical structure. Let us look further at the
word 'trance' in our attempts to understand the dramatic process:

trance from transir: depart, be benumbed:

1. a state of extreme apprehension of doubt or surprise.

2. an unconscious or insensible condition; a swoon, a faint; more
   modern – a state characterized by a more less prolonged suspen-
   sion of consciousness and inertness to stimulus; a cataleptic or
   hypnotic condition.

3. an intermediate state between sleeping and waking; a stunned or
   dazed state; a state of mental abstraction from external things;
   absorption, exaltation, ecstasy.

4. to pass away, to die, to swoon, to faint.

From the same root, we get **transit:**

the action or fact of passing across or through; the passage or journey
from one place or point to another.

a passing across.

*(compare with: a lift, a porter, a delivery van, a carrying across of things
or meaning – some of the many meanings derived from the Greek word
metaphora).*

Thus, trance, transit, transition, transitional, transitionary, are all etymologically linked, and are all intrinsically linked with how we manage
movement from one physical or symbolic state to another.

Winnicott (1971) illustrated for all time the importance of the transitional object for the individual child during the transition from total
dependence to some independence. The transitional object, typified by the
security blanket which belongs to Linus in the Peanuts cartoon, is a child's
first symbol, its first ritual object, which represents the absent carer: it also
has many dramatic possibilities. The child names the 'object' and talks to
it, and then answers on its behalf – surely the earliest example of rôle-
reversal.[11] We are capable of rôle-reversal, i.e. taking on the rôle of the
other, from about 18 months old – a significant time in the dramatic

development of human beings. Whereas Winnicott speaks for the individual child, I am interested in transitionary phenomena – to use my generalist term – especially those which occur in healing rituals and drama performances. For example, we could list costumes, masks, fans, drums – the ritual objects which enable a healer or performer or patient to make a transition from everyday reality into dramatic reality. The ritual space, the space-set-apart for play or performances, needs to be clearly defined as the 'empty space',[12] i.e. empty of the everyday expectations we may project into it, so that it can become the symbolic space of the ritual or performance. Transitionary phenomena are known and predictable and therefore recognized by participants. Because of the constancy of transitionary phenomena, it is possible to set in motion various transformative processes. The safety and signposts of the ritual enable the risk to be explored.[13]

The shamanic mode of dramatherapy acknowledges the two realities – dramatic and everyday – and that movement from one to the other and back again is facilitated through transitionary phenomena. It also emphasizes the altered states of consciousness facilitated through dramatic healing rituals. These states of trance or absorption are in fact focused processes which everyone is capable of experiencing in their lives. In the dramatic ritual or healing theatre they are maximized.

I have illustrated three contrasting but connected models of dramatherapy – the para-theatre, the rôle, and the shamanic – which are all based on an understanding of drama and theatre and ritual. Let us now look at what a dramatherapist actually does in a therapeutic setting.

Methodology and Application

Before the actual commencement of any group, it is important that an assessment takes place, both individually and in a group, so that the right kind of dramatherapy intervention may be provided. Patients and therapists need to be able to make an informed decision before embarking on a dramatherapy programme (which of course is part of the wider therapeutic programme). If dramatherapy is indicated, then the assessment will involve the diagnostic use of some basic dramatherapy methods, such as sculpting (see below) in an individual session(s) and bodywork and rôle-play in preliminary group sessions.

Although far more people than we imagine can find dramatherapy helpful, it is not a cure-all or universal panacea, and group composition needs to be handled with care. In my own experience, most people who indicate that they do not want to join a dramatherapy group either have no idea what it entails or have fearful fantasies that they are going to look foolish. A diagnostic time (say an individual session and several group sessions) serves as an introduction and also enables the dramatherapist to gauge the appropriateness of the medium for the individual. For example, people who are primarily concrete thinkers would find many dramatherapy methods confusing and frustrating:

> Mary was sitting at the desk with a pile of small objects; toys, nesting dolls and so on, and had been asked to create a 'sculpt' of her family. She looked confused and cast her eyes around the room. She fingered some of the toys and said that the children had those, and then asked if she could have a magazine. She cut out human figures from the magazine and arranged them around a space, and, through them, described her family. She was then able to use small dolls that were realistic to represent her experience of her family. The ideas of using animals etc. to represent human beings had no meaning for her, and in answer to the question 'if you were an animal, what animal would you be?', she said immediately 'Humans are animals aren't they?

Open any book on actor training[14] and you will find methods that can be applied therapeutically, especially those that involve the development of the body and voice, and drama games (Barker 1977). These techniques may be taught in classes, but in dramatherapy they are an intrinsic part of the group itself. They are part of the preparation of 'the fertile ground' or the warm-up, and come under the category of 'transitionary phenomena' described above. They assist us to develop vocally and physically, which facilitates the transition into dramatic reality. As well as providing a preparation, they are also a focus for the group, and may also act as a stimulus for the imagination. The warm-up produces energy which is then used creatively.

The central part of the dramatherapy group, its development from the warm-up, takes up about three-quarters of the group time. It can involve a whole range of dramatherapy structures of myths, journeys, scenes, sculpts, which can be explored through movement and voice, improvisation, enacted scenes and so on. Here we have made the transition, and are creating and working within the dramatic reality, and are distanced from everyday reality. The scene and the rôles may also be distanced, which can give a further distancing. To put it another way: by dramatizing any event of our lives or playing a game or creating a sculpt as Mary did above, we have created some degree of dramatic distancing, i.e. we are re-creating something in dramatic form which may be a representation of an everyday event, BUT it is not the event itself; thus we are minimally in dramatic reality and therefore distanced. If the dramatization is an ancient myth or we are all animals going on a journey to a new land rather than being ourselves on a journey, we have further dramatically distanced.

The paradox of dramatic distancing is that we come closer to ourselves and indeed get in touch with profound areas of experience that are not accessible in other ways.

The final stage of a group is the return from the dramatic reality; the transition into the everyday; the 'grounding', and the individuation before leaving the group. Group members are able to share their experiences and reflect on the drama, without having to give explanations or receive interpretations. The ending may be non-verbal through relaxation and calming vocalization instead of verbalization. Other groups will want to discuss and process the drama itself, and it is often by doing this that people begin to bring about changes for themselves. The dramatic meta-phor has begun to work and will continue to work in both individuals and the group as a whole, providing we do not move the goalposts and try to interpret people's experience in a different framework.

> George was creating a mask, having struggled for several weeks with the craft aspects of the dramatherapy group. He had made a mask which collapsed and, before that, had been very reluctant to play. This time, the mask was working for him, and he painted it black with vivid red stripes. Wearing his mask, he said, 'I'm a voodoo god, a leader in the community and I sleep with all the virgins before they get married'.

The above vignette could lead to detailed debate and analysis from psychoanalysts and psychotherapists. However, I am reminded of the crucial part that the mask has to play in the transformative drama, where it is able to say what otherwise we would be unable to say. Within the drama, it was important for George to explore this identity. His final mask, some weeks later, was a mask which covered only part of his face, whereas the voodoo mask had completely covered it and the powerful black and red had been transformed into blue and gold.

Tony Harrison (1988) says that the mask is designed for the sort of situations that are impossible to put into words, or when we are speech-less, which is why the mask has an open mouth – *so that it can go on speaking*:

> The mask is designed with an open mouth for those kinds of situ-ations where words might fail us – in extreme situations where a human being might scream.

Let us summarize the main points of this chapter so far. I have introduced the idea of dramatherapy as being an art based on ancient healing rituals and theatre art rather than a science. I have described how dramatic rituals can empower us into action and set in motion deep internal processes through altered states of consciousness otherwise known as trance. The suggestion is made that western people project, onto 'primitive' cultures and actors alike, fantasies about their lives and customs which can mask an understanding both of ritual and theatre. Three contrasting theatre art models of dramatherapy theory and practice have been described, illustrated by case histories in relation to technique and method.

I now want to look at the importance of Shakespeare for dramatherapists in their work.

Shakespeare and Dramatherapy

Shakespeare, probably more than any other playwright apart from the ancient Greeks, is able to tell a story that is relevant to everyone, even today, and to tell it in such a way that it continues to resonate. Because he is able to speak for all of us, he assists us to 're-work' aspects of our own lives by witnessing their portrayal on stage (and how important it is that the plays are enacted for their full effect and not just read!). Most of us, at some time in our lives, need assistance in re-working experiences where we have become stuck, where we are experiencing chaos or where life ceases to have meaning. In traditional societies, it is dramatic ritual that helps us to re-work. Theatre performances can do the same in a preventative way, through the scenario and character, plot and sub-plot, together with the language, metaphor, imagery, structure, i.e. the sheer craft, as well as the artistic creation. If it is too late for the preventative intervention, we need to look at the curative or healing mode. This is where Shakespeare can work, through the dramatherapist to patients in dramatherapy.

Shakespeare is a master of the 'play-within-the-play',[15] and indeed most of the dramatherapeutic devices have been taken, albeit not always consciously, from his plays: re-enactment, sculpting, journeys, chorus, masks, rôle-reversal, disguise, letter-writing, symbolic fighting, for example. I have mentioned the term 'sculpting' several times in this chapter, which is used frequently by dramatherapists (and has been borrowed by many other therapeutic disciplines), where small or large objects (toys or chairs) – or people themselves – are used to represent the dynamics of a situation. Sculpts can be of past, present, or future situations; in miniature or epic size (Jennings 1986). They can represent how we perceive or experience issues, as in a 'my life now' sculpt, or how we would like it to be or what we fear it to be, or an idealized version of our lives. When we create a sculpt, it is as if we have created a scene in a personal theatre, with different characters that can tell the story. The group as a whole may sculpt a scene, or a theme, or the dynamics of the group. There is a superb example of sculpting in *The Two Gentlemen of Verona*.

Launce enters with his dog and describes his sadness at parting from his family in order to travel overseas with his master. He explains the situation to us through a sculpt:

> 'This shoe is my father. No, this
> left shoe is my father. No, no; this left shoe is my
> mother; nay, that cannot be so neither. Yes, it is so, it
> is so; it hath the worser sole. This shoe with a hole
> in it is my mother'

(II.3.14-17)

Launce is interrupted by Panthino who comes to tell him he is late for the boat and will miss the flood, the voyage, his master and his service if he does not make haste. Launce makes a wonderful transition from *concrete expression* to *poetic* when he says:

> 'Lose the tide, and the voyage, and the master, and
> the service, and the tied? Why, man, if the river
> were dry, I am able to fill it with my tears; If the
> wind were down, I could drive the boat with my
> sighs.'

(II.3.48-51)

This early play of Shakespeare's is so full of dramatic devices – lovers, kidnaps, letters, journeys, disguises, rescues (as well as the inaccuracies and inconsistencies) – that I find it reassuring that Shakespeare took so many years to get it right. The play is also a superb example of how it is possible to 'overload the dramatic framework': i.e. there is too much for the dramatic structure to sustain. It is very easy for dramatherapists to fill their sessions with as much technique and action as possible. We also overload the dramatic framework when we are drawn into the guts of our clients. We want too much to happen too quickly; we want to see it happening, rather than allowing the dramatic process to evolve. Of course, overloading the dramatic framework could have disastrous results in a forensic setting; people in our groups have usually had an overload of drama in their lives. Cox (1992a) discusses the creative tension between dramatherapy and forensic psychotherapy and the need for clarity and structure.

I describe in some detail the dramatherapeutic use of *A Midsummer Night's Dream* (Jennings 1990), where all the major themes of the play were developed during an intensive training course to provide structures for people to work with patients. I want now to describe just one of the ways in which *Hamlet* can be a vehicle for dramatherapeutic work.[16] In Shakespearean criticism and debate, the very first scene is rarely discussed, i.e.

the scene before we first see Hamlet in person. This scene takes place on the battlements of the Danish castle at Elsinore where soldiers are on guard because there is a threat of invasion from Norway. The soldiers have seen a ghost on the previous nights and are telling the disbelieving Horatio about it when the ghost itself appears.

In this structure, groups set up improvisations on the theme of border-guards, the threat of invasion, the camaraderie between soldiers, the hierarchy and so on. I introduce the idea of an apparition – who saw it? What was it like? When did it appear? And would they do anything about it? We then look at the text, and use the improvisation as a way into the text and the play (my sub-text for this theme is 'threat of invasion', which is a multiple-metaphor). My interest was stimulated by the variety of responses which depended on geography. The group in Tel Aviv were the most volatile, and frightened, and needed a very strong structure to stop them flipping into everyday reality in a state of chaos. The group in Norway could not get into the theme at all, and it had to be abandoned. The response in Israel mirrors research that has been done on dreaming[17] (children in Tel Aviv have more nightmares about the war and fear of attack although they live a distance from the tense border zones, than the children on the border who live under the daily fear of attack). The Norwegian group were unable to relate to it at all – it was too far removed from their own recent experience.

Dramatherapy in a Forensic Setting

At present, to my knowledge, there is one trainee and two trained dra-matherapists working in forensic settings. Forensic settings (as well as psychiatric) may be described as marginal institutions for marginal people – people who have undergone an individual loss of identity, rights and freedom, by offending against society, or by suffering from mental ill-ness.[18] What might be the rôle of dramatherapy in these situations?

First, it is possible for people to 're-work' their experience, as has been described above, through the dramatic distance of the drama. Some offender patients are too near the drama of their own lives to be able to understand them. One of the reasons that theatre is so important is that it enables us to see things more clearly *because* it can encapsulate our lives as a whole in manageable form.

Second, it can re-shape affective material and integrate it in new and constructive ways, as illustrated in the para-theatre approach described by Mitchell (op cit).

Third, it can expand and develop rôle repertoire and replace unhelpful and destructive rôles with more socially-acceptable and life-enhancing rôles.

Fourth, Grainger (op cit), has demonstrated that people with thought disorder are able to think more clearly after a period in a dramatherapy group (this contradicts the commonly-held assumption that people who are confused become more confused by doing drama).

Fifth, by developing boundaries between everyday reality and dramatic reality, it may be possible to assist people for whom there does not appear to be a differentiation between fantasy and reality, such as those people who seem permanently to inhabit dramatic reality, such as some psychotic patients who take on new identities or those offenders who live their lives as a never-ending Greek tragedy.

Sixth, we may describe many offender patients as people with an over-fixed script, at times almost like a pre-scripted play (see 1 and 3 above). Rather than working with a 'free script' as in improvisation, it may be possible to work more effectively with the fixed dramatic script within dramatic reality.

However, there are serious caveats. Many forensic institutions are themselves volatile, and any dramatherapeutic work would have to be applied with extreme care. Dramatherapy would need to have the acceptance of all concerned if such work was not to be undermined and create even greater conflicts. Work would need to be thought through judiciously in terms of the relationship between the three frameworks – societal, institutional and dramatic – and whether 'overloading' is more likely to happen. Such institutions are hierarchical with a clear-cut structure of professional expertise which attempts to balance the punishment with the therapy. Although many people working in forensic settings might regard psychotherapy and group work as the soft option in a situation where people are supposed to be punished, nevertheless psychotherapy and psychoanalysis have moved from their original marginal status to an authenticating position.

There are attempts to move dramatherapy from its marginal status to a more central position with the proposal to set up state registration. Whether this is the right move, I am not sure, since it may be changing the actual nature of dramatherapy itself. There is a certain power, such as that of the shaman, to be gained from staying marginal. Maybe there are also ways in which we are especially adept at working with marginal people, since we occupy this position ourselves.

However, there is a bigger question – whether society will allow dramatherapists to change position/status.

To understand the marginal status of dramatherapists, let us remind ourselves of the marginal status of theatre people. It would seem that actors have almost always had marginal status in our society (from the days when the churches threw the drama out onto the streets when improvisation had become too bawdy within the celebration of the Easter Mass),[19] and have been equated with vagabonds and thieves, travellers and tinkers. Vilified by Plato, lauded by Shakespeare (who frequently uses the metaphor of the actor and the stage to illustrate life's truths),[20] society's attitude towards actors continues to be ambivalent. For example, most insurance companies still refuse to insure actors and other members of the theatrical profession; drama is not included in the new curriculum, unlike music and art; there has only been the creation of two theatre lords – Laurence Olivier and Bernard Miles. If dramatherapy is a part of theatre art, then it must also come within this marginal category.

Shakespeare and Broadmoor

I attended all the three professional performances of Shakespeare plays at Broadmoor, and was a part of the small group facilitation. There is no doubt that, as theatre, we were all experiencing something quite remarkable which was, and still is at times, difficult to put into words. *Hamlet*, the first performance, left actors and audience alike in a state of some shock. I attended another performance at The Royal Shakespeare Theatre two days after Broadmoor, and the play had changed: there was more electricity, and the closet scene between Mark Rylance and Clare Higgins was the most painful I had seen. The actors themselves had difficulty returning to their ordinary lives, and referred to 'the Broadmoor experience'. It took a large group meeting to ground the experience for the actors. Everyone talked through their experiences – from the moment when they were first asked if they would like to go to Broadmoor, right through to the actual journey there itself, the performance, and the journey back a dramatherapeutic technique which helps to ground an experience. This illustrates the distance that the actors needed to achieve in order to conduct their everyday lives.

The performance of *Romeo and Juliet*, some months later, suffered from the anxiety of whether it could live up to the first performance, and of course, nothing could. The *Hamlet* was once and for all time. However, despite the need for many understudies and some people having to work from the book, it was a performance which went from boisterousness to pathos. The most remarkable scene for me was the bawdy interchange between Juliet's Nurse and Mercutio, which acted as a rôle-model for sexual innuendo and even provocation, in a dramatic frame which could be acceptable both dramatically and in everyday life. The scene showed how such behaviour could be managed.

A group of actors, together with Ron Daniels, the director of *Hamlet*, returned to Broadmoor for a workshop on *Hamlet*. The patients had expressed interest in several scenes, including 'get thee to a nunnery' which they called the rape scene because in this production it was so violent; the gravedigger's scene and Ophelia's funeral. The actors started with a performance of Act I Scene 2 for everyone to get into the story and idiom again, which was an excellent focus to bring everyone into the dramatic framework. There was some discussion about Ophelia not responding to Hamlet but obeying her father, so an improvisation was set up whereby Ophelia stayed in her closet and Hamlet tried to persuade her to come out and talk. Rylance started off, and then various Broadmoor staff and patients asked to try and persuade Ophelia, using ruses such as shouting and ordering her to come out, tricking her to come out. As one person said as he walked away, 'Well, violence doesn't work.'

This is a very effective method of exploring possible outcomes, and on this occasion it did not go beyond the raising of the issues. It would have been useful to continue exploring the outcome and with some resolution. Jimmy Gardner, as the gravedigger, did the supreme test of whether people would accept the dramatic reality, by showing a Broadmoor broom as his shovel and several plastic cups as the skulls from the grave. Everyone in the room was then asked to step forward in rôle as someone at Ophelia's funeral. This scene was very moving and brought everyone together within the dramatic scene. As a dramatherapist, I had my concerns that there was no de-roling or distancing at the end, but these were my obsessions – this was a theatre workshop and not a dramatherapy group!

I want now to mention briefly some of the outstanding moments for me of the *King Lear* performance. I had seen the production several times before, and also, as with *Hamlet*, saw it immediately afterwards. There was much more attention paid to theatrical convention in the *King Lear* Broadmoor production. For example, exits and entrances, simple lighting, cues and props, were created as near as possible to the conception of the original production. With *Hamlet* it was a bare minimum of costume, furniture and props, with no lighting, and, for example, when Hamlet had dragged Polonius off the stage, the actor then got up and sat in the audience. This was accepted by the audience, whose attention was always on the acting area. There were moments when the actors surpassed their previous performances; certainly Regan in the blinding of Gloucester, and Kent, the Fool, Lear and Edgar when they leave the hovel, 'Child Roland to the dark tower came'. Previously it had been a ragged and uneven scene.

All the moments between Lear and the Fool were superb, and I wondered about the dual rôle-models for patients – of foolishness and madness.

Unfortunately, there was only a brief time after this performance in which the actors were asked a lot of questions. I was left in no doubt that all these three performances had produced powerful therapeutic affect.

So, what can I contribute to this debate? The Broadmoor Shakespeare performances have had a profound affect on actors, staff and patients alike. Perhaps I could liken it to a 'depth charge'; and a depth charge enables a shaking and a stirring. Cox and Theilgaard (1987) quote the following from Bachelard (1969):

But the image has touched the depths before it stirs the surface.

The productions served to heighten consciousness in a dramatic way by bringing all those present into the one 'world' of the theatre and, through Shakespeare, bringing everyone into contact in a very raw way with their extreme fears and fantasies. I am more aware of the major changes it has brought about for staff and actors. As Higgins says:

I felt completely different at Broadmoor. I felt Regan was completely 'at home' . . . in a psychiatric sense I suppose . . . as a character I felt she would be 'at home' there. I did not have the qualms I'd had the first time I went, in displaying violence, sexuality, complicated states of mind in front of those patients . . . I felt much more at home.[21]

These occasional performances rest between the psychotherapy groups on the one hand, and the drama classes on the other, and no doubt serve as a stimulus for both.

Nevertheless, dramatherapists do have a rôle to play in the dynamic relationship between clinicians and actors in forensic work such as at Broadmoor.

Until I saw you with that skull, I never really thought about the actual corpse.

(patient)

'That he should weep for her'

(Hamlet II.2.557)

Notes

1 This is another attempt to define dramatherapy. The British Association for Dramatherapists is already attempting its third definition for the profession.

2 The professions of art, music, dance and dramatherapy, have implemented a policy of calling themselves 'the creative arts therapies' in order to distinguish themselves

from the creative therapies, which can be applied to many forms of psychotherapy and groupwork.

3 The Institute of Dramatherapy inaugurated the annual Dramatherapy & Shakespeare Symposium at Stratford-upon-Avon, and also in 1990 at Elsinore, Denmark.

4 This was a spontaneous entering of a character in the final scene of the *Hamlet* workshop at Broadmoor. When a patient identifies very strongly with a rôle or character, it is very important to de-rôle.

5 Although dramatic rituals have a predominantly social function in helping to define individuals in relation to their stage in life or social group, the ritual itself can have a profound effect on individuals and groups which is not necessarily uniform.

6 It is not an uncommon projection of psychoanalysts onto actors to suggest they are portraying 'the false self'. One clinician said to me, 'Why do actors make such bad patients?' Interestingly enough, in the 1988 conference called Shakespeare & Mind, in the dramatherapy workshop that I led, it was the psychotherapists and psychoanalysts who wanted to take on key Shakespearian rôles and the actors who tried to behave like psychotherapists!

7 Several anthropologists have conducted extended fieldwork with the Senoi Temiar. My own doctoral fieldwork with the same people, found no evidence for a notion of the formalized 'dream clinic' at breakfast-time. In fact, breakfast was not usually a communal family meal, as very often various members of the household would be out before dawn. However, the Temiar do pay close attention to their dreams and, etymologically, there is a direct connection between their word for dreaming and their word for trancing.

8 It is curious that with art, music and drama, we only need one word to indicate the art-form; we do not need to describe the locus of the art- form. However, it is not enough for us to say only the word 'drama', we have to use the word 'theatre' as well. I prefer to use the term theatre-art.

9 Clare Higgins gave an extended interview for the journal of *Theatre & Therapy*, volume 1, number 2. The extracts quoted in this chapter have not been previously published.

10 Part of my research into the therapeutic nature of theatrical performances, has been studying audience reaction to certain plays. Last year I attended some 50 performances of the same production of *A Midsummer Night's Dream*, and almost the same number of *Hamlet*. An extended description of this work will appear in *Shakespeare: Therapeutic Journeys*, in a chapter entitled 'Shakespeare: The Play Within'.

11 rôle-reversal is often considered a sophisticated adult technique. It is often used in psychodrama. However, if we consider Napier's view quoted earlier in this chapter – 'Pretending, whether it be something about ourselves or about the outside world, is basic to our apprehension of change' – illustrates the importance of this development in human beings from a very early age.

12 Peter Brook refers to 'the empty space' in his seminal work of the same name (Brook 1974).

13 I have described elsewhere (Jennings 1987) the ritual/risk paradigm in dramatherapy. The ritual is the known, the repetitive, the predictable and safe, which allows for the risk of exploration, the new, the danger.

14 See, for example, Cicely Berry's book *Voice and the Actor*.

15 See 10.

16 It is possible to work therapeutically with the play of *Hamlet*, with the play as a whole, or just two lines. One can start with themes and then go into text, or vice versa. It is important to remember to keep a clear theatre structure, especially if one is departing from the structure of the text.

17 Mooli Lahad described the Israeli phenomenon on dreaming in connection with his work and research in stress prevention – in preparation.

18 It continues to be a subject of debate as to whether people suffering from an illness should be deprived of their liberty by law (see, for example, Szasz,1974).

19 It is generally accepted that the first formalization of a play was in a dialogue in the Easter Mass between Mary and the Angel at the grave. Over the years, more and more characters were added to the play, until the Church authorities decided to expel the actors from the churches.

20 Although most people would refer to Shakespeare's 'all the world's a stage' in *As You Like It*, almost every play mentions actors and the stage, and many of them use the device of the play-within-the-play.

21 See 9.

Epilogue

Reporting to the
'Yet unknowing world'

The prologue started with words borrowed from Horatio 'How these things came about' and, 250 pages further on, we have rejoined this text. It is 'to the yet unknowing world' that this book speaks. And to the world that knows.

Encountering 'the wealth of human experience' and 'a great accumulation of experience' were phrases chosen by theatre directors to describe one aspect of their visit. This was the impact of being, for a while, within dramatic therapeutic space beneath 'such mirrors as will turn'. We need to remember that 'The Performance of Tragedy in a Secure Psychiatric Hospital' is the book's sub-title.

It is to be hoped that fresh lights and enhanced insights will bring about a greater readiness to try to understand the things which, as Horatio said, 'came about'. He spoke:

> 'Of carnal, bloody, and unnatural acts,
> Of accidental judgements, casual slaughters,
> Of deaths put on by cunning and forc'd cause'

> (*Hamlet* V.2.386)

One of the unexpected benefits of the actors coming hither and holding the mirror up to nature has been the intensity of their new-found role of reporting to the yet unknowing world. They have indeed proved to be the abstract and brief chronicles of the time.

I hear an echo from one of Shakespeare's major primary sources, something about leading captivity captive and giving gifts unto men.

> It is a very active mirror.
> It is a very strong mirror.
> It is a mirror as will turn.

> 'One touch of nature makes the whole world kin.'

> M.C.

Appendix A

Forensic Psychiatry and Forensic Psychotherapy

Forensic Psychiatry is a specialty within the wider field of general psychiatry. Its particular concerns are those aspects of psychiatry directly or indirectly involving legal issues. Initial contact with the patient for assessment and/or treatment usually takes place in one of three time zones. These are pre-trial, during the trial and post-trial. If they have not been acquitted, patients seen after the trial may be on probation, serving a prison sentence (which may be suspended) or be the subjects of hospital orders. Only a small proportion of patients in Broadmoor Hospital, although having been sufficiently disturbed in the past to justify their transfer, has not been tried for an offence. Nevertheless, all are legally detained under one of the sections of the Mental Health Act 1983 (see *Principles and Practice of Forensic Psychiatry* (edited by Bluglass and Bowden 1990) which deals with every aspect of the subject).

Forensic Psychotherapy, the child of forensic psychiatry and mainstream psychotherapy, refers to psychotherapeutic endeavours undertaken with patients who are usually, but not always, 'offender-patients'. Such therapy may take place in an out-patient or an in-patient setting. But in relation to the specific issues raised in this book, forensic psychotherapy implies the psychotherapeutic opportunities which present themselves within the particular setting provided by Broadmoor Hospital.

It is an emergent discipline which is just finding its feet (Cox 1992b). In 1990 the first one-year day-release course in forensic psychotherapy, directed by Dr Estela Welldon, was held at The Portman Clinic in London, under the auspices of the British Postgraduate Medical Federation. In 1991 The International Association for Forensic Psychotherapy was inaugurated at a meeting in Leuven, Belgium.

Theoretically, its approach is inevitably eclectic, as it draws heavily on individual and group psychodynamics; each may be analytic, existential and/or supportive.

Group analysis (see Foulkes 1964 and Pines 1985) frequently stands the best chance of rebalancing the inner world of the individual patient, because of its attention to the group matrix. Offences 'against the person' are so often due to a reactivation of earlier pathological matrices in which the patient was enmeshed. The word *matrix* has a dual connotation: it refers to 'mother' and to other communicational networks in which an individual is embedded.

It may also include cognitive and behaviour modification techniques when these are specifically indicated. Forensic psychotherapy should be regarded as an integral part of a comprehensive therapeutic strategy. This may involve medication, and a wide variety of occupational and expressive therapies, as well as physical treatments when these are clinically called for. Within a secure hospital, such as Broadmoor, no single approach can possibly have a monopoly of therapeutic initiatives. Malan's (1979,74) comment on the basic principles of dynamic psychotherapy is equally applicable to forensic psychotherapy: 'The aim of every moment of every session is to put the patient in touch with as much of his true feelings as he can bear.'

Throughout this volume there have been various references to the way in which the performance of tragedy within a special hospital could be linked to conventional, formal, structured psychotherapy. It therefore seemed appropriate to describe in outline a few of the overlapping conceptual frames and *foci* of attention which guide the thinking of the forensic psychotherapist. It needs to be emphasised that this is merely a highly condensed thumb-nail sketch.*

Intrapsychic Phenomena

The endeavour to reconcile Unconscious and Conscious motivation is never far from the therapist's mind. As with all ventures of this nature, there is the fundamental problem of trying to discern what is essentially new and what is merely the rebalancing and realignment of well established approaches. An obvious instance of the latter is the indubitable significance of the psychoanalytic emphasis on *unconscious motivation*. This is a crucial and central component in the psychodynamic assessment of many forensic patients. Nevertheless, the necessity of a balanced approach becomes clear when the importance of *conscious motivation* also needs to be underlined. It would be an equally serious error of clinical judgement to say that unconscious motivation is *always* the central dynamic issue, as to say that it *never* is. It is not hard to explain why Gloucester's words 'And that's true too' (*King Lear* V.2.11) are in my mind

---

* These observations are personal and do not necessarily reflect the rapidly differentiating *corpus* of forensic psychotherapeutic opinion. They should be regarded solely as the current views of a 'jobbing forensic psychotherapist', based on 25 years' experience in prison, out-patient department and special hospital. Like all other modes of clinical experience, they are never static but are constantly being reappraised in the light of fresh challenges

just now. Let us consider the psychopathology of two patients who are both arsonists, and their therapeutic needs. The first may have complex, 'deep' unconscious motivation for an offence, involving 'inexplicable' impulses to set fire to his own most treasured possessions. The second may have easily understandable 'reasons' – transparently conscious motivation – for setting fire to a rival's house; an offence 'fired' by speedy, easy-to-execute destructive revenge. (There is, of course, a series of subsidiary questions, such as why a particular kind of fire, at a particular time, etc?) Therapy with both these patients would, sooner or later, deal with their inner world phenomena, their dreams and fantasy-life.

The *fons et origo* of forensic psychotherapy is Freud's (1916,332–333) paper entitled 'Criminals from a Sense of Guilt'. Here he writes: 'Paradoxical as it may sound, I must maintain that the sense of guilt was present before the misdeed, that it did not arise from it, but conversely – the misdeed arose from the sense of guilt' (309–332).

Interestingly enough, this exceedingly short article (only two printed pages in length – yet limitless in terms of forensic significance) follows his study of Macbeth and Lady Macbeth in a section entitled 'Those Wrecked by Success'. Together with comments upon Richard III in 'The Exceptions', they constitute 'Some Character-Types met With In Psycho-Analytic Work'.

The implications of Freud's paper are extended and amplified in a monograph by Tuovinen (1973) *Crime as an Attempt at Intrapsychic Adaptation*. These papers discuss that which takes place within the mind of the patient during three time zones, although these are not the same as those relating to the trial, just described under the heading of forensic psychiatry. We are here concerned with intrapsychic dynamics before, during and after the offence. Like all dynamic psychotherapy, forensic psychotherapy endeavours to facilitate the process through which unconscious material enters consciousness and is subsequently integrated and accepted by the patient. This is something very different from transient *catharsis*, which, though it may give temporary relief, will not lead to lasting intrapsychic change.

Here it is pertinent to underline how often *catharsis* has been mentioned in these pages by representatives of the theatre world. A psychoanalytic study of *catharsis* is to be found in *Purgation through Pity and Terror* (Binstock 1973). Another key psychoanalytic text is *The Roots of Crime* (Glover 1960).

Mention has already been made of the complex process of *projective-identification* (p.166). It underlies many 'offences against the person'. During forensic psychotherapy, the therapist may become the recipient of the patient's projective-identifications which, prior to therapy, were transiently, though crucially, invested in the victim. This implies that the victim thus carries the dislocated and relocated parts of the assailant's original inner world. *Object Relations Theory* also throws much light on other forensic phenomena – 'throwing' being a metaphor with many clinically concrete implications. Greenberg and Mitchell (1983,404) state: 'The relational model establishes relational configurations as the bedrock of existence; all other human behavior and experiences . . . are relational derivatives'. Cashdan (1988,23) writes: 'The "stuff" of which mind is made has less to do with libidinal impulses and psychic energy than with the internalization of relationships. To understand what motivates people and how they view themselves, one needs to understand how relationships are internalized and how they become transformed into a sense of self'.

Interpersonal Phenomena: Contextual Imprinting

In addition to unconscious motivation, endopsychic processes and personality structure, forensic psychotherapy also concentrates upon the interactional aspects (the sociology of deviance) of the patient's story. Reference has already been made to the work of Becker (1963), and Matza (1969), who respectively described and developed the concept of the 'controlling identity' (see page XXX). The ambient circumstances, the context, 'imprint' an impression of 'self' which influences self-esteem regulation. The offence may therefore be part of a 'self'-fulfilling prophecy.

It is often patently clear why a particular individual committed a particular crime. But sometimes offences seem to defy explanation, so that neither unconscious motivation nor the study of social interactions at the material time (the time of the offence), seem to yield solid explanatory ground on which to stand. When such a sociological survey has been made, and conventional psychoanalytic work – which includes transference, interpretation and dream analysis – seems to have drawn a blank, an illuminating light has been known to shine from an unexpected quarter.

Existential Obligations: Invisible Loyalties

In *Invisible Loyalties* (Boszormenyi-Nagy and Spark 1973) the authors describe an interesting phenomenon known as 'transgenerational existential obligations'. It implies that behaviour, which is inexplicable in one generation, can be due to the fact that the patient is living out the un-lived life of a previous generation. In other words, that which appears to be inexplicable, in terms of current intrapsychic dynamics and interactional exchanges, does make sense in terms of completing an action which had only been anticipated – or perhaps initiated and stopped in its tracks – by a member of a previous generation. It is here that the title of the book is so important. The offender is loyal to that which is presently invisible, because it is loyalty to a previous generation. There are numerous clinical examples of this phenomenon. The behaviour of young Hamlet is 'over-determined' with many unconscious influences prompting him to act as he does, though he is ultimately loyal to the visible/invisible-to-his-mother ghost of his father.

Existential obligations have always been with us, as myth and classical Greek drama demonstrate. In the opening lines of *Antigone* we find these words:

> 'Tell me this: are there any evils coming from Oedipus that
> Zeus does not fulfill through us – the two still living?'
>
> (Sophocles: Wertenbaker 1992,91)

Though many invisible loyalties are experienced as being beneficient, rather than conveying 'evils'.

These three components, namely, intrapsychic phenomena, inter-personal phenomena and the possibility of existential obligations enable us to understand the majority of offences, although it is inevitable that in daily clinical work there are numerous variations on the theme. These include the wide range of precipitating factors such as alcohol and other drugs, as well as the whole gamut of possible physical or 'organic' factors.

In this book we have found many passages in which Shakespeare's language – although poetic/dramatic – is no less precise than that of the present-day clinician. His account of Hamlet's mother not seeing the ghost, seen by Hamlet, is redolent of many clinical accounts in which distorted perception, due to mental disorder, has led to a distorted con-struction of events.

> HAMLET: Do you see nothing there?
> QUEEN: Nothing at all; yet all that is I see.
>
> (III.4.132)

Reference has been made to the process of *internalization*, whereby that which was originally 'outside' is taken in and incorporated. This means that it becomes integrated as part of the structure of the personality – so different from becoming an isolated psychological 'ghetto' or 'enclave', which might suddenly break free. This, again, features in the psychopa-thology of many violent offenders.

Shakespeare's paraclinical precision vividly presents these dynamics. The newly crowned Henry V says:

> 'This new and gorgeous garment, majesty,
> Sits not so easy *on* me as you think .–
>   .   .   .
> Sorrow so royally *in* you appears,
> That I will *deeply* put the fashion *on*,
> And wear it *in* my heart.'
>
> (*II Henry IV* V.2.44,52. Italics added.)

This brief survey of forensic psychotherapy ends with many important issues – such as impulsivity and the 'over-controlled personality' who suddenly 'explodes' – still unmentioned. Though we cannot conclude without referring to the frequent initial need for *supportive* psychotherapy for disturbed/disturbing patients, especially those whose personality structure is precarious and whose endopsychic fragility can lead to further capricious behaviour. In supportive therapy the patient's defences are strengthened and reinforced. Analytic therapy cannot gain a foothold until adequate inner and outer stability has been achieved. The particular modifications of generic forensic psychotherapy called for by the psychotic, the borderline or the patient with a treatable psychopathic disorder are important, *per se*. But they are beyond the scope of this survey and have no direct link with our guiding subtitle

Attention has been drawn to a crucial time zone where clinical attention is focused:

> 'Between the acting of a dreadful thing
> And the first motion.'
>
> (*Julius Caesar* II.1.63)

In *Oedipus Revisited* Hillman (1991,50) has caught a subtle moment of transition when that which is under question changes from 'what happened to *where are we now*' (his italics). Paradoxical as it may sound, this polarity is perpetually present in forensic therapeutic space. There is a constant oscillation of attention from 'what happened' to 'where are we now'. Only when both focal points are sharply defined can the future be seen in perspective.

The forensic psychotherapist spends much of his time and energy waiting and witnessing, while his patients try to unravel that vitally important nodal point of experience 'between the acting of a dreadful thing/And the first motion'. It is here, in the waiting, that intrapsychic, interpersonal and existential wavelengths converge.*

Psychopathology: Though this term has only been mentioned twice (pp.255, 257), it has in fact been implicit throughout this Section. In collaboration with his colleagues, the forensic psychotherapist endeavours to establish an appropriate therapeutic policy for an individual patient. This depends upon discerning a 'dynamic formulation' which, itself, depends upon the underlying psychopathology.

---

* For an overview of current psychotherapeutic practice, see *Textbook of Psychotherapy in Psychiatric Practice* edited by J. Holmes. Although the word 'forensic' does not appear in the index, P. Gallwey (1991,359–381) has written an authoritative chapter on social maladjustment which covers much of the same ground.

Appendix B

Shakespeare, Psychiatry and the Unconscious

This was the title of a meeting of the Psychiatric Section of The Royal Society of Medicine held at Stratford on 19 June 1987. The event was reported in the journal of The Royal Society of Medicine and the theme was introduced in an editorial under the heading 'From Wimpole Street to Stratford' (Cox 1988) – Wimpole Street being the home of The Royal Society of Medicine. The published papers, all in the same edition of the journal, included material by both psychiatrists and Shakespeareans. See Trethowan, Bristow and Brockbank (1988b) in the bibliography.

Bibliography

Allderidge, P. (1974) *Richard Dadd*. London: Academy Editions.

Archer, W. (1888) 'Masks and Faces' in Johnstone, K. (1981) *Impro: Improvisations and the Theatre*. London: Methuen.

Atkinson, M. (1984) *Our Master's Voices*. London: Methuen.

Auden, W.H. 'The Sea and the Mirror' in Mendelson, E. (ed)(1976) *W.H. Auden: Collected Poems*. London: Faber and Faber.

Bachelard, G. (1969) *The Poetics of Space*. Boston: Beacon Press.

Baker, J. (1902) 'Female Criminal Lunatics: A Sketch'. *Journal of Medical Science* 48, 13–25.

Barker, C. (1977) *Theatre Games*. London: Eyre Methuen.

Becker, H. (1963) *Outsiders*. New York: The Free Press of Glencoe Inc.

Beckerman, B. (1990) *Theatrical Presentation: Performer, Audience and Act*. London and New York: Routledge.

Bennett, S. (1990) *Theatre Audiences: A Theory of Production and Reception*. London and New York: Routledge.

Bennett, S. (1991) Personal Communication.

Berry, C. (1973) *Voice and the Actor*. London: Harrap.

Berry, C. (1975) *Your Voice and How to Use It Successfully*. London: Virgin/W.H. Allen.

Berry, C. (1987) *The Actor and His Text*. London: Virgin/W.H. Allen.

Bettelheim, B. (1954) *Symbolic Wounds: Puberty Rites and the Envious Male*. Illinois Free Press.

Binstock, W.A. (1973) 'Purgation Through Pity and Terror'. *International Journal of Psycho-Analysis* 54, 499–504.

Blatner, A. and Blatner, A. (1988) *The Foundations of Psychodrama: History, Theory and Practice*. New York: Springer.

Blau, H. (1987) 'Odd, Anonymous Needs: The Audience in a Dramatised Society'. *Performing Arts Journal* 10.1, 34–42.

Bluglass, R. and Bowden, P. (eds)(1990) *Principles and Practice of Forensic Psychiatry*. Edinburgh: Churchill Livingstone.

Boszormenyi-Nagy, I. and Spark, G.M. (1973) *Invisible Loyalties: Reciprocity in Intergenerational Family Therapy*. New York: Harper & Rowe.

Bristow, C. (1988) 'Canst thou not minister to a mind diseas'd? Shakespeare, the Theatre and the Elizabethan Psyche'. *Journal of the Royal Society of Medicine* 81, 193–195.

Brockbank, J.P. (ed)(1988a) *Players of Shakespeare 1*. Cambridge University Press.

Brockbank, J.P. (1988b) 'Shakespeare's Language of the Unconscious'. *Journal of the Royal Society of Medicine* 81, 195–199.

Brook, P. (1972) *The Empty Space*. London: Penguin.

Bruscia, K. (1989) *Defining Music Therapy*. Phoenixville, Pennsylvania: Barcelona Publishers.

Bruscia, K. (1990) *Case Studies in Music Therapy*. Phoenixville, Pennsylvania: Barcelona Publishers.

Cashdan, S. (1988) *Object Relations Therapy: Using the Relationship*. New York: W.W. Norton & Company.

Clemen, W. (1951) *The Development of Shakespeare's Imagery*. London: Methuen.

Cox, B. (1991) *Salem to Moscow: An Actor's Odyssey*. London: Methuen.

Cox, M. (1978) *Structuring the Therapeutic Process: Compromise with Chaos*. Oxford: Pergamon. Reprinted 1988 with a new preface by Murray Cox. London: Jessica Kingsley Publishers.

Cox, M. and Theilgaard, A. (1987) *Mutative Metaphors in Psychotherapy: The Aeolian Mode*. London: Tavistock.

Cox, M. (1988)(Editorial) 'From Wimpole Street to Stratford: Shakespeare, Psychiatry and the Unconscious'. *Journal of the Royal Society of Medicine* 81, 187–188.

Cox, M. (1992a) 'The place of metaphor in psychotherapy supervision: creative tensions between forensic psychotherapy and dramatherapy' in Jennings, S. *Dramatherapy Theory and Practice* 2. London: Routledge.

Cox, M. (1992b) 'Forensic Psychotherapy: an Emergant Discipline' in Casselman, J. et al (eds) Law and *Mental Health in International Perspective*. Proceedings of the XVIIth International Congress of the International Academy of Law and Mental Health, Leuven, Belgium, May 26–30, 1991. Leuven.

Cox, M. and Theilgaard, A. (1993) *Shakespeare as Prompter: The Amending Imagination in Theatre and Therapy*. London: Jessica Kingsley Publishers.

Davis, D.R. (1992) *Scenes of Madness: A Psychiatrist at the Theatre*. London: Tavistock/Routledge.

Devereaux, G. (1956) 'Normal and Abnormal: The Key Problem of Psychiatric Anthroplogy' in Lewis, I.M. (1971) *Ecstatic Religion: An Anthropological Study of Spirit Possession and Shamanism*. Harmondsworth: Penguin.

Domhoff, G.W. (1985) *The Mistique of Dreams*. Berkeley, Ca. & London: University of California Press.

Driscoll, J.P. (1983) *Identity in Shakespearean Drama*. London and Toronto: Associated University Presses.

Drury, N. (1989) *The Elements of Element, Shamanism*. London: Element.

Elsass, P. (in press) 'The Healing Space: A comparative analysis of psychotherapy and theatre'. *New Theatre Quarterly*. Cambridge University Press.

Esslin, M. (1990) *The Theatre of the Absurd*. London: Penguin.

Foulkes, S.H. (1964) *Therapeutic Group Analysis*. London: George Allen & Unwin Ltd.

Fox, J. (ed)(1987) *The Essential Moreno*. New York: Springer.

Freud, S. (1916) S.E. **XIV** *Some Character-types Met Within Psycho-Analytic Work*. London: The Hogarth Press and the Institute of Psycho-Analysis. 309–333.

Friedman, N. (1953) 'Imagery: From Sensation to Symbol'. *Journal of Aesthetics and Art Critisism*12, 25-37.

Gallwey, P. (1991) 'Social Maladjustment' in Holmes, J. (ed) *Textbook of Psychotherapy in Psychiatric Practice*. Edinburgh: Livingstone Churchill.

Gaylord, K. (1983) 'Theatrical Performances: Structure and Process, Tradition and Revolt' in Kamerman, J.B. and Martorella, R. (eds) *Performers and Performances: The Social Organisation of Artistic Work*. New York: Praeger.

Glover, E. (1960) *The Roots of Crime: Selected Papers on Psycho-Analysis Vol II*. London: Image Publishing Company.

Goffman, E. (1961) *Asylums: Essays on the Social Situation of Mental Patients and Other Inmates*. New York: Anchor Books.

Grainger, R. (1990) *Drama and Healing: The Roots of Drama Therapy*. London: Jessica Kingsley.

Greenberg, J.R. and Mitchell, S.A. (1983) *Object Relations in Psychoanalytic Theory*. New York: Basic Books.

Gurr, A. (1970) *The Shakespearean Stage 1574–1642*. Cambridge University Press.

Hapgood, R. (1988) *Shakespeare the Theatre-Poet*. Oxford: Clarendon Press.

Harrison, T. (1988) 'Facing up to the Muses', lecture to the Classical Association in Bristol. *Proceedings of the Classical Association*.

Haugsgjerd, S. (1990) *Lidelsens karakter i ny psychiatri*. Oslo: Pax.

Hillman, J. (1991) 'Oedipus Variations: Studies in Literature and Psychodynamics' in Hillman, J. and Kerenyi, K. *Oedipus: Two Essays*. Dallas: Spring Publications.

Holland, N.N. (1964) *Psychoanalysis and Shakespeare*. New York: McGraw-Hill.

Holmes, J. (ed)(1991) *Textbook of Psychotherapy in Psychiatric Practice*. Edinburgh: Churchill Livingstone.

Holmes, P. and Karp, M. (eds)(1991) *Psychodrama: Inspiration and Technique*. London: Tavistock/Routledge.

Honigmann, E.A.J. (1976) *Shakespeare: Seven Tragedies. The Dramatist's Manipulation of Response*. London: Macmillan.

Irwin, E. (1985) Externalising and Improvising Imagery through Drama Therapy: a Psychoanalytical View. *Journal of Mental Imagery* 9, 33–42.

Jackson, R. and Smallwood, R. (1988) *Players of Shakespeare* 2. Cambridge University Press.

Jameson, F. (1972) *The Prison House of Language*. Princeton: Princeton University Press.

Jennings, S. (1986) *Creative Drama in Groupwork*. Bicester: Winslow Press.

Jennings, S. (ed)(1987) *Dramatherapy: Theory and Practice for Teachers and Clinicians*. London: Routledge.

Jennings, S. (1990) *Dramatherapy with Families, Groups and Individuals: Waiting in the Wings*. London: Jessica Kingsley.

Jennings, S. (ed)(1992) *Dramatherapy Theory and Practice* 2. London: Routledge.

Johnson, D.R. (1982) Developmental Approaches in Drama Therapy. *Arts in Psychotherapy* 9, 183–190.

Johnstone, K. (1981) *Impro: Improvisations and the Theatre*. London: Methuen.

Kandinsky, W. (1913) *1901–1913*. Berlin: Der Sturm.

Kaufmann, R.J. (1965) 'Ceremonies for Chaos: The Status of Troilus and Cressida'. *English Literary History* 32, 139–59.

Kher, J.N. (1974) *The Landscape of Absence: Emily Dickinson's Poetry*. New Haven & London: Yale University Press.

Klein, M. (1946) 'Notes on some schizoid mechanisms' in (1975) *The Writings of Melanie Klein*. London: The Hogarth Press.

Knill, P.J. (1978) *Intermodal Learning in Education and Therapy*. Cambridge, Mass.: Lesley College Arts Institute.

Kott, J. (1965) 'Der Hamlet der Jahrhundermitte' in Kaiser, J. (ed) *Hamlet Heute: Essays und Analysen*. Frankfurt am Maine: Insel Verlag.

Kozintsev, G. (1977) *King Lear: The Space of Tragedy*. London: Heinemann Educational Books.

Laing, R.D. (1960) *The Divided Self*. London: Tavistock Publications Ltd.

Landy, R. (1991) 'Role as a Primary Bridge between Theatre and Drama Therapy'. *Dramatherapy*, Spring 1991.

Lewis, I.M. (1971) *Ecstatic Religion: An Anthropological Study of Spirit Possession and Shamanism*. Penguin, Harmondsworth.

Levi Strauss, C. (1968) *Structural Anthropology*. London: Allen Lane.

Lidz, T. (1975) *Hamlet's Enemy. Madness and Myth in Hamlet*. Madison, Connecticut: International Universities Press.

Mack, M. (1968) 'The World of Hamlet'. *Casebook Series on Hamlet*. London: Macmillan.

Macquarrie, J. (1972) *Existentialism*. New York: N.Y. World Publishing.

Malan, D. (1979) *Individual Psychotherapy and the Science of Psychodynamics*. London: Butterworths.

Marineau, R. (1989) *Jacob Levy Moreno 1889–1974*. London: Tavistock.

Matza, D. (1969) *Becoming Deviant*. Englewood Cliffs, New Jersey: Prentice-Hall.

McCully, R.S. (1987) *Jung and Rorschach*. Dallas: Spring Publications.

Merleau-Ponty, M. (1962) *Phenomenology of Perception*, translated by C. Smith. London: Routledge & Kegan Paul.

Meyer, M.A. (1988) 'Growing by doing. Expressive Therapy applied to psychotic women in an outpatient setting'. *Tidskrift for Norsk Psykologforening* 25, 604–611.

Meyer, M.A. (1990) Expressive Therapy applied to substance abusers. *EL IXIR*, Journal for the Norwegian Art Therapy Ass. and the Norwegian Psychodrama Ass., 11-13.

Miller, A. (1990) *The Untouched Key*. London: Virago Press.

Mitchell, S. (1992) 'Therapeutic Theatre: A para-theatrical model of dramatherapy' in Jennings, S. *Dramatherapy Theory and Practice 2*. London: Routledge.

Moreno, J.L. (1972) *Psychodrama Vol I*. New York: Beacon Press.

Moreno, J.L. (1973) *Theatre of Spontaneity*. New York: Beacon House Press.

Moreno, J.L. (1978) *Who Shall Survive*. New York: Beacon House Press.

Moreno, Z.T. (1965) Psychodramatic Rules, Techniques and Adjunctive Methods. *Group Psychotherapy and Psychodrama*, 18, 73–83.

Moreno, Z.T. (1975) The Significance of Doubling and Role-Reversal for Cosmic Man. *Group Psychotherapy and Psychodrama*,28, 55–59.

Napier, A.D. (1986) *Masks Transformation and Paradox*. Berkeley, Ca. & London: University of California Press.

Ogden, T.H. (1982) *Projective Identification and Psychotherapeutic Technique*. New York: Jason Aronson.

Ogden, T.H. (1986) *The Matrix of Mind*. Northvale, New Jersey: Jason Aronson.

Parker-Lewis, P. (1989) A Jungian/Object Relations Approach in Drama Therapy Assessment and Process. Paper delivered at the NADT Conference, Pittsburgh.

Partridge, R. (1953) *Broadmoor*. London: Chatto & Windus.

Pedder, J.R. (1977) The Role of Space and Location in Psychotherapy, Play and Theatre. *International Review of Psycho-Analysis* 4, 215–223.

Pedder, J.R. (1979) Transitional Space in Psychotherapy and Theatre. *British Journal of Medical Psychology* 52, 377–384.

Pfister, M. (1988) (English Translation) *The Theory and Analysis of Drama*. Cambridge University Press.

Pines, M. (1982) Reflections on Mirroring. Sixth S.H. Foulkes Annual Lecture of the Group-Analytic Society. *Group Analysis* 15, Supp. 1–26.

Pines, M. (ed)(1985) *Bion and Group Psychotherapy*. London: Tavistock/Routledge.

Pitzele, P. (1991) 'Adolescent inside out: intrapsychic psychodrama' in Holmes, P. and Karp, M. (eds) *Psychodrama: Inspiration and Technique*. London: Tavistock/Routledge.

Raine, K. (1976) Personal communication.

Reibetanz, R. (1977) *The Lear World: A Study of King Lear in it's Dramatic Context*. London: Heinemann Educational Books.

Robins, A. (1986) *Expressive Therapy*. New York: Human Sciences Press.

Røine, E. (1978) *Group Psychotherapy as Experimental Theatre*. Oslo: Aschehoug. English translation in preparation.

Rose, G.J. (1980) *The Power of Form: A Psychoanalytic Approach to Aesthetic Form*. New York: International Universities Press.

Schattner, G. and Courtney, R. (eds)(1981) *Drama in Therapy. Volume II: Adults. Humanizing Offenders Through Acting Therapy*. New York: Drama Book Specialists.

Siirala, M. (1978) in Cox, M. *Structuring the Therapeutic Process: Compromise with Chaos*. Oxford: Pergamon. Reprinted 1988 with a new preface by Murray Cox. London: Jessica Kingsley Publishers.

Slade, P. (1954) *Child Drama*. London: University of London Press.

Slater, A.P. (1982) *Shakespeare the Director*. Brighton: The Harvester Press.

Snell, P. (1990) Behind Bars: Serving Theatre in the Prisons. *Theatrum*, 11.

Sophocles 'Antigone' in Wertenbaker, T. (Tr)(1992) *The Thebans: Oedipus Tyrranos, Oedipus at Colonus and Antigone*. London: Faber and Faber.

Spurgeon, C.F.E. (1979) *Shakespeare's Imagery and What It Tells Us*. Cambridge: Cambridge University Press.

Stanislavski, K. (1980) *An Actor Prepares*. Tr. by E. Reynolds Hopgood. London: Methuen.

Styan, J.L. (1967) *Shakespeare's Stagecraft*. Cambridge University Press.

Stafford-Clark, M. (1989) *Letters to George: the account of a rehearsal*. London: Nick Hern Books.

Szasz, T. (1974) *The Myth of Mental Illness*. London: Granada.

Thomson, P. (1983) *Shakespeare's Theatre*. London: Routledge and Kegan Paul.

Tillich, P. (1952) *The Courage to Be*. New Haven: Yale University Press.

Trethowan, W.H. (1988) 'Psychiatry and the Seven Ages of Man'. *Journal of the Royal Society of Medicine* 81, 189–193.

Tuovinen, M. (1973) *Crime as an Attempt at Intrapsychic Adaption*. Finland: University of Oulu.

Vandenbroucke, R. (1985) *Truths the Hand Can Touch: The Theatre of Athol Fugard*. New York: Theatre Communications Group.

Velz, J.W. and Teague, F.N. (1986) *One Touch of Shakespeare: Letters of Joseph Crosby to Joseph Parker Norris, 1875–1878*. Washington: Associated University Presses/Folger Books.

Weatherhead, A.K. (1967) *The Edge of the Image*. Seattle: University of Washington Press.

Wilshire, B. (1982) *Role-playing and Identity: the Limits of Theatre as Metaphor*. Bloomington: Indiana University Press.

Winnicott, D. W. (1971) *Playing and Reality*. London: Tavistock.

Yeats, W.B. 'He Wishes for the Cloths of Heaven' in Albright, D. (ed)(1990) *W.B. Yeats: The Poems*. Everyman Series. London: J.M. Dent & Sons.

Yochelson, S. and Samenow, S.E. (1976) *The Criminal Personality, Volume 1: A Profile For Change*. Northvale, New Jersey: Jason Aronson.

The Contributors

Dominic Barber is currently Resident Theatre Director at the Wilde Theatre, South Hill Park Arts Centre, Bracknell. He has been the Drama Tutor at Broadmoor Hospital for the past two-and-a-half years, taking weekly acting workshops with patients. He trained at Dartington College of Arts and was Assistant Director at the Maddermarket Theatre, Norwich and Community Drama Director at the Wyvern Theatre, Swindon. A passionate believer in 'arts for all' he is a Trustee of The Ark, a creative centre for students with learning difficulties with whom he takes weekly drama workshops.

Ann Barker, Consultant Forensic Psychiatrist at Broadmoor Hospital, reached forensic psychiatry through a childhood in Africa, an initial training in modern languages prior to medicine and a decade as a magistrate, and feels fully qualified as an 'alienist' to work among the 'alienated'. Primarily interested in the language or meaning of behaviour – the thoughts and feelings expressed through deeds – she finds Shakespeare a perfect biographer of dark misdeeds; and would like to help her patients ultimately to understand and compose their own biographies.

Ian Bayne spent two years working as a trainee civil engineer, both in the private sector and in local government, before making a career move into nursing. He started work at Broadmoor Hospital in 1966 as a student nurse and worked in a wide variety of wards and departments, completing his training in 1970. In 1981 he was promoted to senior nurse manager, initially involved in direct patient care before moving to Post Basic Education and, in 1989, to the Creative department, where he is responsible for organising the social and recreational programme for some 500 patients currently receiving inpatient treatment.

Cicely Berry joined the RSC in 1969 and is now Voice Director, responsible for all the voice and text work within the company. She is involved in numerous projects, including much work with the company's Education Unit, work in HM Prisons Long Lartin and Dartmoor, and as Patron of both Northumberland and Leicester Youth Theatres. She has travelled extensively, working with theatre groups in the USA, Europe, India, Australia, China and Zimbabwe. She also runs her own Teacher Weekend workshops, aiming to help teachers find new ways of teaching Shakespeare to students. In 1985 she was awarded the OBE for services to the theatre.

Brian Cox's most recent theatre work includes an award-winning *King Lear* with the Royal National Theatre and *Titus Andronicus* at the RSC, for which he won a 1988 Olivier Award. In 1984 he won both the Olivier and Drama Magazine Awards for his performance in *Rat in the Skull*. Television appearances include *Shoot For The Sun* and *The Cloning of Joanna May*. His films include *Manhunter, Hidden Agenda,* and *Red Fox.* As a director, his work includes *The Crucible* at the Moscow Arts Theatre, which initiated an exchange of students with the West.

Murray Cox's interest in Shakespeare ran parallel with pre-clinical studies at Cambridge. As a medical student, subsequently becoming a GP, Shakespeare's capacity to capture clinically significant detail took hold of him. Having entered psychiatry, Shakespeare's grasp of inner world phenomena, and its implications for psychotherapy, became an abiding, affectionate obsession: 'I see a strange confession in thine eye'. An interest in the aesthetic imperative and the edges of language led to collaborative publications with Alice Theilgaard. Other publications include books, chapters and professional papers.

Ron Daniels was born in Brazil, where he was a founding member of the Teatro Oficina in Sao Paulo. He moved to Britain in 1964, acting at the Byre Theatre and with the Victoria Theatre company before joining the RSC in 1977 as Artistic Director of The Other Place, Stratford-upon-Avon. His productions have included *The Tempest, Julius Caesar, Pericles, Timon of Athens* and *Hamlet,* as well as the world premières of works by writers such as David Edgar, David Rudkin and Stephen Polikoff. He is an Honorary Associate Director of the Royal Shakespeare Company and currently Associate Artistic Director of the American Repertory Theatre in Cambridge, Massachusetts.

Rob Ferris, Consultant Forensic Psychiatrist at Broadmoor Hospital and Honorary Consultant in Forensic Psychiatry at St George's Hospital, London, trained and worked as a psychiatrist in Adelaide, South Australia. There, and in the Northern Territory, he developed an interest in forensic psychiatry, and started work at Broadmoor in 1989. A longstanding interest in the theatre, and psychotherapy, led him to collaborate with Sue Jennings in running a one-day workshop on dramatherapy with offenders. Another is planned for March 1992.

Harvey Gordon has been a Consultant Forensic Psychiatrist at Broadmoor Hospital since 1984 and has been its Director of Medical Services since 1989. Previously he had been training in general and forensic psychiatry at the London Hospital and the Maudsley Hospital. He regards forensic psychiatry as calling for a careful balance between maximising attempts to meet the needs of the patient whilst concurrently addressing issues of public safety.

Saul Hewish became a founder member of Geese Theatre Company after a brief spell studying drama at Warwick University. Between 1987 and 1989 he developed his skills as a performer and workshop leader working exclusively in prisons and probation services in Britain, Ireland and America. He has trained extensively with John Bergman, founder of Geese Theatre USA and one of the top dramatherapists working in the US penal system. In 1989 he was promoted to Director. Current work includes training prison and probation staff in Geese Company techniques and the development of drama based offending behaviour programmes with emphasis on violent and sexually abusive offenders.

Clare Higgins was brought up and educated in Yorkshire, and trained at LAMDA. She has worked extensively in theatre, television and film. Her work includes Katherine in *The Secret Rapture* (1989), Regan in *King Lear* (1990-91), Elizabeth in *Richard III* (1990-91) and Amalia in *Napoli Milionaria* (1991) at the Royal National Theatre; and Titania in *A Midsummer Night's Dream* (1989-90) and Gertrude in *Hamlet* (1989-90) at the Royal Shakespeare Company. She created the rôle of Leah in the world première of Arthur Miller's *The Ride Down Mount Morgan* (1991). She is a founder member of the Institute of Dramatherapy.

Sue Jennings, actor, author and dramatherapist, has spent most of her life working between theatres and clinics. Her doctoral research on shamanic healing and midwifery took her to the Temiar people of the Malaysian rain forest. She is Senior Research Fellow at the London Hospital Medical College, Director of Dramatherapy Consultants and founder of the Institute of Dramatherapy. She is also Honorary Research Fellow, The Shakespeare Institute, The University of Birmingham.

Ian McKellen was born and bred in south Lancashire, where he first acted in school. After University he spent three years with regional repertory companies, before joining Laurence Olivier's National Theatre company at the Old Vic. Throughout his thirty years as an actor, he has concentrated on the theatre, working in a wide range of plays. With the National, the RSC, the Actor's Company and in his solo show *Acting Shakespeare*, he has regularly toured abroad. The *King Lear* which visited Broadmoor was partnered by *Richard III*, both of which he produced for the National Theatre

Melinda A. Meyer studied in both Norway and the USA, graduating with an MA in Expressive Therapy. She has been Chairperson of the Norwegian Psychodrama Association since it was founded in 1985, has worked for UNICEF in Nicaragua and, since 1986, has taught and supervised at the Norwegian Psychodrama Institute. In 1991 she became a Psychodrama Director in Norway. She is a senior staff member at the Scandinavian Institute for Expressive Therapies and co-leader of an education pro- gramme in expressive therapies in Oslo. She has completed a training programme in bioenergetics, and is currently working at the Psychosocial Centre for Refugees at the University of Oslo.

Eva Røine was born in Norway in 1929. She studied at The Webber Douglas School of Dramatic Art in London, and was an actress, a journalist and critic of television and theatre, and Head of Public Relations at the National Theatre in Oslo before completing her PhD in history of the theatre, criminology and psychology. She went on to become a psycholog- ist, specialising in clinical psychology. She is founder and Head of the Norwegian Psychodrama Institute, a member of the Nordic Board of Examiners, and Vice President of the Psychodrama Institute for Europe.

Mark Rylance is an associate actor of the RSC and Artistic Director of Phoebus Cart Theatre Company. A graduate of RADA, he has worked with, among others, the Glasgow Citizens Theatre, Shared Experience, the Royal Court, the Scottish Ballet and the London Theatre of Imagination, playing roles such as Iago, Puck, Percy Bysshe Shelley, William Blake and Arturo Ui. His film work includes *Hearts of Fire, Prospero's Books* and *The Grass Arena*. He is a Friend of the Francis Bacon Research Trust and an Associate Director of Sam Wanamaker's project to rebuild Shakespeare's Globe Theatre on the South Bank of the Thames.

Rebecca Saire's theatre work includes *Hamlet* and *Nicholas Nickleby* (RSC), *The Ticket-of-Leave Man* (National Theatre), *The Glass Menagerie* (Redgrave Theatre, Farnham) and *Thunder in the Air* (Gate Theatre, London). Her television appearances include Juliet in the BBC's 1978 production of *Romeo and Juliet, Love in a Cold Climate*, Amelia Sedley in *Vanity Fair*, Theresa Nolan in P.D. James' *A Taste for Death*, Aline Hemingway in *Jeeves and Wooster* and guest appearances in *A Bit of Fry and Laurie*. She played Cecily in the film *The Shooting Party*. Rebecca is a writer and has published various articles and short stories.

Jessica Saunders is a registered dramatherapist and a performer. Trained in both contemporary dance and acting, she has worked extensively as a professional actress in theatre, film and radio. She qualified in dramathe- rapy in 1989 and since then has worked in the fields of forensic psychiatry, eating disorders, psychiatry and dramatherapy training. She currently works as a dramatherapist at HM Prison Holloway and is to begin work at Broadmoor Hospital in January 1992. She spends a day a week in her studio, currently working on a dance performance she is giving in August 1992. Her theatre company, The Theatre of Reflection, hopes to launch its next production early in 1993.

Georgia Slowe has been working in film, theatre and television for fourteen years. On the screen she has had major roles in productions as diverse as *I'll Take Manhatten*, *The Company of Wolves* and *The Attic*. Her performance as Juliet for the RSC earned her nominations for both the Manchester Evening News and Olivier awards in 1990. She has recently completed a four hour drama series for the BBC. Georgia, whose greatest pleasures are friends, films, fiction and her dog Poppy, lives in North London.

Oliver Taplin teaches at Magdalen College, Oxford, and has a special interest in Greek drama and narrative poetry in performance. His book *Greek Fire* was published by Jonathan Cape in 1989, and *Homeric Soundings* is to be published by Oxford University Press in 1992.

Alice Theilgaard, DrMedSc., Professor of Medical Psychology, The University of Copenhagen; Honorary Research Fellow, The Shakespeare Institute, The University of Birmingham; Member, Danish Society for Psychoanalytic Psychotherapy. Author or co-author of over 80 publications, including *Mutative Metaphors in Psychotherapy* (1987) and *Shakespeare as Prompter* (1993) with Murray Cox. In the creative field her particular interest is in the complementarity of dramatic art and clinical phenomena. She is keen to explore the limits of the translatable.

Trevor Walt was born in 1952, the son of a Durham miner. He came to work at Broadmoor in 1971, one week after his marriage to Anne. Having qualified and worked as a psychiatric nurse he later trained as a nurse tutor and was involved in both basic nurse training and the provision of advanced courses for qualified staff. He commenced theological training in 1983 and was ordained in 1986. He was licensed initially as an Honorary Assistant Chaplain, whilst working as a nurse tutor. In 1989 he was appointed as Broadmoor whole-time Anglican Chaplain. Anne also works at Broadmoor as Senior Lecturer in the Patient Education Department, and they have two teenage daughters.

Deborah Warner trained at the Central School of Speech and Drama and in 1980 formed the Kick Theatre Company. She directed the first Bengali speaking production of *The Tempest* for the British Council in Dhaka, Bangladesh. Her 1988/89 production of *Titus Andronicus* for the RSC won her the Evening Standard and Olivier Awards for Best Director. She is an Associate Director of the Royal National Theatre, where in 1989/90 she directed *The Good Person of Sichuan* and *King Lear*. In 1991 she directed *Hedda Gabler* in Dublin and London, and *Electra* in London and Bobingny, France.

Peter Wight studied English Literature at Oxford University and worked for ten months in the United States before embarking on an acting career which began in community theatre in South London and has since included work at various provincial theatres including the Sheffield Crucible and the Royal Exchange, Manchester as well as at the National Theatre and the Royal Shakespeare Company. He has worked with directors including Mike Alfreds, Mike Leigh, Di Travis, Richard Eyre, Bill Gaskill, Peter Gill, Nick Hytner, David Jones and Michael Boyd. He has also appeared in various television plays and series.

Hamlet

Francisco	William Oxborrow
Barnardo	Ben Miles
Marcellus	Neil Richardson
Horatio	Jack Ellis
The Ghost	Russell Enoch
Claudius	Peter Wight
Gertrude	Clare Higgins
Hamlet	Mark Rylance
Valtemand	Mark Brignal
Cornelius	Peter Carr
Polonius	Patrick Godfrey
Laertes	John Ramm
Ophelia	Rebecca Saire
Reynaldo	Andrew Havill
Rosencrantz	Andrew Bridgmont
Guildenstern	Patrick Brennan
First Player	Russell Enoch
Second Player	Katherine Stark
Third Player	Roger Tebb
Violinist	William Oxborrow
Fortinbras	Jared Harris
Lady	Hilary Tones
Sailor	Michael Howell
First Gravedigger	Jimmy Gardner
Second Gravedigger	William Oxborrow
A Priest	Neil Richardson
Osric	Paul Lacoux

Other parts played by members of the company

Directed by	Ron Daniels
Designed by	Antony McDonald
Stage Manager	Jasper Gilbert
Music by	Claire Van Kampen

Romeo and Juliet

Chorus .... Rob Heyland
Sampson .... Francis Johnson
Gregory .... Jared Harris
Abraham .... Ben Miles
Balthasar .... William Oxborrow
Benvolio .... Patrick Brennan
Tybalt .... Vincent Regan
Capulet .... Bernard Horsfall
Lady Capulet .... Linda Spurrier
Montague .... Michael Loughnan
Lady Montague .... Katherine Stark
Escalus .... Rob Heyland
Romeo .... Mark Rylance
Paris .... Michael Howell
Peter .... Evan Russell
Nurse .... Margaret Courtenay
Juliet .... Georgia Slowe
Mercutio .... David O'Hara
Old Capulet .... Griffith Jones
Lady .... Hilary Tones
Lady .... Jennie Heslewood
Friar Laurence .... Patrick Godfrey
Apothecary .... Griffith Jones
Friar John .... Ben Miles
Paris' Page .... Richard Doubleday
First Watch .... Peter Carr
Servants, guests, citizens of Verona and musicians

Directed by .... Terry Hands
Designed by .... Farrah
Stage Manager .... Jondon Gourkan
Music by .... Claire Van Kampen

King Lear

The Earl of Kent	Ian McKellen
The Earl of Gloucester	Peter Jeffrey
Edmund	Hakeem Kae-Kazim
Lear	Brian Cox
Goneril	Susan Engel
Regan	Clare Higgins
Cordelia	Eve Matheson
The Duke of Albany	Richard Bremmer
The Duke of Cornwall	Richard O'Callaghan
The Duke of Burgundy	Mark Strong
The King of France	David Collings
Edgar	Derek Hutchinson
Oswald	Nicholas Blane
Third Knight	Peter Sullivan
Lear's Fool	David Bradley
Curan	Stephen Marchant
Gentleman	Colin Hurley
First Servant	Mark Strong
Second Servant	Stephen Marchant
Third Servant	Richard Simpson
Old Man	Sam Beazley
Messenger	Phil McKee
Doctor	Brian Purchase
Captain	Mark Strong
Herald	Richard Simpson

Knights, officers, servants, attendants, messengers, played by members of the company

Directed by	Deborah Warner
Designed by	Hildegard Bechtler
Stage Manager	John Caulfield
Music by	Domonic Muldowney

Measure For Measure

Duke	Peter Pearson
Angelo	Mike Snelgrove
Claudio	Trevor Leek
Escalus	Hugh McCartan
Lucio	Jeremy Radburn
Pompey	Julian Hirst
Abhorson	Nick Leftwich
Froth	Richard Simpson
Elbow	Richard Fieldhouse
Provost	Chris Bowring
Friar Thomas	Guy Riggs
Bernadine	Bob Atte La Crouche
First Gentleman	David Rhodes
Second Gentleman	Rob Kemp
Justice	John Grady
Servant	Dean Smith
Messenger	Clive Haynes
Isabella	Robbie Morgan
Juliet	Nicky Bevan
Mariana	Diane Moreton
Mistress Overdone	Linda Blakely
Francisca	Lola Irvine
Nuns/Whores etc	Katherine Webb
	Natalie Cutler
	Val Pollard
	Joyce Ferrar

Directed by	Dominic Barber
Designed by	Sue Lawson-Dick
Stage Manager	Sally Little
Music by	Oliver R. Ashmore

Cast lists as supplied

Subject Index

Name Index

References in notes to the main text are indicated by 'n'.

Page numbering in bold type indicates quoted material.

Quotations from Shakespeare's Plays